THE WORLD CHAMPIONS

The World Champions

GIUSEPPE FARINA TO JACKIE STEWART

by
Anthony Pritchard

MACMILLAN PUBLISHING CO., INC.
NEW YORK

Copyright © 1972, 1974 by Anthony Pritchard

All rights reserved. No part of this book may be reproduced or transmitted in any form or by any means, electronic or mechanical, including photocopying, recording or by any information storage and retrieval system, without permission in writing from the Publisher.

Macmillan Publishing Co., Inc.
866 Third Avenue, New York, N. Y. 10022

Library of Congress Cataloging in Publication Data

Pritchard, Anthony.
    The world champions: Giuseppe Farina to Jackie Stewart.

    1. Automobile racing—Biography.   I. Title.
GV1032.A1P74 1974   796.7'2'0922   73-15147
ISBN 0-02-599210-4

FIRST AMERICAN EDITION 1974

Printed in the United States of America

Contents

	Introduction	vii
1.	*The First Champion* GIUSEPPE FARINA, 1950	1
2.	*The Greatest Argentinian* JUAN MANUEL FANGIO, 1951, 1954–7	14
3.	*Champion Son of a Champion* ALBERTO ASCARI, 1952–3	35
4.	*The First British Champion* JOHN MICHAEL HAWTHORN, 1958	54
5.	*The Champion Who Never Was* STIRLING MOSS	74
6.	*Australian Champion* JACK BRABHAM, 1959–60, 1966	95

7.	*Yankee Champion* PHIL HILL, 1961	111
8.	*The Man Who Rowed* GRAHAM HILL, 1962, 1968	125
9.	*The Greatest Champion of Them All?* JIM CLARK, 1963, 1965	148
10.	*Champion on Two Wheels and Four* JOHN SURTEES, 1964	168
11.	*The Kiwi King* DENIS HULME, 1967	180
12.	*A Champion of Our Times* JOHN YOUNG STEWART, 1969, 1971	191
13.	*The Fastest Champion* KARL-JOCHEN RINDT, 1970	213
14.	*The Black Prince* EMERSON FITTIPALDI, 1972	237
	Appendix: The Drivers' World Championship, 1950–73	247

Introduction

IN THIS STUDY of the World Champions I have endeavoured to give an appreciation of their talents and abilities but it must be remembered that the standards by which judgments of drivers are made must to some extent be purely subjective. The World Championship is in itself a very rough and ready yardstick as to ability. To win the Championship a driver must be at the wheel of a car that is at least as fast and handles as well as any of its rivals.

It is equally important that the team's standards of preparation are beyond reproach—much of Jackie Stewart's very considerable success is attributable to the high standards of preparation of the Tyrrell team—and the winning driver needs more than a fair share of luck. Many drivers of very great ability and with an impressive record of success in individual races have failed to win the Championship, notably Stirling Moss, to whom a chapter of this book is devoted. Tony Brooks and Jacky Ickx, on the basis of merit, would also have been worthy Champions, but they happened to be driving the wrong cars at the wrong time.

I am certainly of the view that to attempt to compare drivers of different eras is in itself a perilous occupation.

Driving techniques with heavy, front-engined cars of immense speed in a straight line (the Alfa 159 driven by Fangio was capable of 200 mph), but with primitive suspension and wheels of great diameter and very narrow tire width that severely restricted cornering speed, were very different from those needed with today's highly sophisticated designs with the engine mounted ahead of the rear axle, great emphasis on aerodynamics, immense cornering power from tires of remarkable adhesion, but with which the margin between safe negotiation of a corner and rebounding off the Armco barrier is so narrow. If Fangio 'over-cooked' a corner with the Alfa 158, a firm wrench on the steering wheel would almost certainly have it all under control again and fatal accidents, when they occurred, most frequently arose from freak road or weather conditions and the subsequent violent contact with a wall or tree. Modern racing accidents have in the main resulted from loss of adhesion through the driver misjudging a corner. It is of course dangerous to generalise too freely about motor racing accidents as each is different, many are totally unexpected and several have led directly to new safety arrangements.

An equally uncertain yardstick of ability is to add up and compare the number of Grands Prix won by different drivers. Nowadays there are twice as many rounds in the World Championship as there were at its conception in 1950. Although Jim Clark and Jackie Stewart topped the number of Grand Prix wins scored by Fangio, it must be remembered that Fangio drove in less Grands Prix in each year than his modern rivals.

As I have indicated elsewhere in this book, any nominations for the greatest driver of all times are very much within the realm of idle speculation, but I am going to stick out my own neck, by listing my own personal 'top ten' made up on the basis of achievement, style, speed, tenacity, determination to finish when the odds were against them and, of course personal prejudice. There is no significance in the

Introduction

order other than that the list is chronological according to the dates at which the drivers were racing:

Giuseppe Campari
Tazio Nuvolari
Bernd Rosemeyer
Rudolf Caracciola
Achille Varzi
Jean-Pierre Wimille
Giuseppe Farina
Juan Manuel Fangio
Stirling Moss
Jim Clark

No book can be written without a great deal of help from many people, not only those who supply information, but the 'backroom' people who usually do much of the work. I am especially grateful to Kathleen Harvey for deciphering my hand-written notes and typing the manuscript; I am also grateful to Keith Davey for reading the manuscript and for his valuable advice and to Nigel Snowdon for his assistance in finding so many of the photographs that illustrate the book.

AP.

THE WORLD CHAMPIONS

1

The First Champion
GIUSEPPE FARINA
1950

TWENTY-THREE YEARS after he won the first World Championship, Nino Farina is both a legend and something of an enigma. When Farina was racing, drivers simply got on with the job of driving, only if they had journalistic leanings did they pen their own autobiography and it was rare indeed for a driver to collaborate with a journalist, rarer still for him to have a close enough friend to write his biography. Very little of what Farina felt about racing ever became known, there was no explanation for his harsh, forceful driving that sometimes bordered on ruthlessness or for his moods that on occasion resulted in him giving up the race in the middle of a chase and made life so difficult for his team-manager.

Farina was born in Turin on 30th October 1906. He took his doctorate in political economy at Turin University and was related to Pinin Farina, the greatest of all Italian coachbuilders. In Turin, in the Corso Tortona, he ran with his brother his own coachbuilding company known as Stablimente Farina. The business flourished in post-war days and was responsible for a number of bodies fitted to early Farraris, but as Ferrari turned to the Pininfarina concern more and more for new coachwork for his cars, the fortunes of Stablimente Farina gradually faded.

Giuseppe Farina is best remembered for his style of driving; the relaxed, inclined position and outstretched arms that was to influence a whole generation of drivers. Even in post-war days, when Farina was driving for the Alfa team, many of his contemporaries still sat crouched, fighting with the wheel. While the great stylist Farina applied art and intelligence to the driving of his car, the 'Pampas Bull,' Argentinian Froilan Gonzalez, would hunch over the wheel of his Ferrari and urge it along with great heavings of his ponderous frame.

Farina's parents had comfortable financial means; there was always a car in the family and before he was ten years old he was a rabid motoring enthusiast. Although his parents tried to steer him towards a more academic career, young 'Nino' was determined to become a racing driver. His first race, of a very unofficial nature, came in 1921 when he was only fifteen years old. He and his brother raced through roads near Turin with a brace of Temperino 1200 cc cycle-cars—there is, however, no record as to who won, but that this race did take place was substantiated by a photograph in Farina's family album.

While at University twenty-year-old Farina decided to buy a racing car without his family knowing. The only problem was money and Nino tried to raise this by speculating on the stock exchange. Soon he had accumulated almost all the money needed, but then disaster struck, his final speculation failed and he found himself hopelessly in debt. There was now only one thing that he could do—tell his father the full story. By this time Farina senior had become reconciled to his son's plans to become a racing driver. He paid off all the debts and agreed to buy Nino the Alfa Romeo he wanted, but on the understanding that he, too, should have one so that they could compete together.

Their first event was the 1927 Aosta-Gran San Bernardo hill climb. Nino's run was first, but in a burst of over-exuberance he lost control at a corner, turned the car over and was taken off to hospital with a broken shoulder. At this point Farina senior put his foot down and decreed that Nino could forget cars and racing and concentrate on his studies. It was not until 1933 that Nino could afford another car for competitions work, an 8C-2300 Alfa, which he drove into third place in the Naples Grand Prix. The following year he crashed again in a hill climb, hitting a wall at the first corner, less than two hundred yards from the start. This accident helped to tame his wild driving. He took his racing more seriously and later in the year switched to a Maserati 1500 cc Voiturette, with which he scored a number of successes including a win in the Circuit of Masaryk in Czechoslovakia and third place in the Circuit of Biella, a minor Italian 'round the houses' race. Both of these successes were gained at the wheel of cars entered by Gino Rovere on behalf of the works and he continued to drive for this entrant the following year.

In the early part of the 1935 season he handled a 3.7-litre version of the new 6-cylinder Maserati that had made its debut in the hands of the great Tazio Nuvolari at Monza the previous year. This car proved hopelessly unreliable, as did the 4.4-litre V-8 Maserati which he handled later in 1935. Perhaps Nino's best drive of the year was in October in the Donington Grand Prix (the first international Grand Prix to be held on a true road circuit in England) which he led on a rain-soaked course for the first hundred miles until his V-8 Maserati expired with a broken half-shaft. Farina had become friendly with Tazio Nuvolari and the great Italian helped and encouraged the young Maserati driver.

Farina's driving greatly impressed Enzo Ferrari who later wrote of him: 'He was a great driver, but I could never help feeling apprehensive about him, especially at the start of a race and one or two laps from the end. At the start, he was not unlike a highstrung thoroughbred, liable to break through the starting tape in its eagerness. When nearing the finish, he was capable of committing the most astonishing follies, although it must be admitted in all justice that he risked only his own safety and never jeopardised that of others. As a consequence he was a regular inmate of the hospital wards.' *

Ferrari's remarks are of considerable interest, but it is impossible not to question whether one can trust what he wrote of Farina, any more than one can trust his undoubtedly prejudiced descriptions of Fangio or Fangio's equally prejudiced comments on Farrari! Certainly Farina was involved in many accidents, so many that he could not remember them all, but his moments of folly came mainly in later years when both he and Ascari were driving for Ferrari (to be beaten by the younger man was more than his pride could stomach). In pre-war days Farina appeared to be gripped by a ruthless determination to succeed, a man who had made a scientific study of motor racing and drove with forethought and precision. If he took a risk, it was a calculated risk and not a chance.

Enzo Ferrari invited the slim, austere Farina to join the Scuderia for 1936. At this time Italian motor racing was in a very sick state. Since the introduction of the 750-kg Grand Prix Formula at the beginning of 1934, a Formula imposing a maximum weight but no maximum engine size, the German teams, Mercedes-Benz and Auto Union, had been racing cars of considerable technical complexity. Their annual racing budget was many times greater than that of Alfa Romeo, the leading Italian contender that had dominated racing in the early 'thirties. The outcome of so much effort applied was inevitable; there was a Teutonic stranglehold on Grand Prix racing that the Italians could rarely break and Farina's chances of success in Grand Prix racing with Alfa Romeo were slim.

Farina's first drive for Scuderia Ferrari was in the Mille Miglia road race in April and at the wheel of one of the new 2.9-litre supercharged Alfa sports cars, closely based on

---

* The Enzo Ferrari Memoirs (Hamish Hamilton Ltd., 1963).

the design of the team's Grand Prix machinery. He finished a bare half-minute behind team-mate Brivio whose car had covered the last twenty-five miles of this 992-mile race, the latter stages run in the dark, with smashed head-lamps. In Grand Prix racing he achieved a fourth in the Eifelrennen at the Nürburgring and thirds at Milan, Modena and Barcelona, but his year was marred by a horrible accident in which he was not blameless. In the Deauville Grand Prix, in the absence of opposition from the German teams, Farina was leading the race with his 8-cylinder Alfa Romeo when he collided with the ERA of Marcel Lehoux which he was lapping. The accident cost the life of Lehoux whose car caught fire.

For 1937 Farina remained with Scuderia Farrari, finishing second in the Mille Miglia with a 2.3-litre unsupercharged Alfa Romeo, taking other second places in the Circuit of Turin and Milan and winning at Naples. Alfa Romeo decided to resume racing cars on their own behalf in 1938 and Farina now drove for this works team proper which was given the name of Alfa Corse. 1938 started badly for Farina; he crashed in the Mille Miglia and at the Tripoli race he was involved in yet another fatal accident when he collided with the Maserati of Laszlo Hartmann who was killed. In this first year of a new Grand Prix Formula the latest German cars were not entirely *au point*, and it was for this reason rather than any other that Farina achieved more Grand Prix successes than in the past. In the Coppa Ciano at Leghorn he took second place to Hermann Lang's Mercedes, a fortnight later he finished second to Caracciola's Mercedes in the Coppa Acerbo at Pescara, he was fifth in the Swiss Grand Prix and second again in the Italian race. For the second year running he was the winner of the Italian Championship.

From an Italian point of view the most significant event of 1938 had been the introduction of the new Alfa Romeo Tipo 158 1500 cc Voiturette which, after teething troubles in its early days, was to enjoy a run of racing success that persisted until the end of the 1951 season. In 1938 these cars had appeared in four races and won two of them, but Farina did not drive a 158 until 1939 when all major Italian races were held for 1500 cc racing cars and the Tipo 158 spearheaded the Alfa attack. At Tripoli the 158s were trounced by two new Voiturettes from the Mercedes factory, cars that no one knew existed until shortly before the race. After an early effort in which he held second place ahead of Caracciola's Mercedes, Farina retired with engine trouble.

The new Mercedes only appeared the once and in the remainder of the year's Voiturette races Alfa Romeo had a comparatively easy time. The Dottore won the Coppa Ciano, after leading the race for the whole distance, took third place in the Coppa Acerbo and won the Voiturette class of the Swiss Grand Prix. Farina drove a fantastic race at Bremgarten, for in the final in which the Voiturettes and Grand Prix cars ran together, he was in second place to Lang's Mercedes at the end of the first lap and it took seven laps before Caracciola could force his Mercedes past into second place. At the finish he was still leading a works Mercedes and a works Auto Union. In the whole of his career this was the race that gave Farina the greatest satisfaction. One final victory in 1940 before Italy entered the war and Farina joined the army, came in the Tripoli Grand Prix in which he again drove a Tipo 158.

Little is known of Farina's military service, but it is recorded that he served as a tank commander in the North African desert. Rodney Walkerley (formerly 'Grande Vitesse,' the sports editor of the London magazine *Motor*) has recently commented that like so many Italians Farina was reluctant to talk of his wartime experiences. When Walkerley met Farina in Milan after the war, he found that 'Nino was a changed man, embittered, Communistic in outlook and felt the Italian switch of sides very deeply.' He recalled having met Farina's wife in London in 1933, but when he enquired as to her health, Farina denied that he had ever been married.

Alfa Romeo—and Giuseppe Farina—returned to racing in June 1946, in the St Cloud Grand Prix run through the streets of a Paris suburb and incorporating a half-mile long tunnel—much longer than the tunnel at Monaco. The Alfas were driven by Farina and Jean-Pierre Wimille, but both retired with clutch trouble, a direct result of the cars' long hibernation during the war years. What was remarkable about this failure was that it was the only post-war defeat of the 158s until Gonzalez pushed Fangio back into second place at the 1951 British Grand Prix.

The Alfas' second outing was at the Grand Prix des Nations, on a street circuit at Geneva, the following month and here Farina's team-mates were Wimille and Achille Varzi, two of the greatest drivers of all time, and Count Felice Trossi. The race was run in two heats and a final, and at the end of the first lap Nino came round in second place behind Nuvolari's Maserati, gesticulating wildly and it was apparent to everyone that Tazio had been baulking him every inch of the way! Farina pushed his way past on the next lap and won the heat from team-mate Trossi. In the final, Nuvolari succeeded in ramming Wimille's leading Alfa which spun off and rejoined the race in third place and Farina was the winner, again leading Trossi home.

Farina retired with transmission trouble on the very first lap of the Turin Grand Prix and the race was won by another Alfa driven by Varzi. At this time there was a great deal of dissension in the Alfa team because the company insisted on picking the winner, and quite often signalled the leading Alfa driver to ease off and let another Alfa driver overtake him. The usual practice when teams were running three or four cars for fairly evenly matched drivers would be to let them sort out their placings for themselves in the opening laps and then signal them to hold position, a much fairer arrangement. At Turin, Wimille was forced to ease off to let

Varzi win and as result of the altercation after the race he was dropped from the team at the Milan Grand Prix. In this race Farina finished first on the road in his heat, but was penalised a minute for jumping the start and classified third. It seems that Trossi was supposed to win the final and after a few laps Achille Varzi let him through to the front. A furious duel between Varzi and Farina developed in which Varzi appeared more concerned in stopping Farina from going after Trossi than holding on to second place. Farina's brakes began to play up and when he spun at one of the corners, instead of carrying on in a safe third place he retired in a 'huff' because he was not being allowed to win. 'During the evening after the race, in the cafe in the Galleria della Duomo,' wrote John Eason Gibson, 'Farina put on a terrific act: aloof and sulky.'

The net outcome of these nursery antics was that Farina was told by Alfa Romeo that they no longer required his services, thank you very much, and when Farina failed to appear on the circuits in 1947 everyone concluded that he had retired. Nino bounced back again in the South American Formule Libre races early in 1948 and won the Mar del Plata Grand Prix with a 3-litre Maserati. In European races he drove Maserati 4CLT/48 cars for two seasons and soon revealed that he had lost none of his old sparkle. In 1948 he won the Grand Prix des Nations at Geneva and the Monaco Grand Prix, but despite driving really hard in 1949 his only success was second place in the *Daily Express* Trophy race at Silverstone. He appeared at the 1949 Italian Grand Prix at Monza at the wheel of a new version of the Maserati known as the 'Milano,' one of two cars built by the Scuderia of that name to win the special starting money prize of six million lire (£3000) offered to any entrant of two new cars. The Milano, with an engine much more powerful than that fitted to standard Maseratis, proved really fast, but it still lacked the speed to catch the latest Ferraris which were also making their debut in this race. Yet again Farina's difficult and disagreeable temperament let him down. He was in third place when he retired in a 'huff,' merely because he could not catch the two leading Ferraris—one of these retired and if only he had had the sense to keep going, he would have finished second!

After a year's absence Alfa Romeo returned to racing for 1950 and there is no doubt that they were desperately short of drivers. Of their old team, both Varzi and Wimille had been killed in motor racing accidents and Count Trossi had died of cancer. At the time Alfa Romeo must have felt that they were scratching about rather when they signed up promising Argentinian Juan Fangio, who had but one season of European racing behind him; veteran Luigi Fagioli who was another driver thought to have retired; and, as team-leader, Nino Farina who was given another chance.

As events turned out, this trio proved to be one of the most successful that had ever raced together, and more than a match for the Ferrari opposition driven by Ascari and Villoresi. Just as in 1947 and 1948, the Alfa team won every Grand Prix entered and Farina took the Drivers' Championship, newly inaugurated for that year, with victories in the British, Swiss and Italian races. Nino also scored victories in non-Championship races at Bari and Silverstone. At Monaco he spun on water that had broken over the sea-wall, hit the wall and rebounded broadside across the road where his Alfa was rammed by Gonzalez's Maserati. This triggered off the multi-car accident that eliminated half the entry. He fell back with gearbox trouble to finish fourth at Spa and after fuel pump trouble was classified seventh in the French race. At the Grand Prix des Nations he crashed his car into the straw bales to avoid Villoresi who had lost control, hit a curb and was thrown out.

In 1950 Farina was at the peak of a career which now went into a gradual decline. The following year he won his heat of the *Daily Express* Trophy race at Silverstone, but the final was abandoned because torrential rain flooded the track. At the Swiss Grand Prix, another race run in heavy rain, he drove a car which bulged with supplementary tanks to get him through the race without refuelling. All the extra tankage affected its handling and he fell back to finish third behind team-mate Fangio and Taruffi with one of the new 4.5-litre Ferraris. A minor victory in the Ulster Trophy race in Northern Ireland followed, and setting the pace right from the start, he won the Belgium Grand Prix at Spa.

His Alfa was delayed by tire trouble in the French Grand Prix and with his car crippled in the closing stages of the race by a faulty magneto, he finished fifth, banging his fists in frustration on the sides of the car as he tried to snatch fourth place on the last lap from Parnell's 'Thin Wall' Farrari which had been slowed by transmission problems. His car expired with an under-bonnet fire in the British race, the gearbox failed at the Nürburgring and at Monza his Alfa retired after only five laps. Farina took over team-mate Bonetto's car and started a frantic chase after the leading Ferraris. When he stopped to refuel, the Alfa was stationary for two minutes, an inordinately long time, all the ground he had gained was lost, but once more he began to fling his Alfa round Monza in vain pursuit of Gonzalez's Ferrari. His car had developed a fuel leak, he stopped again for the tanks to be topped up and as he accelerated away from the pits, fuel could be seen spewing from the tail of the Alfa. Despite the fire risk, the Alfa was not black-flagged, and after one of the most gallant and hard-fought races of his career Farina took third place. In the last round of the Championship at Barcelona he again finished third.

When Alfa Romeo withdrew from racing at the end of the 1951 season, Giuseppe Farina signed up with the Ferrari team. For the next two seasons he fought a personal battle to beat Ascari, a battle that he was bound to lose, for Ascari was by far the better driver; more controlled, faster and more precise. At forty-five Farina found that his ability was waning, he could not match Ascari's lap times, and time and time again he threw away good placings by overdriving his car. At Marseilles in 1952 he took the lead when Ascari stopped for new tires and carried on at undiminished pace until he shot into the straw bales and wrecked his front suspension; at Montlhéry in the Paris Grand Prix he was overtaken by team-mate Taruffi and while trying to regain the lead, he ended up in a ditch and was disqualified for receiving help in getting the car back on the track; at les Sables d'Olonne he was eliminated in a multi-car crash that was no more his fault than anybody else's; and he crashed again at La Baule in August. His best performances during the year were wins in the Naples and Autodrome Grands Prix, and in Championship races he finished second at Spa, Rouen, the Nürburgring and Zandvoort.

1953 was to be Farina's last full racing season. At the beginning of the year he was involved in a horrible accident in the Argentine Grand Prix when his Ferrari mowed down a crowd of spectators who had strayed over the safety barriers to watch the race from the edge of the track. Ten onlookers lost their lives. After such a terrible accident, however little he was to blame personally (the real fault was lack of crowd control) many a driver would have felt unable to carry on driving. But only a fortnight later Farina reappeared at the same circuit with a Ferrari and won the Buenos Aires City Grand Prix. Shortly afterwards another accident, albeit of a minor nature, cost Farina a race; he was leading at Pau when he 'over-cooked' a corner, spun off, stalled and buckled a wheel. Once the European Championship season, as such, was under way Farina seemed to take a grip on himself and his driving became more restrained. He finished second to Ascari at Zandvoort, retired with engine failure at Spa, crossed the line in fifth place at Reims (which meant that in this close-fought race he was only a couple of seconds behind the winner) and took a sound third place at Silvertone.

At the Nürburgring, generally recognised as being the

most difficult of European circuits, Farina drove with rare brilliance, displaying much of his skill of earlier days. After Ascari's leading Ferrari had lost a wheel, the Dottore sped past Fangio's Maserati and team-mate Hawthorn to score his first World Championship race victory since the 1951 Belgian Grand Prix and the last in his career. He followed this up with another good drive in the Swiss race in which he finished second, and he was second again in the Italian race after Ascari had spun at the last corner of the last lap. In sports car racing in 1953 he co-drove with Ascari the winning Ferrari in the Nürburgring 1000 kilometres race.

For 1954 Farina remained with the Ferrari team, finishing second in the Argentine Grand Prix, co-driving the winning car with Maglioli in the Buenos Aires 1000 kilometres sports car race and winning at Siracusa in the first European Formula One race of the season. In the Mille Miglia he drove one of the new and monstrous 4.9-litre Ferrari sports cars, but crashed into a tree not long after the start while trying to avoid a spectator who had run on to the road. Farina's injuries included a broken arm and although he reappeared two months later at the Belgian Grand Prix he was not really fit. He had another bad crash during testing at Monza and did not race again until 1955. After running without conspicuous success during the first few months of 1955, Farina was still badly troubled by leg burns and once again withdrew from racing. He was entered with one of the Lancia V-8s which Ferrari had just acquired at that year's Italian Grand Prix, but non-started after tire trouble in practice.

Farina was now approaching his forty-ninth birthday, older even than Fangio when he retired, but, admittedly, not as old as that motor racing wonder Tazio Nuvolari who drove in his last Grand Prix at the age of fifty-six. He decided that the time had come to hang up his crash helmet for good and he never raced again. He had hoped to round off his career by running at Indianapolis, a life-long am-

Giuseppe Farina

bition, but failed to qualify in 1956 or 1957 when he appeared with cars entered by American Ferrari concessionaire Luigi Chinetti.

Giuseppe Farina was not a great driver by the standards set by Nuvolari, Fangio, Moss and Clark, but he was a very fast driver of great courage and determination. He was too audacious and too temperamental perhaps for his own good, sometimes too obstinate when the odds were weighted heavily against him, sometimes throwing in the towel before the race was lost. Farina died on 30th June 1966 when he lost control of his Lotus-Cortina on a slippery road near Chambery in France while driving to the French Grand Prix. His car went off the road and demolished two telegraph poles, and Nino was killed outright.

2

The Greatest Argentinian
JUAN MANUEL FANGIO
1951, 1954-7

OF THE SCHOOL of Argentinian drivers, sponsored by their government, who invaded the European circuits in the early fifties, the slow-speaking, completely relaxed Fangio was their finest graduate. With five World Championships to his credit and an almost complete domination of Grand Prix racing for four successive seasons, Juan Manuel Fangio set a motor racing record that remains unmatched. His total of World Championship race victories has now been topped by Jim Clark with his Lotus cars and by Jackie Stewart, but when Fangio was racing there were far fewer rounds in the Championship and many more non-Championship Formula One races in which he scored more than his fair share of victories.

South American interest in motor racing has always been strong and particularly so in the Argentine where it was actively promoted and sponsored by dictator Juan Peron. The dictator encouraged a winter series of races, those at Buenos Aires being named after him and his wife. He was responsible for the magnificent Buenos Aires Autodrome opened in 1952 and the Argentine Automobile Club sponsored a team of drivers to Europe in 1949–50. When Juan Fangio was chosen as a member of that team he had already proved himself in South American cross-country Grands Prix and in local Formule Libre races against European opposition.

Fangio's own devotion to motor racing and the close relationships which he built up so quickly with the Italian teams for which he raced in later years is more easily understood when one remembers that he was a first generation Italian emigré; his father was born in Italy, a country where motor racing is a national and passionately supported pastime, and emigrated with his parents to Argentina at the age of seven. Loreto Fangio settled at Balcarce, some 220 miles from Buenos Aires, became a house painter, married Erminia. Juan Manuel, the fourth of six children, was born on 24th June 1911. The Fangio family income was enough to feed the eight mouths and very little else and Juan Manuel's dreams of becoming a racing driver had every prospect of remaining unfulfilled.

Juan Manuel gained his early mechanical experience working at a local garage and in due course became a fully experienced mechanic of no small ability. His career in the motor trade was interrupted at the age of twenty-one by military service, but when he returned to Balcarce, he started his own small motor repair business in partnership with a friend. His share of the partnership capital came partly from his own savings and partly from a small loan from his father. Now that he was working on his own in a business that was proving successful, Fangio was able to turn his thoughts to racing. At this time most motor racing in South America took the form of long-distance cross-country road races for highly modified production cars, the faster examples usually sponsored by the concessionaires for the make. He could see that it was within his financial means and the resources of his own workshop to modify a car that he could race, but whether he would ever have a car that would be competitive—and it would cost much more to build—seemed doubtful.

For his first race Fangio borrowed a car, but much to its owner's chagrin it suffered a broken crankshaft, and he had to repair this before he could start work on his own car. Fangio's first competition car was a Model A Ford but in his early racing days he achieved no success and it was not until 1939 when he was at the wheel of an elderly, but highly modified Chevrolet that his fortunes began to change. In the so-called Extraordinary Grand Prix, a race in which he received some sponsorship from the Chevrolet agent in Cordoba, he had been well up with the leaders in the opening stages but then he crashed and overturned his car; however, with the help of friends the car was repaired and Fangio carried on to finish fifth overall and highest-placed Chevrolet driver. Later in the year he finished third in the Argentine Thousand Miles race. A year later Fangio scored a magnificent victory with another Chevrolet in the thirteen-stage International Grand Prix of the North, defeating many better known rivals. Juan won another six Argentinian cross-country races during 1941–2, but because of the war racing was then abandoned in Argentina. Now he was forced to settle down to a quiet life in Balcarce with Andreina, the woman with whom he lived for almost twenty years before they parted in 1960. Fangio devoted his efforts to his garage business and did not race again until 1947 when, still at the wheel of a Chevrolet, he scored another three victories.

So far all Fangio's racing efforts had been entirely self-financed, but for the 1948 series of South American Formule Libre races the Argentine Automobile Club bought two 4CL Maseratis for local heroes to drive against the European opposition and the men chosen were Fangio and the man against whom he had raced so many times, Oscar Galvez. Fangio had no previous experience of circuit racing, but he used the races against the Europeans to good advantage, closely studying their styles and technique. Although he was out of luck, his best performance being a fourth place in the Mar del Plata Grand Prix, the experience gained was of inestimable value. During the year the Automobile Club paid for Fangio to travel to Europe and he drove a Simca-Gordini in Coupe des Petites Cylindrées at Reims, but retired with engine trouble.

Then it was back to the Argentine again to drive his Chevrolet in another cross-country race, the 6,000-mile Grand Prix of South America over a course running from Buenos Aires to Caracas in Venezuela, right to the north of the great subcontinent. Near Trujillo in Peru Fangio 'misread' the road at a particularly difficult point and crashed; travelling with him as second driver was his close friend Daniel Urrutia who suffered fatal injuries. When he learned of his death, Fangio was completely broken, vowing never to race again and blaming himself entirely for the accident. Later, when objective reasoning replaced the passion of grief he realised that he was too dedicated to give up racing. He had made a terrible mistake that had cost his friend's life, but mistakes were inevitable in motor racing, and the best means of reducing the risk of an accident was always to be prepared for the unexpected, an attitude of mind belied by his calm appearance, but one which he put to good advantage in many European races.

Once again, in February 1949, Fangio drove a Maserati against the European opposition in his home country and scored a victory in the Mar del Plata Grand Prix. Then instead of whiling away the Argentine winter and thinking of the racing ahead in the spring, Fangio embarked on a full European season with Maseratis entered by the Scuderia Argentina. In memory of the great Achille Varzi, the Italian driver who had been killed at the wheel of an Alfa Romeo in practice for the 1948 Swiss Grand Prix and at the invitation of Varzi's father, the team's cars were entered under the name of Squadra Achille Varzi. The team based itself at Varzi's house and workshops at Galliate and Guido Bignami, Varzi's former assistant, acted as team manager. When Fangio appeared at European circuits, he impressed everyone immediately with his precise, relaxed style, his apparent impeturbability no matter what went wrong and his very considerable speed—his lap time with his 4CLT 'San Remo' Maserati matched those of the best European drivers with the same model.

Although the Argentine team returned home before the end of the 1949 European season, Fangio enjoyed an impressive run of successes. His first race was the San Remo Grand Prix, held on the Ospedaletti circuit on the Adriatic coast of Italy, and he drove immaculately, taking the lead early in both heats and staying in front until the chequered flag. The news might not yet have percolated to England, but in Italy the Argentinian was already regarded as a hero. Next came the Pau Grand Prix, held over a tight little street circuit in the shadow of the snow-clad Pyrenees. This was a true driver's circuit with difficult cambers and corners, cobbles and lamp-posts as would be met in any French provincial town. It was a long, tiring race, lasting over three-and-a-half hours, which demanded stamina as well as skill. Fangio scored another fine victory from other Maseratis driven by the Swiss Baron Emmanuel de Graffenried and team-mate Benedicto Campos. In the heat of the moment, heady with success, Fangio vowed that he would not be satisfied until he won a National European Grand Prix. It was not idle talk and such a victory was only thirteen months away.

Yet another victory followed at Perpignan and he won the Marseilles Grand Prix with one of Amedée Gordini's Simca cars. He retired at Rome and Spa, but for the Formula Two Autodrome Grand Prix at Monza the Argentine Club provided Fangio with a brand-new V-12 Ferrari. Fangio drove a fast, consistent race and, despite the presence of works Maranello cars driven by Ascari and Villoresi, scored his fifth victory in his European tour. Next on the calendar was the Albi Grand Prix, held on a very fast, tree-lined circuit. The race was run in blazing sunshine and oppressive heat which affected a number of drivers, but not Fangio who seemed to revel in racing when the weather was at its hottest. In the early part of the race Farina with another Maserati chased Fangio hard, but when the Italian stopped to refuel, his engine refused to fire again on the starting handle (in this race push-starts were forbidden) and so the Argentinian was unchallenged. He went on to score his sixth European victory from Siamese driver Prince Birabongse.

Fangio's last race, before returning to Argentina, was the Formula Two Coupe des Petites Cylindrées at Reims (the race in which he had retired in 1948). Again he was eliminated, this time with a broken accelerator on his Ferrari. When he returned to Buenos Aires, Fangio was given a hero's welcome. Greeted by a vast mob of supporters at the City airport he was then rushed to the Casada Rosada for an audience with Dictator Peron. Celebratory banquets and receptions followed and it was days before Fangio could escape home to Balcarce.

After reappearing at the wheel of his Chevrolet in the Grand Prix of the Republic in which he took second place, once again in the Argentine summer of 1949–50 Fangio met up with the European drivers escaping from the Continental winter. He finished second in the Eva Peron Cup race in December 1949 but otherwise success eluded him. But the disappointments he suffered in the Argentine races—especially in the Mar del Plata Grand Prix in which Villoresi cut across the front of his Ferrari on one of the corners, causing both cars to crash—were soon forgotten when Fangio received an invitation to go to Milan for talks with the Alfa Romeo directors. After a year's absence from the circuits, the Alfa Romeo team was returning to racing with its elderly, but now even more powerful 158 cars.

That year's Alfa team, the three 'F's, was one of the strongest ever to race together. The trio, Farina, Fangio and veteran Italian Luigi Fagioli, backed up at many races by Alfa chief tester Consalvo Sanesi, were formidable opponents indeed. Fangio was a driver with remarkable self-discipline and he was an ideal recruit for the Alfa Romeo team which was unmatched at the time for the high standards of its race preparation work, the efficiency of its race management and its effective control of its drivers from the pits.

Fangio's first race for Alfa Romeo was in the middle of April, but by then he had already driven in two European races, at Marseille where he finished third with a Ferrari and Pau which he won with a Maserati for the second year in succession. The Argentinian drove his first race for the Milan team at San Remo where he was the only Alfa driver entered. On a rain-soaked circuit he carefully reigned back the 350 bhp of his powerful but heavy car that was such a tremendous handful in these conditions, accelerating and braking sensibly, lapping at a steady pace, while Ascari drove flat-out at the wheel of his Ferrari with apparent disregard for the conditions until he spun off (the Commendator must have badly wanted to win that day). The Argentinian, very much on trial in this race, went on to score a good victory.

The following month Alfa Romeo ran in two important races. At Silverstone the team competed in the British Grand Prix, the first round in the newly inaugurated Drivers' World Championship. Alfa Romeos took the first three places, but Fangio, his car distinguished by a yellow radiator cowl, was out of luck and retired eight laps from the finish because of a broken connecting rod. Out of luck is the correct expression and there can be no imputation that the Argentinian's car was in any way prepared to a lower standard than those of his team-mates. Fangio has written of the British Grand Prix: 'For me this race was a source of great bitterness. Mechanical trouble, which I still do not understand, forced me to retire.' Later Fangio was to make a similar insinuation,

Juan Manuel Fangio

but in more direct terms, about the preparation of Ferraris he drove in 1956. It is an insinuation that Enzo Ferrari goes to considerable pains to refute in his memoirs. It seemed that once in a while Fangio would become almost obsessional about some mechanical failure on his car or mistake made by another driver which had no real significance. Ferrari goes even further and suggests that Fangio, whom he quite obviously disliked, had a persecution complex.

A week later was the first post-war Monaco Grand Prix, the second round in the Championship. The use of intelligence in the heat of the moment brought Fangio a fine victory, the sort of victory that illustrates one aspect of a true champion's character and helps to distinguish him from lesser drivers. Fangio made a brilliant start and led away from the rest of the field, but, behind him, there was a repeat of the pile-up that had occurred on the first lap of the 1936 race. At Tobacconist's corner by the harbour Farina, in third place behind Villoresi, spun on water that had broken over the sea-wall. The Dottore hit the wall, bounced backwards across the road and his Alfa was run into by Gonzalez. Other cars became involved in the incident, but until he emerged from the tunnel and saw a yellow danger flag being waved by a marshall, Fangio had no reason to suspect that any accident had happened. On seeing the flag he had a mental picture of the 1936 accident and immediately braked hard. As he reached the mêlée, a marshall directed him round the wrong side of the tangled cars so that his Alfa was blocked in. With his powerful, beefy arms Fangio heaved on the back wheels of his Alfa, slowly reversing the car and then accelerating round the stationary cars and on with the race. For the remaining ninety-eight laps of the 1.95-circuit he was completely unchallenged and he won from Ascari's Ferrari.

Fangio drove to the same consistently high standards during the remainder of the season—there were no 'off' days for him. He scored victories for Alfa Romeo in the Belgian and French rounds of the Championship, won non-Championship races at Geneva and Pescara and finished second at Bari and in the *Daily Express* Trophy race at Silverstone. He retired in the Swiss and Italian Grands Prix, both of which were won by Farina and took second place in the Championship with twenty-seven points to the thirty gained by his team-mate.

Fangio's first contact with Mercedes, for whom he was to drive for two brilliantly successful seasons in 1954-5, came in Argentina in 1951. He was invited to drive one of the 1939 3-litre supercharged cars that had been brought out of retirement to give the Stuttgart staff some experience under actual racing conditions before tackling their first post-war season the following year. Unfortunately the very complex German cars were plagued by carburation problems and were no match for the Ferrari driven by another Argentinian, Froilan Gonzalez. Fangio finished a poor third in one of the Peron Cup races and retired in the other.

The Argentinian remained with the Alfa Romeo team in 1951 and won the World Championship by a narrow margin. Throughout the year the Alfas were hard pressed by the new unsupercharged Ferraris and such was the pressure that at a couple of races even Fangio began to do some very un-Fangio-like things. He started the season well with a fine victory in the Swiss Grand Prix at Bremgarten. In the Belgian race there occurred an incident which at the time Fangio thought could well affect his chances in the World Championship.

It was caused by sheer bad luck, but the incident illustrated Fangio's remarkable patience and control. When he made a routine stop for a wheel-change, one of the rear wheels could not be removed because a spoke-head had jammed behind the hub splines. Eventually team manager Battista Guidotti decided to take the old tire off the rim; a new one was fitted and blown up. The stop lasted nearly fifteen minutes and while his chances of victory completely evaporated, Fangio watched with a calm, inscrutable expression, occasionally wiping his goggles or the Alfa's aeroscreen. If the driver had been Italian, he would almost certainly have been talking ceaselessly, urging the mechanics on and jumping up and down in agitation! In later years Fangio admitted that however unruffled an exterior he retained on such occasions, inside he was seething and that it was only with the greatest difficulty that he maintained a facade of apparent calm. Fangio rejoined the race to set fastest lap and finish ninth.

The Argentinian scored another victory in the French Grand Prix, but he had to share his championship points with Luigi Fagioli whose car he had taken over. At Reims the Alfas had been very nearly beaten and at the next race at Silverstone the Maranello cars finally tipped the scales and defeated their Milanese rivals. Gonzalez led initially with his Ferrari, but then Fangio forged ahead, endeavouring to gain enough time to compensate for the two fuelling stops he needed to the Ferrari's one. But the Ferrari driver was not easily beaten and he closed up again on Fangio who, losing control slightly under pressure, clipped the straw bales and lost enough time to allow Gonzalez to draw even closer. When Gonzalez swept by into the lead, the race was lost and all Fangio's valiant efforts, with arms see-sawing at the wheel, some beautiful four-wheel drifts and some not so elegant or efficient tail-sliding, were to no avail. At the end of this epic and significant race Fangio was still in second place, soundly beaten by his compatriot.

By the German race at the Nürburgring, it seemed that the aura of efficiency surrounding Alfa Romeo was beginning to crack under the strain. After practice the team was reduced to a state of near-panic; the mechanics frantically repairing damage to Fangio's car after an accident and carrying out a last-minute instruction to change all the axle ratios, while the technicians were almost wringing their hands in despair because the Alfa drivers had been unable to match

Ferrari practice times. Only Fangio seemed aloof from the confusion and unaffected by the nervous excitement that gripped the Italian team as their cars lay spread out like a collection of spare parts. Fangio realised that his chances of defeating the Ferraris were slight, but he had planned a race that would bring him more points to add to his Championship score and outright victory should the fastest Ferraris break; right from the start he drove at a fast, regular pace, well within his car's rev limits, leading for a while, but falling back to second place after his second refuelling stop. Fangio finished second to Ascari's Ferrari, set fastest lap and added seven points to his Championship score—the other three Alfas all retired.

A morale-boosting victory for Fangio and his Alfa followed at the minor Bari Grand Prix and both he and Farina appeared at Monza with new and even faster versions of the Alfetta. On this high-speed course, so well suited to Alfa Romeo engine characteristics, the Milan team started firm favourites despite their two earlier defeats. Fangio retired with mechanical trouble, Ascari scored Ferrari's third successive World Championship victory and with one race to go the Argentinian still headed the Championship table with twenty-eight points to the twenty-five scored by Ascari. The last race was the Spanish Grand Prix at Barcelona, the Ferraris were plagued by tire troubles and as a result of Maranello misfortunes, Fangio scored a fine victory to clinch the World Championship.

As reigning Champion Fangio was at the peak of his career, but at the start of 1952 he was in a dilemma. In 1951 the Alfa Romeo 158, whose racing career dated back to 1938, had finally bitten the dust and if the Milan company was to carry on racing a new design was urgently needed. Government aid to Alfa was refused and the company withdrew from Grand Prix racing. As a direct result of Alfa's decision all 1952 Championship Grand Prix races were to be held to 2000 cc Formula Two rules and Fangio had to find a suitable

Formula Two car to drive during the coming season. Teammate Farina had joined Ferrari where, in theory at least, all the drivers were of equal status. For Fangio this would not have been good enough. Rightly or wrongly, and in my view wrongly, Fangio felt that at times there had been a conflict of interests within the Alfa Romeo team and that because of Farina's Italian nationality he had on occasions been given preferential treatment. Fangio wanted to be number one driver without any ifs or buts and it was on this basis that he eventually signed up to lead the Maserati team. Maserati were entering Formula Two with the new A6GCM 6-cylinder car, but this was not ready at the beginning of the season.

Early in 1952 Fangio enjoyed a clean sweep in the South American races with his 2-litre supercharged Ferrari, winning all six races he entered. On returning to Europe he handled one of the very fast, but very unreliable BRMV-16 cars at the invitation of Raymond Mays. His drives with the British cars were completely fruitless and led indirectly to the accident that completely wrecked Fangio's 1952 season. While he was in Belfast for the third of his races with BRM, the Ulster Trophy on the Dundrod circuit, he received a telegram from Maserati asking him to be at Monza the day after the Irish race to drive the new Formula Two car in the Autodrome Grand Prix. As soon as he had retired his BRM in the Ulster Trophy, he flew to Paris where he was hoping to catch a connection to Milan.

At Le Bourget Fangio was curtly informed that all flights to Italy were cancelled because of bad weather; a glance at the railway timetable was enough to reveal that if he went by train, he would arrive after the race was over. The only possibility was to drive the 500 miles. He borrowed a Renault from French driver Louis Rosier, but as he set off, he felt that sinking feeling that we all experience when we embark on something that is more than we can really cope with. An exhausted Fangio arrived at Monza an hour before the race started, far too tired to compete and looking grey and ashen. He was allowed to waive practice and started from the back of the grid, picking up places on the first lap; on the second lap he made a terrible error of judgment that would never have happened had he been fresh. He misjudged a corner completely, struck the curb and was hurled out of the car. The World Champion lay unconscious on the grass verge, neck broken, while other competitors passed only a couple of feet away. Fangio's recovery from that accident was slow and painful and he did not drive again until the 1953 season.

Fangio stayed with the Maserati team for 1953 and his first race following his accident was in the Argentine Grand Prix at the beginning of the year. The latest and improved Maseratis were not yet ready and with the old 1952 car he chased the Ferraris hard, showing that his accident had cost him nothing of his old skill and sparkle. He was in second place when his engine blew up. His first outing in Europe was in the Mille Miglia, the 1,000-mile road race round Italy in which he handled one of the 'Disco Volante' Alfa Romeos that the Milan company had been developing since they gave up Grand Prix racing. Fangio drove a fine race, holding back in the early stages, and moving up into the lead after the retirement of his team-mates Sanesi and Kling. By Florence, with four-fifths of the race over, Fangio was all set for victory. Another dramatic incident in Fangio's career came over the next section of the course at the mountainous and tortuous Futa Pass. As he hurled his car through the tight bends, he suddenly discovered to his horror that only one front wheel was responding to the steering (the cause was drag-link failure). A lesser driver would have called it a day there and then, for the consequences should the steering fail on the other wheel were unthinkable.

The Argentinian decided to press on, however, obliged to crawl through some corners and before the end of the race he was passed on time by privateer Giannino Marzotto at the wheel of a Ferrari. A week later Fangio drove one of Amédée Gordini's lightweight Formula Two cars into third place at Bordeaux. He continued to race works Alfas during 1953, but the cars were out of luck and his sole success was a win in the minor Supercortemaggiore Grand Prix in September.

His year had started in earnest, however, at Naples in May where he drove the latest Maserati for the first time and, despite a stop for a wheel-change, finished second to Farina's works Ferrari. The remainder of the season developed into a close duel between the two Italian marques which culminated in a victory for Fangio in the last round of the Championship at Monza. Fangio retired in the Dutch race, retired in the Belgian race, but took over another team car and crashed in the last lap, and in the French Grand Prix was beaten into second place by a matter of feet after a race-long battle. Other second places followed for Fangio at Silverstone and the Nürburgring. In the Swiss race at Bremgarten he handed his crippled car over to team-mate Felice Bonetto, took over Bonetto's car and drove it so hard in his chase back through the field that the engine expired in a bank of smoke thick enough to cause other drivers to reduce speed. When he came into the pits particles of aluminium from the engine were all over the splash-guard. In the final round of the Championship at Monza, the Argentinian battled wheel to wheel for the whole 313 miles with the Ferraris of Ascari and Farina; at the last corner of the last lap Ascari spun, Farina took to the grass to avoid his teammate and the wily Fangio sneaked by on the inside to score his only Championship race victory of the season. Ascari was World Champion for the second year in succession, but Fangio took second place with 28 points to Ascari's 34½.

For 1954 Fangio was invited to lead the Mercedes team which was re-entering Grand Prix racing for the first time since pre-war days. The Stuttgart team spent more money on their racing programme than any other; the new W196 cars represented the then ultimate in automobile engineering and were faster in a straight line than any of their rivals. And Mercedes' attention to detail in both pre-race preparation and race management was likewise superior to that of other teams. As events during 1954 were to prove, the Achilles' heel of the Mercedes was its road-holding, but by the end of the year even this problem had been resolved.

The Mercedes was not ready to race at the beginning of the season and in the Argentine and Belgian races Fangio drove Maseratis and won both events. The new streamlined German car made its debut in the French Grand Prix held on the very fast Reims circuit and Fangio, with team-mate Karl Kling close behind, ran away from the opposition, setting the pattern for what was to be two seasons of almost complete domination of Grand Prix racing. On the difficult Silverstone circuit the weaknesses of Mercedes' roadholding revealed itself and the streamlined bodywork which concealed the front wheels, made it difficult to place the car for corners, many of which were marked only by oil drums. Fangio had a thoroughly miserable race, unable to match the speed of the Ferraris of Gonzalez and Hawthorn and the Maserati driven by Stirling Moss. He fell further and further back; the bodywork of the Mercedes was battered and split by contact with oil drums, the gears were jumping out of engagement, the brakes were failing and oil was leaking. But Fangio pressed on—a Farina would have retired—determined to get the car to the finish as a matter of honour and at the end of this ninety-lap ordeal he was rewarded with fourth place.

By the German Grand Prix the Mercedes team had ready a new unstreamlined version of the W196, and both at this circuit and the Bremgarten course the Argentinian scored comparatively effortless victories. In the Italian race Fangio again drove a streamlined car to victory, but it was another hard race for him. Even on this high-speed circuit the cornering of the W196 was far from right and Fangio was taking to the grass on the outsides of the bends in a perilous manner; he had to battle with the Ferraris of Ascari and Gonzalez, he was bettered by the Maserati of Stirling Moss until the Englishman's car ran into mechanical trouble and he finished the race oil-soaked and in a state of near-exhaustion. The last race of the season at Barcelona proved a repetition of Silverstone.

Fangio played a waiting game, leaving his attack until later in the race when the sprinters who had led away from the start had tired. It was to no avail, for the Mercedes was overheating as a result of waste paper sucked into its air intake. Both water and oil overheated and as the race neared its end, the exhaust note of the German car became flatter and flatter until it was little more than a painful groan. The Argentinian crossed the line in third place, the cockpit of his car almost awash with oil, but with six Grand Prix victories to his credit he had again won the World Championship after an interval of two years.

By the Argentine Grand Priz in January 1955, the Mercedes engineers had resolved all the problems that had troubled the cars the previous year: the roadholding was much improved, the engines were more reliable and the oil leaks that had caused Fangio so much discomfort were completely cured. At only one race in 1955 did the Mercedes team fail, at Monaco, the first race of the European season, where the cars of both Fangio and Moss retired with engine trouble. Fangio enjoyed a clean sweep of victories at Buenos Aires in both the Argentine Grand Prix and the Buenos Aires City Grand Prix, at Zandvoort and Spa. He finished second to Moss at Aintree and, in a season much curtailed after the Le Mans disaster, won the final race at Monza, the only event in 1955 at which the streamlined cars were used. With a Championship score of forty points, Fangio took the drivers' crown for the second year in succession.

When Mercedes withdrew from racing at the end of 1955, Fangio for the first and only time in his career, signed to drive for Ferrari. It was not a happy year for the Argentinian, who felt that his cars were not always as well prepared as they should have been, and he left the team again at the end of the year. Although 1956 gave Fangio his fourth World Championship, with a little more luck and a little more speed Stirling Moss at the wheel of his Maserati would have beaten him. At the beginning of the year Fangio broke his own car and took over team-mate Luigi Musso's to win the Argentine Grand Prix and he scored clear victories in both the Buenos Aires City Grand Prix and at Siracusa, but three months elapsed before he scored another win.

At Monaco his driving fell far short of the expected Fangio standards; he spun his ill-handling Lancia-Ferrari early in the race and in his efforts to rejoin the contest caused both team-mate Musso and Vanwall driver Harry Schell to go off the track. As he hurled the Maranello car round Monaco in vain pursuit of Moss's Maserati, constant contact with barrier and curbs reduced it to a shattered wreck and he finally took over Peter Collins's car to finish second. His performance at Monaco was totally out of character and can only be attributed to the frustrations of driving a car he disliked for a team for which he had little affection.

He retired at Spa with transmission trouble and finished fourth at Reims after a pit stop. As Silverstone in the British race he won only after the Maseratis of both Stirling Moss and Roy Salvadori had retired with mechanical trouble, but in the German race he displayed much of the old Fangio style to soundly trounce the Maserati opposition. At the last Championship race of the season at Monza the Championship still hung in the balance. The Lancia-Ferraris were plagued by tire trouble and steering arm failures. It was steering trouble that caused Fangio's retirement and he owed his victory in the Championship to British driver Peter Collins. When Collins brought his second-place car in for a routine tire check, he agreed to hand it over to Fangio, knowing that it would tip the scales between Championship success and failure, with the comment: 'I've got plenty of opportunity in the future.' With the three points gained from a shared second place Fangio beat Moss with thirty points to twenty-seven.

It was with a great sense of relief that Fangio returned to Maserati for 1957 after an interval of three years. His contract with the Modena company was on a race to race basis and he limited his Formula One appearance to Championship races plus the Buenos Aires, Reims and Moroccan Grands Prix. In South America Fangio scored runaway victories in both the Argentine and Buenos Aires City Grands Prix. On his return to Europe his first race was at Monaco and he was given victory on a plate when race-leader Moss crashed on the fourth lap and eliminated himself and the Lancia-Ferraris of both Hawthorn and Collins.

Moss and the Vanwall were Fangio's greatest threat in 1957, but at the next round in the Championship at Rouen (there was no Belgian or Dutch race that year) Moss was out of the Vanwall team because of sinus trouble. Unchallenged for victory, Fangio gave a brilliant virtuoso display of driving over this difficult course which incorporated 150 mph bends, 100 to 120 mph downhill swoops requiring tremendous confidence to take them at optimum speed, and tight hairpins. It was the first time that Fangio had driven at the circuit, but his driving, much of it in full-throttle four-heel-drifts, outshone the rest of the entry. 'His cornering under full power in long controlled slides,' wrote Denis Jenkinson, 'being a poem of mechanical artistry. He continually threw the car into deliberate slides on his approach to the fast open bends and drove round on full power, judging the slide to a nicety so that it finished a few inches from the curb.' He won the race by fifty seconds from Luigi Musso's Lancia-Ferrari.

At Reims, when his brakes locked up in the closing stages of the race, he aimed his car at what looked like innocent straw bales but they concealed an earth bank which wrecked the Maserati's front suspension. He retired with engine trouble in the British race, but came back in true Fangio style at the German Grand Prix. At this race the Maseratis started with half-full tanks and when they came into refuel at half-distance, the rear wheels would be changed if necessary. The idea was that without full tanks, which would have adversely affected the handling, the cars could be driven hard from start to chequered flag. Although this sort of strategy sounds fine in theory, it rarely works in practice and experience has shown that a driver usually cannot build up a big enough lead to make a pit stop without losing it. And it is certain that but for Fangio's brilliance the plan would have mis-fired in 1957. Although the Lancia-Ferraris of Hawthorn and Collins led initially, Fangi soon went ahead. He consistently lowered the lap record and when he stopped at the pits at the end of lap twelve he had a lead of twenty-eight seconds. Refuelling the car and changing the rear wheels took fifty-two seconds and with slowing off for the stop and restarting Fangio lost around another twenty-five seconds.

It seemed that his chances of catching Hawthorn and Collins were very slim. During the first three laps after his pit stop, Fangio made no impression on the leaders and this had the affect of lulling the Ferrari pit into a state of false security. Then he began to speed up, progressively lowering the lap record still further and by the time the Ferrari pit had been able to warn their drivers of what was happening Fangio was right on their tails. Fangio swept past the Ferrari drivers and although Hawthorn chased the Maserati all the way to the chequered flag, he was unable to get to grips with the Argentinian. The Vanwalls were out of the picture at the Nürburgring because of roadholding problems, but in the remaining two Championship rounds at Pescara and Monza, the British cars came out on top and Fangio had to settle for second place at both races. He took his fifth World Championship with forty points to the twenty-five of Stirling Moss.

Maserati withdrew from racing at the end of the 1957 season and Fangio was beginning to think that it was time that he hung up his crash helmet. His racing manager, Marcello Giambertone, made arrangements for him to drive a Maserati in the 1958 Argentine races, but he failed to appear at the beginning of the European season. It seemed that Fangio had retired, but he made two further appearances to round off his career. The Argentinian was hoping to drive the Dean Van Lines Special, a true Indianapolis car, in the Monza 500 Miles race—a race that was intended to bring together on one banked course the fastest European and Indianapolis machinery. The car failed to start in the first two heats because of mechanical trouble and retired in the third after only a single lap. A week later he drove the latest lightweight Maserati in the French Grand Prix, finishing fourth after a pit stop. Fangio never raced again.

Juan Manuel Fangio was one of the greatest drivers ever to race. He combined speed, precision and a mastery of cornering technique with powers of tremendous endurance and a will to carry on to the finish regardless of the odds. He won four World Championships at an age when most drivers have retired, and when he won his fifth Championship in 1957 at forty-six his powers as a driver were in no way diminished. Fangio was a motor racing phenomenon, a member of that select group of true Champions whose greatness has never been excelled.

After his retirement, Fangio returned home to the Argentine where he runs a successful motor business. He stayed fully involved in motor racing, making frequent visits to European circuits and helping to organise the present successful South American series of races. In his own racing days scant attention was paid to safety precautions, but Fangio has succeeded in keeping apace with the times and has co-operated fully in the installation of safety requirements at the Buenos Aires Autodrome. And passengers who have been lucky enough to ride with him on his visits to Europe consider that his road driving still displays a flair and brilliance that is almost unique.

3
Champion Son of a Champion
ALBERTO ASCARI
1952-3

No OTHER WORLD Champion has had such a great reputation to live up to, no other has followed so closely in his father's tragic footsteps. Born at Milan on 13th July 1918, young Alberto celebrated his seventh birthday less than a fortnight before his father's death in a motor racing crash. There was no World Championship when Antonio Ascari was racing, but he was certainly in the top echelon of drivers racing at the time. The short, stout Ascari had been driving Alfa Romeo cars since 1920; when he joined the team, he was its least experienced member, but he rapidly became one of its most famous and most successful drivers. He enjoyed close friendships with other members of the team, especially racing manager Enzo Ferrari and fellow-driver Giuseppe Campari, both of whom nursed ambitions to be opera singers—when they sang, Antonio accompanied them on his guitar.

In 1924 Alfa Romeo raced the brilliant new straight-eight P2 2-litre supercharged model designed by Vittorio Jano, a car which incorporated many features innovated at Fiat where Jano had previously worked. The P2 was sleek, purposeful and fast, and on its debut in the Circuit of Cremona with Ascari at the wheel it covered the long ten kilometre straight at close to 125 mph. Ascari won that race, retired while leading the European Grand Prix at Lyon shortly afterwards and rounded off the season with a magnificent victory in the Italian Grand Prix at Monza. The following June Ascari won the European Grand Prix at Spa-Francorchamps in Belgium. The team's next race was the French Grand Prix held on the new track at Montlhéry, fifteen miles from Paris, which had been opened in October 1924. The Grand Prix was to be a strenuous marathon, over eighty laps of a difficult 7.8-mile circuit incorporating part of the banked track and making a total length of 621 miles—longer than any other single-day Grand Prix in the history of racing to that time.

Despite the very considerable length of the race, all the drivers intended to complete it single-handed and 1925 was the first year in which riding mechanics were not carried. Ascari took the lead at the rolling start and drew further and further away from the opposition and his team-mates. Drizzle had begun to dampen the circuit and although he had a comfortable lead of more than two minutes, Ascari did not preceptibly slacken his pace. Then disaster struck. Perhaps because of a momentary loss of concentration, Ascari entered the long left-hand bend some five kilometres from the start/finish line at much too high a speed for the conditions. The Alfa went into a vicious slide and Antonio, almost notorious for the gay abandon with which he used to slide his cars through the corners, could not on this occasion regain control. Despite the driver's efforts, the P2 went off the edge of the road, careered along, demolishing 130 yards of fencing, and when the wheels sank into soft earth, the car overturned into a ditch. Ascari was gravely injured and died in a military ambulance that was taking him to a hospital in Paris.

Alberto was old enough to understand how his father had died but too young to appreciate the motivation that had driven him to greatness and lured him to his death. No

Alberto Ascari

father has been more respected by his son and Alberto's only desire was to emulate his father's greatness. Family pressures not to pursue a motor racing career were great, but the lure of speed and the desire to succeed were greater. The young Ascari began his racing career in a modest enough style, riding motor cycles, and at the age of eighteen he was a member of the works Bianchi team. From two wheels he graduated to four, a pattern of development more commonly followed by Continental drivers than British, and raced a Tipo 6CM Maserati, the 6-cylinder Voiturette introduced in 1936 and by 1939 superseded by the Maserati brothers' new 16-valve 4-cylinder cars.

A great help and encouragement to Ascari throughout his racing career was his close friend Luigi Villoresi. A fellow-citizen of Milan, Villoresi, born in 1908, raced works Maserati cars, while his brother Emilio drove the latest Tipo 158 Alfa Romeo 'Alfetta' Voiturettes. Emilio was killed while testing an improved version of the Alfetta at Monza in July 1939 and although this did not deter Luigi from racing he would never drive for Alfa Romeo. Luigi Villoresi recognised that Alberto Ascari had great potential talent, a natural skill combined with restraint and self-discipline. For Ascari was placid and gentle, largely lacking in that fiery and unpredictable temperament that characterised the driving of so many Italians. The generous-natured Villoresi advised and coached the younger man. The plump, genial Ascari listened and learned, and so Villoresi played a vital role in the development of Ascari as a driver.

Alberto Ascari's first real break in the motor racing world came in 1940 when Enzo Ferrari offered him a drive in his new competition car. In 1938 Ferrari had parted company with Alfa Romeo on whose behalf he had entered the works cars in the name of his own team, Scuderia Ferrari, and because his severance agreement with the Milan company prevented him from reconstituting Scuderia Ferrari for a period of four years, he was unable to use his own name for the first cars he built. These were 1500 cc sports cars entered in the 1940 Brescia Grand Prix as being the products of Auto-Avio Costruzioni, a small firm which Ferrari had founded in Modena. The Brescia Grand Prix was a substitute for the Mille Miglia, normally held as a long-distance road race, and was run over nine laps of a 103-mile closed circuit. On the first lap young Ascari, partnered by Minozzi, led the 1500 cc class, but then retired because of a broken valve spring. The Brescia race was run on 28th April and on 10th June, Benito Mussolini, knowing that France was defeated and suing for peace, in the words of William Shirer: 'hopped into the war . . . to try to get in on the spoils.' So Ascari's career was interrupted by a war that, like so many of his countrymen, he was strongly opposed to. He did not race again until he was twenty-eight.

It was not until 1947 that Ascari's driving achieved prominence. Italy's motor industry had not been as badly ravaged as most of Europe's and most of the racing cars and equipment had survived the hostilities unscathed. The Alfettas had been carefully stored and Alfa Romeo re-entered racing in 1946, as did Maserati whose cars were raced for them by a private team known as Scuderia Milano. A certain Count Dusio had conceived grandiose plans for manufacturing on a large scale small, light racing cars powered by Fiat 1100 cc-based engines and with a top speed of around 110 mph which were given the name of Cisitalia. Early in 1947 fifteen Cisitalias were shipped from Italy to the Middle East for a series of races to be run on a commercial basis. It was hoped they would bring in a substantial return in profits for the sponsors. The cars would then carry on for a world tour. A number of leading Italian drivers competed in the first race held in March on Gezireh Island, Cairo and in the final Ascari drove a fine race to finish second to Franco Cortese. The Cairo race proved a financial disaster and the remaining races planned to take place at Heliopolis and Alexandria were cancelled.

In early post-war days the Maserati factory did not field a works team as such, but entrusted their cars to private teams. From 1947 onwards the team responsible for the representation of the Modena concern was the Scuderia Ambrosiana and when Luigi Villoresi received an invitation to lead the team, he suggested that Alberto Ascari should be second-string driver. This was the biggest opportunity offered to the up-and-coming Italian so far in his career and he accepted with alacrity. The 4-cylinder 4CL Maserati being raced at this time were virtually unchanged from pre-war days, but they were no real match for another pre-war design, the Alfa Romeo 158. Fortunately for Maserati, the Alfas ran in only four races in 1947 (and won them all) and this gave the Ambrosiana drivers plenty of scope for success. Driving in the same team as Villoresi and at the wheel of an almost identical car immeasurably increased the value of the lessons learned by the younger man. For the first time Ascari was driving for a team that was at the forefront of racing and he so rapidly improved in judgment, confidence and speed that his lap times at many circuits were soon faster than Villoresi's.

During the 1947 season Ascari failed to win a single Formula One race; he suffered rather more than his fair share of mechanical troubles, troubles that were in no way attributable to cockpit shortcomings. At Nice his car caught fire and in the Italian Grand Prix at Milan he held third place ahead of one of the all-conquering Alfas until a succession of pit stops, to secure loose fuel tank retaining straps, dropped him back to fifth place. One small consolation during the year was his first International race victory, albeit a victory marred by circumstances beyond his control. In the Sports Car Circuit of Modena held on 28th September, Maserati entered two brand-new 6-cylinder 2-litre cars with potent twin-cam motors and a top speed of around 140 mph. Ascari and Villoresi were heading the field when the race was stopped after only forty-eight miles because another competitor had gone off the course and crashed into a spectator enclosure.

Both Ascari and Villoresi continued to drive for the Scuderia Ambrosiana in 1948. In June of that year at the San Remo Grand Prix held on the Adriatic coast of Italy there appeared a much improved Maserati, officially designated the 4CLT/48, but soon to be tagged the 'San Remo.' There was not much in the way of opposition in this race apart from other and older Maseratis, but one of these driven by the great Giuseppe Farina led the field until its throttle linkage broke and the Dottore was forced to retire. Now Ascari's steady driving came into its own and he went on to score his first Grand Prix victory, well clear of his teammate Villoresi who had been forced by mechanical trouble to make a couple of pit stops.

The team's next race was the Swiss Grand Prix held at Bremgarten near Berne; a circuit that ran through dense forests and was made up of a succession of difficult and dangerous fast bends. There was nothing significant in Ascari's drive in this race—he finished fifth—but the race was over-shadowed by a particularly tragic accident. During a wet practice session, when light mist was drifting across the course, Achille Varzi, one of the world's greatest drivers, lost control of his Alfa Romeo on the lethally slippery surface at a bend. The car bounced and rebounded off the wooden barriers, turned over and crushed the head of its driver who was wearing only a linen helmet. This sad loss badly affected many of the leading drivers who had known Varzi for so long, but it was a tragedy with a pay-off for Ascari.

The Alfa Romeo team had made three entries at the French Grand Prix to be held on the high-speed Reims circuit on 18th July and they were now a driver short. Alberto Ascari was invited to handle the third car, an invitation which he gladly accepted. At this stage in its development the 'Alfetta' was only some 20 bhp more powerful than the latest Maseratis to which Ascari was accustomed,

Alberto Ascari

but enough to give it a definite edge in top speed and acceleration. The cars were also superbly prepared and run with a team organisation and discipline unmatched in racing at that time. At the start of the race Jean-Pierre Wimille (perhaps *the* greatest driver of the time) went straight into the lead with his Alfa and with Ascari close behind. Villoresi moved up into third place with his Ambrosiana Maserati in hot pursuit, and as 'Gigi' chased his usual team-mate, it was obvious that both drivers were deriving a great deal of amusement from racing against each other instead of running as a team. But the chase proved too hot for the over-driven Maserati, which was forced to make several pit stops. As the race drew on, Ascari in accordance with team orders, eased back to third place behind the other Alfa driven by Consalvo Sanesi. This was the only occasion on which Ascari appeared for the Alfa team, but within a couple of years he was at the wheel of a car that could meet them on level terms.

During the remainder of the season little success came Ascari's way and his best performances were a fourth place in the Italian Grand Prix and second to Villoresi in the British race at Silverstone in which the Maseratis faced little opposition. In sports car racing Ascari drove one of the new 2-litre Maseratis in the arduous and dangerous Mille Miglia 1000-mile road race; he led the race on time as far as Padua, but retired with mechanical trouble.

At the 1948 Italian Grand Prix, held at Turin in September, Enzo Ferrari raced his new V-12 supercharged Grand Prix cars for the first time. Almost needless to say, the race was won by an Alfa Romeo, and Villoresi's Maserati finished second, but he was chased hard all the way by one of the new Ferraris driven by Frenchman Raymond Sommer. Although the new Ferrari was less powerful than the Alfa Romeo and its handling and braking were suspect, it clearly had tremendous development potential, a potential that Ferrari was well capable of exploiting. In the few races in which the new Ferraris appeared in 1948, the Commendatore engaged drivers on a one-race only basis, but he needed a regular team of top-line drivers. 'Would you be interested in driving Ferraris?' Enzo asked Villoresi and Ascari. In the absence of any proper development programme at the Maserati factory, the long-term prospects with Scuderia Ambrosiana looked bleak indeed. The Maserati drivers accepted Ferrari's offer and they remained with the Scuderia until the end of the 1953 season, driving both racing and sports cars. For Ascari it was a particularly happy relationship for he had known Enzo Ferrari since his childhood.

Alfa Romeo withdrew from racing before the start of the 1949 season, and Formula One racing became a duel fought between Ferrari and Maserati with the occasional intervention of the French racing blue in the shape of an unsupercharged Lago-Talbot. Under the then current Formula One regulations cars of up to 1500 cc supercharged and up to 4500 cc unsupercharged competed together. At this time all the Italian cars were supercharged, incredibly thirsty beasts, consuming alcohol-based fuel at around three miles per gallon; in a full-length Grand Prix the supercharged cars needed at least one and often two refuelling stops according to the race length and efficient pit-work could tip the balance between winning or losing. The Lago-Talbots were conspicuously slower than both the Ferraris and Maseratis, but consumed fuel at half the rate. So a tortoise and hare situation developed in which the Lago-Talbots, running through races without refueling stops, could sometimes steal a march on their faster opponents.

Such a situation arose in Ferrari's first Grand Prix in 1949, the Belgian race run on the fast and difficult Spa-Francorchamps circuit. The Ferraris led until they stopped to refuel and Louis Rosier's ponderous blue Talbot built up such a lead that the Italians could not catch it before the finish. When the chequered flag fell Villoresi was trailing in second place by fifty seconds and Ascari was a disappointed third.

This was not the only occasion in 1949 on which the fuel economy of the Lago-Talbots was to give the Ferrari team cause for anxiety, but after the Spa race Maranello fortunes improved considerably. In the Swiss Grand Prix at Bremgarten, Ascari seared away at the start into a lead that he retained throughout the race to score Ferrari's first Grand Prix victory. Later in the year he won the *Daily Express* Trophy race at Silverstone after a tussle with Farina's Maserati, and driving a new and improved Ferrari he galloped away from the opposition to score another victory in the European Grand Prix at Monza. Driving in Formula Two races for cars of up to 2000 cc unsupercharged, Ascari scored victories in 1950 at Bari and Reims. During the winter months Ascari and Villoresi competed in the series of races held in South America. These were Formule Libre races and the cars they drove were 2-litre Formula Two models fitted with superchargers. The Ferraris dominated the series and Ascari won the first race, the Juan Peron Cup, held at Buenos Aires on 18th December, and the Mar del Plata Grand Prix early in 1950, but the latter race only after Villoresi and Fangio had collided.

There had now been a major change of design policy at Maranello and although Ferrari continued to race the supercharged cars for the time being, the team was working hard to get ready a new unsupercharged 4500 cc V-12 car that would match the speed of the Alfas with almost the economy of the Talbots. Alfa Romeo returned to racing in 1950 with faster cars and and a particularly strong team of drivers consisting of Nino Farina, Juan Fangio and veteran Italian driver Luigi Fagioli. Over the next two seasons, as the Ferrari on-slaught increased in strength and reliability, motor racing witnessed a titanic struggle during which the mighty Alfa Romeo team, which had only been beaten once since the war, was gradually toppled from power.

Alberto Ascari was never very enthusiastic about sports

car racing which made different demands on a driver than Grand Prix racing, with less scope for individual displays of brilliance and greater emphasis on team tactics and endurance. Both he and Villoresi, however, drove cars with Ferrari's new unsupercharged engine in interim 3.3-litre form in the Mille Miglia in April. But the new engines were too powerful for the chassis and the cars were plagued by tire failures, and over-strained transmissions caused their eventual retirement. Although it has been Ferrari's practice never to nominate a 'number one' driver as such, Ascari was now that man and Ferrari was relying on him rather than Villoresi to produce results. The first unsupercharged single-seater Ferrari was entrusted to Ascari at the 1950 Belgian Grand Prix, but it had only a 3.3-litre engine and was hopelessly underpowered; despite Ascari's hardest driving, the best that he could manage was fifth place. By the Grand Prix des Nations at Geneva at the end of July Ascari was at the wheel of a new and much faster 4.1-litre version of the Ferrari. For fifty of the sixty-eight laps he chased the Alfas hard, throwing the Ferrari round the corners of the difficult Geneva street circuit right on the limit. He was lying second only to Fangio when the Ferrari broke under the strain of hard driving and expired with water running out of the exhaust pipes.

The Ferrari team did not run again until the Italian Grand Prix at Monza in September and here Ascari drove the full 4500 cc version of the Ferrari. Monza is a very fast circuit where the performance of the car is all-important and the skill of different drivers appears more equal than on more testing and arduous circuits. In the early laps of the race Ascari was sandwiched in second place between the Alfas of Farina and Fangio, poised to take the lead when the thirstier red beasts from Milan stopped to refuel; for two laps Ascari held the lead, but then his engine expired out on the circuit in a cloud of blue smoke and a very disconsolate Alberto returned to the pits on foot.

Alberto Ascari

In this race the Alfas had to make two refuelling stops and the Ferraris only one; when Dorino Serafini, Ferrari's chief test driver brought his sixth-place Ferrari into the pits for fuel and tires, Ascari took the wheel and, with no need to make a further pit stop, began to carve his way back through the field. At the end of this 313-mile race Ascari was only just over a minute behind the winning Alfa Romeo of Giuseppe Farina. It was only too clear to the Alfa Romeo directors that Ascari and the Ferrari were now a very serious threat to Milanese supremacy. The last Formula One race of the 1950 season was the Penya Rhin Grand Prix held at Barcelona, but Alfa Romeo did not compete in this and Ascari scored an easy victory. In Formula Two in 1950 Ascari and Ferrari were uncrowned kings and scored a total of six wins, including a victory in the first post-war German Grand Prix.

In preparation for the intense struggle that was expected in 1951 both Alfa Romeo and Ferrari made improvements to their cars and the first clash between the two teams came at the Swiss Grand Prix in May. Ascari had burnt an arm badly on the exhaust of his car in a Formula Two race, this was still giving him a great deal of pain at Bremgarten and he was very off-form; in the race he was never in the picture and finished a poor sixth. Another defeat for Ascari and Ferrari followed in the Belgian race where the best they could manage was second place, three minutes behind Farina's winning Alfa and the fight did not really warm up until the French Grand Prix on the fast Reims circuit in July. Here the race proved a close battle right from the start and although Ferrari was defeated by a narrow margin, a victory for Maranello was now a matter of inevitability. In the opening laps Ascari chased the leading Alfa driven by Fangio, but his Ferrari soon succumbed to gearbox trouble. New recruit to the Ferrari team Froilan Gonzalez, now in second place was called into the pits. Ascari took over his car and resumed the chase, but was still a minute behind Fangio's Alfa at the end of the race.

When the defeat of the Alfas was finally achieved in the next Championship race at Silverstone, the man who defeated them was Froilan Gonzalez. Ascari retired with gearbox trouble and when Gonzalez came into the pits to refuel, Ascari, recognising that this was Gonzalez's day, declined to take over the Argentinian's car and contented himself with giving the 'Pampas Bull' a reassuring slap on the back. But Ascari's turn soon came and he defeated the Alfas in both the German Grand Prix over the difficult and tortuous 14.2-mile Nürburgring circuit and in the Italian race at Monza. The Ferrari driver was now a close second in the World Championship and the outcome would be settled in the Spanish Grand Prix at Barcelona in October. In this race the Ferraris carried enough fuel to run through non-stop, but were running with smaller diameter rear wheels than those usually fitted. On the bumpy, rough Pedralbes circuit the Ferrari tires were cut to ribbons. Ascari was forced to stop for new rear tires every ten laps or so and lost all chance of winning the World Championship. The race and the Championship were won by Fangio. Ascari finished fourth in the race and took second place in the Championship with twenty-five points to the thirty-one gained by his Argentinian rival.

Alfa Romeo withdrew from racing at the end of the 1951 season and if Grand Prix racing had carried on in its existing form, it would have been little more than a Ferrari landslide. It was eventually decided that all Championship races and most others would be held to Formula Two, a category in which many different makes were competing. As events turned out, the new Tipo 500 4-cylinder Ferrari coupled with Ascari's considerable skill proved more than a match for the rest of the opposition. During the previous two seasons Ascari had handled cars that at first were marginally

Alberto Ascari

inferior and later marginally superior to the dominant Alfa Romeos and he had to fight hard for every success gained, inevitably on occasions over-driving his car as he tried to stay with the race-leader.

Now that he was driving cars that were superior to the opposition, the sheer brilliance of Ascari's driving style became apparent. Some drivers are like animals on the hunt for prey; preferring to sit on a rival's tail, pushing him every inch of the way to encourage errors of judgment under pressure. But Ascari was happier out in front, driving with precision and accuracy, knowing within the finest limits how exactly close he was to the car's ultimate performance and limits of adhesion, and able without apparent effort to increase his speed at any stage to match the tempo of the race. Because Ascari knew so precisely his own and his car's limitations the number of accidents in which he was involved were very few. It was rare indeed for him to finish other than completely relaxed and without signs of fatigue.

The following passage from the magazine *Autocourse* sums up well the domination of Ascari and Ferrari in 1952 Grand Prix racing. Ascari was leading the Dutch Grand Prix, but Giuseppe Farina, now also a member of the Ferrari team, had set the fastest lap for which a World Championship point was given. This is how *Autocourse* described Ferrari's reaction to the situation: 'The supremacy of the present Ferraris was rubbed in by the almost insolent ease with which Ascari, after a casual signal from Meazza (*Ferrari head mechanic*), produced the fastest time on the penultimate lap at 1 min 49.8 sec or 85.362 mph. It was most instructive to study the driving of Ascari during this race, in which he was not in any way pushed. One might have thought that he had been studying the dicta of the famous Sunbeam driver Kenelm Lee Guinness, who held that if one drove over a sixpence on the first lap when cornering, one should do it every lap until the end of the race. If *il com-*

panissimo was not doing this he must be one of the greatest natural drivers, because he was in fact taking the same line, lap after lap, with a precision that was fantastic.'

There were seven Championship races in Europe in 1952, but Ascari competed in only six. Both Ferrari and his leading driver had long nursed the desire to compete in the Indianapolis 500 Miles race on the banked track, a race last won by a European car in 1940. Ascari travelled out to drive the latest 4.5-litre Ferrari and because of qualifying at Indianapolis, was forced to miss the Swiss Grand Prix. In the American race he was in twelfth place when he retired with a seized rear hub. In each of the remaining six Championship races during the season, the Belgian, French, British, German, Dutch and Italian Grands Prix, Ascari won with consummate ease and set fastest lap. Only at Monza in the Italian race did Ascari meet opposition worth his mettle; Froilan Gonzalez with a new Maserati led in the early part of the race, but his car was fitted with a small fuel tank and he was forced to make a refuelling stop which cost him all chance of victory. In this race Gonzalez shared fastest lap with Ascari.

An additional series of Formula Two races in 1952 were the Grands Prix de France; there were eight races in the series, Ascari competed in six and won four. In one he retired with mechanical trouble, but in the race at Reims he and the rest of the Ferrari team were soundly thrashed by French Motor Cycle Champion Jean Behra at the wheel of a Gordini. On this one occasion in its career the Gordini was able on this high-speed circuit to run away from the Ferrari and on this one occasion in his career Ascari was thoroughly demoralised. Unable to pass the Gordini, he slip-streamed it closely until his engine overheated and then he stopped at the pits. When the car was ready for him to rejoin the race, he threw in the towel and let Villoresi take over; later in the race he took the car again to finish third. The whole incident was very much out of character with

Ascari's normal behaviour and the only logical explanation is that he was not feeling well, for his driving in past years had shown that he was quite capable of fighting hard even when the odds were against him.

Ascari drove in no more sports car races than he could help, but at Le Mans in 1952 he set a new lap record with a 3-litre Ferrari shared with Villoresi before retiring with clutch trouble. Later in the year in the Carrera Panamericana Mexico race, a 1934-mile grind across Mexico, he made a rare mistake and crashed his 4.1-litre Ferrari. In the previous year's race, co-driving with Villoresi, he had finished second with a 2.6-litre car.

Ferrari continued to race his very successful 4-cylinder cars in 1953, but Maranello now faced strong opposition from Maserati with a team of new cars and Juan Fangio as number one driver. In the early part of the season, before the Maseratis were fully developed, Ascari had things much his own way and scored easy victories in the first two rounds in the Championship at Buenos Aires and Zandvoort in Holland. It was in the Belgian race at Spa that Ascari first found the Maseratis were more than he could cope with; Gonzalez and Fangio hurtled into the distance, leaving the World Champion trailing, badly, until engine troubles brought their fast runs to an end. Ascari won the race, but in the next round of the Championship at Reims, he was outpaced once again and it was Hawthorn, the youngest and newest member of the Scuderia who saved the day, narrowly beating Fangio and Gonzalez. The reigning World Champion had to settle for fourth place.

Both the Belgian and French races were run on very fast circuits on which the Maserati's extra engine power more than compensated for its roadholding deficiencies. In the British race at Silverstone, a much slower circuit, Ascari scored an easy win, but in the next race at the Nürburgring luck was against him and in his struggle against mechanical misfortune he showed all the perseverance and determination that are an essential characteristic of a true Champion. By the end of the first 14.2-mile lap Ascari had already pulled out a ten-second lead, but towards the end of the second lap, one of the knock-on eared hub caps came off, the wheel followed it and he completed the lap on three wheels and a brake drum. A new wheel and hub cap were fitted and Ascari rejoined the race in ninth place.

In accordance with their standing arrangement, Villoresi was signalled to come into the pits to swap cars with the World Champion. By the time of the swap at the end of lap ten, Villoresi was fourth and Ascari had risen to fifth place. Ascari stopped, jumped into Villoresi's car and was away in a matter of seconds, hurling his new mount at his very hardest down the dips, through the difficult bends and over the jumps on the bumpier parts of the circuit. He turned in a lap within three seconds of the outright lap record which had stood since 1939 to the credit of Hermann Lang's 3-litre supercharged Mercedes. He was rapidly closing up on team-mate Hawthorn and third place when one of the Ferrari's pistons failed and he crawled into the pits with blue smoke pouring out of the cockpit. As a very weary-looking Ascari climbed out of the car, took off his familiar blue crash-helmet and picked up his canvas hold-all used by his father nearly thirty years before, he knew, like his thousands of supporters, that he had driven the hardest and, in some ways, the finest race in his career.

Another victory followed in the Swiss Grand Prix at Bremgarten, but at the last Championship race of the season at Monza Ascari's race ended in a complete débâcle. For 313 miles Ascari and team-mate Farina battled wheel-to-wheel with Fangio's Maserati and, tagged on to this group to give moral support to his team leader, was another Argentinian, Onofre Marimon, whose Maserati was several laps in arrears after a pit stop. As the cars started their last lap, it seemed as though Fangio would be beaten back into third place, but the Maserati drivers kept up the pressure every inch of the way and at the very last corner of that lap, only a matter of yards from the finishing line, Ascari made the mistake that his rivals were hoping for. The World Champion's Ferrari spun viciously, Farina swerved on to the grass to avoid his team-mate, Marimon rammed the spinning Maranello car and Fangio squeezed by on the inside to score his only Championship race victory of the season. Never in his career had Ascari made such a crucial mistake, but despite this accident the Italian won his second World Championship with 34½ points to the 28 gained by Fangio.

For 1954 a new Grand Prix Formula with a maximum capacity limit of 2500 cc unsupercharged was introduced. It was common knowledge that Mercedes would be re-entering racing, the old-established Turin company Lancia was developing a new contender to the design of that great man of motor racing, Vittorio Jano who had been responsible for all the classic Alfa Romeos of the 'thirties, but both Ferrari and Maserati were racing developed versions of their existing cars. Ascari realised only too well that the new Mercedes would be a stiff opponent and both he and Villoresi pledged their trust in Jano's ability by leaving Ferrari after five successful seasons to drive the new Lancias.

The D.50 Lancia was the most advanced car of its time, many of its roadholding problems were attributable to the fact that its chassis design was five years ahead of tire evolution and it pioneered the idea of using the engine as a stressed chassis member. Development work on the new car was protracted; it was not ready to race until the end of 1954, but Lancia meanwhile raced the sports cars that had first appeared the previous year.

The 1954 season saw Ascari's career at its nadir and its zenith. His antipathy of the Mille Miglia was such that the thousand-mile race was excluded from his contract with Lancia. Yet when Luigi Villoresi was injured in an accident in training for the Mille Miglia while his mechanic was at the wheel, Ascari stepped into the breach and drove one of the Turin factory's sleek red cars. Opposition in the race came from a strong team of Ferraris including two of the new and monstrously powerful 4.9-litre cars and a trio of Maseratis. While other Lancia drivers went flat out in the early stages of the race Ascari drove cautiously, gradually picking up places as faster cars fell by the wayside. Teammate Piero Taruffi, 'the Silver Fox' of motor racing, led with his Lancia until he went off the road and damaged it too badly to continue, then Ascari went ahead to win the race from the Ferrari of Vittorio Marzotto. Usually, when Ascari finished a Grand Prix, he looked fresh and unfatigued; after the Mille Miglia he was too exhausted to stand, his face was distorted with strain and he had to be helped away from the car.

The Mille Miglia was the zenith and the Formula One races were the nadir. At the French Grand Prix, Ascari was released from the Lancia team to drive a works Maserati. Perhaps striving too hard to assert his position as reigning World Champion, he blew up his engine. He drove a Maserati again in the British race, retired with an over-revved engine, took over Villoresi's Maserati and blew that up too. The story goes that Ascari returned to the Maserati pit, swinging his blue crash helmet, to ask nonchalantly: 'Any more Maseratis?' At Monza he drove a Ferrari and again retired with engine trouble.

The new Lancia raced at Barcelona in October; Ascari set the fastest lap in practice, leading the race for nine laps until he retired with clutch failure. Lancia's next race was the 1955 Argentine Grand Prix where the complete entry of three cars retired and the team returned to Turin without competing in the Buenos Aires City Grand Prix. By the early races in the European season the Lancia team had sorted out most of their problems. Ascari won races at Turin and Naples, but the team was beaten at Pau by Behra's Maserati

Alberto Ascari

after Ascari stopped at the pits for a brake pipe to be changed.

Then came the Monaco Grand Prix, Lancia's first important race of the European season. For much of the race the works Mercedes led, but first Fangio and then Moss retired. When Moss retired, Ascari was on the same lap, striving not to be lapped by the Mercedes driver (he would have had no knowledge until he reached the pits that Moss was out of the race). As he slowed for the chicane the Lancia's brakes locked up, the car bounced off the straw bales and bollards and plunged into Monte Carlo harbour in a shower of spray and steam. Within seconds Ascari's blue helmet bobbed to the surface and he was hauled aboard a boat, apparently unhurt apart from a broken nose and shock.

Ten days later Ascari was dead, killed in circumstances that have never been understood. He was not competing in the Supercortemaggiore Grand Prix, a sports car race at Monza, but he went along to the circuit during practice and at the invitation of Lancia team-mate Eugenio Castellotti decided to try a few laps with the latter's Ferrari. Ascari had never driven without his own crash helmet but for this practice session he borrowed Castellotti's. The exhaust note of the Ferrari could be heard rising and falling as the Lancia team-leader drove round the deserted 3.9-mile circuit. Then there was an eerie silence. Ascari's car had gone straight on for no apparent reason at a bend that was taken nearly flat-out and the driver was dead. It seemed incredible that Ascari should have misjudged a bend he knew so well and the only explanation was that he had not fully recovered from the accident at Monaco and had suffered a black-out. An added irony was that when Alberto Ascari died he was the same age as his father and Alberto, too, left a widow and two children.

4
The First British Champion
JOHN MICHAEL HAWTHORN
1958

No PERIOD OF persistent domination of the Grand Prix scene, no year of victory after victory characterised the racing career of the six foot two, blond, pale-faced Hawthorn. Mike raced for the love of the sport, the battle with a rival on the friendliest possible terms, not with the almost existentialist dedication of Stirling Moss. When his kidney trouble that plagued him all his life was playing up, when he was unhappy with his car, then his driving would match his mood to the point of mediocrity; but when the sun was shining in Hawthorn's world, when his car was behaving as it should and especially when the odds were heavily against him, then Mike's grin would broaden and he would drive with inspiration; it was this inspiration that brought him a magnificent victory in the face of the strongest opposition in the French Grand Prix in 1953 and resulted in his fantastic drive with the primitively-handling D-type Jaguar over the difficult Dundrod course in the 1955 Tourist Trophy. But in 1958, when Hawthorn took the World Championship by the narrow margin of one point, he won only one race, the French Grand Prix, and it was consistent good placings that brought him success.

John Michael Hawthorn

Mike Hawthorn was born at Mexborough in the West Riding of Yorkshire on 10th April 1929, but two years later his father, Leslie bought the Tourist Trophy Garage at Farnham in Surrey and the family moved south. Educated at Ardingly College Sussex, young Mike then took a four-year apprenticeship with Dennis Brothers, the commercial vehicle builders whose works were at Guildford. Later he went to Kingston Technical College and the College of Aeronautical Engineering at Chelsea. From motor-cycles Mike graduated via a Fiat 500 to a Riley Nine saloon and then to a Riley Imp sports model. It was the Imp that he drove in his first motor competition, the 1950 Brighton Speed Trials, an exhilarating dash along the Sussex seafront on Madeira Drive and he won the 1100 cc sports class. Mike was fascinated by fast driving and anxious to race; his father was almost equally anxious to encourage him in a sport which he loved himself, but later in Mike's career his father's anxiety seemed to grow into an ambition that was almost oppressive and at times he pushed Mike too hard to do well.

Rather than tip Mike into the maelstrom of 500 cc Formula Three racing, almost as undisciplined a class of racing as today's Formula Ford, but one from which many first-class drivers emerged, Leslie Hawthorn decided to give his son another, but faster Riley, a 1500 cc TT Sprite model which he had owned himself for some while. Throughout 1951 Mike displayed considerable ability at the wheel of the elderly, but lively Riley, winning the ten-lap sports handicap over the Dundrod circuit that preceded the Ulster Trophy Formula One race and the *Motor Sport* Brooklands Memorial Trophy on the strength of his successes in Club races at Goodwood.

By the end of the year the Hawthorns faced a difficult problem; Mike clearly should progress to a faster and more competitive car for the coming season, but the cost of such a car was more than the family could afford. It was at this critical point in his career that Mike received help that was as invaluable as it was unexpected. A family friend, marine engineer Bob Chase, had read of the new Formula Two Cooper-Bristol announced by Charles and John Cooper and he telephoned Mike, offering to buy one of these new cars, if the Hawthorns would maintain it. The offer was gladly accepted, for the Cooper was the most promising of the British cars built to comply with Formula Two regulations and the decision that all major Grands Prix in 1952 would be held to Formula Two meant that Mike would be able to undertake a full international season.

The Cooper-Bristol with simple box-section chassis, wishbone and leaf spring independent suspension front and rear and an engine developed from the pre-war BMW unit, was a simple and unsophisticated design, but it handled exceptionally well, was extremely forgiving to a novice driver and it was a fairly simple car to maintain. Although racing in 1952 was dominated by Ascari and Ferrari, the combination of Hawthorn's natural talents and the Cooper's good all-round qualities brought them an unexpected degree of success, despite a power deficiency of some 30 bhp compared with the faster Continental cars.

There was a rush to get the new Coopers ready for the start of the season and Mike went along to the works at Surbiton to help to complete his car. Their debut was at the Easter Monday Goodwood International meeting and they appeared with the Cooper in unpainted aluminum and Mike resplendent in white overalls and the bow tie that he always affected when racing and was to lead to the nick-name on the Continent of *le papillon*. His first race was the 6-lap Formula Two Lavant Cup and the silver Cooper snarled away to an easy victory. Another win followed in the Formule Libre Chichester Cup, a race in which most of the contesting cars were elderly British-owned vehicles, and in the 12-lap Richmond Trophy Mike and the Cooper were beaten only by Froilan Gonzalez and the 4½-litre Ferrari

John Michael Hawthorn

'Thin Wall' Special. Overnight Hawthorn and the Cooper were headline news.

In other minor British races during the year Hawthorn maintained the same level of success and, revelling in his newfound fame, he achieved even greater success in Championship races, although the results, misleadingly, indicate otherwise. His first Continental race was the Belgian Grand Prix on the fast and difficult Spa course; in heavy rain and with a car far less powerful than those that finished ahead of him, Hawthorn and his now dark green-painted Cooper took fourth place after a slow pit stop while his leaking fuel tank was refilled from a can. At Reims, where lap speeds were very high and skill could not compensate for lack of power, Hawthorn was a poor seventh. He retired at Rouen, but in the British race at Silverstone he finished third, defeated only by two works Ferraris. The Dutch Grand Prix at Zandvoort followed; in practice Hawthorn lapped faster than one of the works Ferrari drivers and in the race he was again fourth. At Monza he retired early in the race with a sheared magneto drive.

There are few better talent-spotters than Enzo Ferrari and as early as the Dutch Grand Prix overtures had been made to Mike by the Maranello team-manager. He was not too happy about the idea of driving for a foreign team and he realised that to sign up with Ferrari was to commit himself to racing as a fully-fledged professional. He hesitated and Ferrari offered him a trial drive in the non-Championship Modena Grand Prix in the middle of September. Mike accepted and arranged for his Cooper to be driven by Roy Salvadori. In practice for the Italian race he decided to give his usual mount a test run, but, probably because of the sudden change-over of cars, he crashed, injuring his ribs. Neither Hawthorn nor Salvadori was able to start in the race and although Mike seemed to have escaped lightly from this prang, he later contracted fluid on the lung and had to spend a while in hospital. Ferrari was still pressing Hawthorn to sign up with the Scuderia and eventually he agreed.

He was now a full member of the International motor racing circus; travelling out to the Argentine for that country's first Championship Grand Prix in which he finished fourth, bulging out of the Ferrari's cockpit which was really too small for such a bulky driver, and returning to Italy for the Mille Miglia Sports Car race in which he retired. He finished fourth at Zandvoort and was disqualified at Le Mans because his Ferrari was topped up with brake fluid before the minimum permitted distance had been covered. At Spa after a pit stop because of a broken fuel pipe and a nasty slide on a patch of oil, he finished sixth. Mike was enjoying his motor racing, as his jokes and broad grin made clear. But Ferrari was under increasing pressure from the Maserati team headed by Fangio and Gonzalez and the inscrutable Nello Ugolini, the Ferrari team-manager, not really understanding the way in which Mike's mind worked, thought that the young Englishman was not taking his racing seriously enough and, in the words of a million-and-one school reports 'could do better if he tried harder.' Any doubts he nurtured about Hawthorn were, however, completely dispelled at the team's next race.

This was the French Grand Prix at Reims, a circuit on which the Maseratis' top speed came into their own, on which the advantages of the Ferraris' better handling were at a discount and the Maranello drivers had to rely on their slightly better acceleration and brakes; it was also a circuit on which a young and inexperienced driver, throwing caution to the winds and keeping his foot hard down, could pull one across a more experienced *pilote* whose skill was tempered by a greater awareness of danger. In the early stages of the race Gonzalez and his Maserati pulled further and further away from the rest of the tight, scrapping bunch of Ferraris and Maseratis. At half-distance Gonzalez rushed into the pits and his car was refuelled from churns—his advantage over the rest of the entry had been attributable to a lighter fuel load, and now Hawthorn and Fangio headed the field, racing wheel to wheel, locked in combat, the Argentinian gaining a slight advantage on the straights and Mike slightly faster through the curves and making up ground by later braking at the Muizon and Thillois hairpins.

When Fangio moved over to crowd Hawthorn out, Mike, grinning broadly, held his ground and wagged his finger warningly. Lap after lap the two cars crossed the finishing line side-by-side in a red blur, at the end of the last lap but one Hawthorn led by inches, then he dropped back into the Maserati's slip-stream, and leaving his braking to the last possible moment, went ahead of Fangio into the last corner and took the chequered flag a length ahead of the Argentinian. No one was more delighted at this victory than Ugolini, no one was more impressed than Fangio who wrote, 'England had a new and worthy champion.' Hawthorn had been the first British driver to sign up with a leading Continental team since Dick Seaman drove for Mercedes-Benz in 1937–9 and now like Seaman, he had won a major Grand Prix.

The rest of the season, although not without incident, proved more than satisfactory for a driver in his first full season of International racing. In the British Grand Prix at Silverstone, he was still riding high on his Reims triumph and perhaps a shade over-confident, he over-cooked Woodcote bend and revolved his Ferrari twice in full sight of the Maranello pit! After a pit stop for the car to be checked over he finished sixth. In the Belgian 24 Hours race for sports cars he shared the winning 4½-litre Ferrari with Giuseppe Farina and the following month, co-driving with Umberto Maglioli, he scored another sports car victory in the Pescara 12 Hours race. Some weight to the argument that Hawthorn's Reims victory was the result of boldness rather than skill came in the German Grand Prix held at the Nüburgring, the most difficult of all European circuits, on which he was unable to hold either team-mate Farina or Fangio, both of whom passed him while he was leading the race. He rounded off the season with a third place in the Swiss Grand Prix at Bremgarten and a fourth at Monza.

For 1954 Mike Hawthorn remained with Scuderia Ferrari and although in the face of almost overwhelming Mercedes opposition, he turned in some of the finest drives in his career, the season proved to be his unhappiest. After running at Buenos Aires, where he was disqualified in the Argentine Grand Prix for receiving a push-start after spinning off, and retiring on the last lap of the Formule Libre race a fortnight later when his engine seized up, Hawthorn returned home to an adverse press. The great British public, aided and abetted by the gutter British press, were demanding to know how Hawthorn had evaded conscription for National Service; why, anxious mothers asked, should their sons have to drill and march for two years, while Hawthorn gallivanted from country to country, enjoying himself motor-racing? Questions were asked in parliament and the answer was given that Hawthorn had been rejected as medically unfit because of kidney trouble (for which he later had an operation). No one was really satisfied with the answer, and the same criticism, not without some justification, reared its ugly head on several occasions over the next couple of years.

In April 1954 the Ferrari team ran in the Syracuse Grand Prix. The rather wild Argentinian driver, Onofre Marimon, was leading with his Maserati and with Hawthorn hot on his exhausts, when he misjudged a corner, clouted a straw-bale and Mike, his vision obscured by flying straw, hit a wall; the Ferrari's fuel filter sprung open and in a matter of seconds the car was ablaze. Froilan Gonzalez, close behind with his Ferrari, stopped and rescued Mike from the inferno, but the British driver had suffered second-degree burns to his left hand and arm and both legs. Hawthorn spent a long spell in hospital, was not fit enough to drive again until the Belgian Grand Prix in June, and when he did re-appear his

John Michael Hawthorn

burns had not fully healed. But already Mike had suffered another blow. While returning home from the Whitsun Goodwood meeting, Leslie Hawthorn was involved in a road accident at Hindhead and suffered injuries to which he succumbed the following day. Mike now faced the additional responsibility of his father's garage business and the appointment of a manager did not alleviate all his cares.

When Mike returned to racing at Spa, he was looking even paler than before, laughing less readily and, for the time being, had lost a lot of interest in the sport. At Spa he drove well, holding second place behind Fangio's winning Maserati until he was overcome by fumes from an exhaust leak and stopped to hand his car over to Froilan Gonzalez who had already retired. In 1954 both Ferrari and Maserati were racing cars that were developments of the models fielded in 1953, for the time being Italian motor racing development was stagnating and at the next race at Reims the initiative passed to Mercedes whose new straight-eight W.196 cars, developed and built at enormous cost and raced with staff and facilities that none of the other teams could match, dominated racing for much of 1954 and throughout 1955. In the French race the streamlined Mercedes of Fangio and his German team-mate Karl Kling seared away from the rest of the field, and all the Ferrari drivers blew up their engines in pursuit of the 'silver arrow,' as the Mercedes were popularly known. Hawthorn, at the wheel of the newer short-chassis, short-stroke 'Squalo' Ferrari, had his engine blow up on the pits straight, he took to the escape road towards the village of Gueux and only managed to bring the car to rest a matter of inches before a barrier at neck height.

The next battle between the German and Italian teams came at Silverstone and on this flat, dull, former airfield circuit, with many of the corners ill-defined by oil drums, the Mercedes drivers found difficulty in placing their cars and Fangio's Mercedes was soon battered from contact with solid objects. On this circuit the older, better-handling, rather more flexible Tipo 625 Ferraris were in their element and while Gonzalez motored further and further into the distance, Hawthorn acted as a shield, fending off Moss's Maserati for many laps until the privately owned car finally forged by into second place. Moss retired, Hawthorn finished second ahead of Marimon's Maserati and Fangio trailed home fourth with a mechanically ailing car.

By the German Grand Prix the Mercedes team had put its house in order and had introduced a conventional, unstreamlined car that was easier to drive. Fangio won this and the next two Championship races. At the Nürburgring Hawthorn retired his own car with rear axle failure and then took over the second-place car from Froilan Gonzalez who, heart-broken from the death in practice of his compatriot Onofre Marimon, was driving a spiritless race. Mike retired again in the Swiss Grand Prix at Bremgarten, but at Monza, driving a calm, steady race, the sort of race that was to make him Champion four years later, finished second after many of his faster rivals had retired. In the Tourist Trophy race on the Dundrod circuit the following week, co-driving a Ferrari with Frenchman Maurice Trintignant, he averaged the highest speed, but was beaten on handicap by a French 750 cc DB car.

On two occasions Mike had driven Tony Vandervell's 'Thin Wall' Special Ferrari, a much modified 4.5-litre car that had started life in 1950 as a works team car. Now the 'Old Man' invited Mike to drive his latest car at the September Goodwood meeting. This was the 'Vanwall Special,' a new Formula One car built by Vandervell and incorporating many features of Ferrari design practice. Although the car was as yet far from fully developed, in the hands of Peter Collins it had already proved itself a promising contender for Formula One success. Vandervell was hoping that Mike would be sufficiently impressed with his new car to agree to drive it in 1955. The 10-lap Woodcote Cup

Formule Libre race was dominated by Collins with the 'Thin Wall' and Wharton's BRM, but Moss with his private Maserati and Hawthorn battled all the way for third place, the Italian car leading the British over the line by the narrow margin of a fifth of a second. Continuing to dangle the carrot before Hawthorn's patriotic eyes, Vandervell invited him to drive the Vanwall again at Aintree the following weekend and put up a £100 stake between him and Moss. In the 17-lap Formula One race he was beaten by Moss by a margin of eleven seconds and in the Formule Libre event he retired with an overheating engine, after an off-course excursion blocked the air intake with earth and grass.

There was one more race to complete the Championship year, the Spanish Grand Prix at Barcelona on 24th October. Here Hawthorn drove the latest 'Squalo' Ferrari and at Barcelona he was at peak form. Initially Ascari's new Lancia led, but stopped at the pits after nine laps, and then Hawthorn, team-mate Trintignant and Maserati driver Harry Schell, who had started the race with a half-full tank and instructions to break up the opposition, battled for the lead, slipstreaming each other, racing into corners wheel-to-wheel, braking early to deceive their opponents and braking late to gain an advantage; all the while Mike was grinning broadly, for this was to him what motor racing was all about. Behind, a calm, relaxed Fangio played a waiting game. Schell spun off, dropping to fourth place, and Trintignant retired with transmission trouble, leaving Hawthorn in the lead. Now it seemed the fun was over, now the race would begin and Fangio would launch his attack. Despite 'faster' signals from the Mercedes pit, Mike was able to adjust his speed to ward off the Mercedes attack. As the race progressed, a strong wind blew up along the main straight, litter thrown down by the spectators was sucked into the air intakes of the cars and most of them began to overheat; the Mercedes was running ever more roughly, Fangio was being soaked with oil and Hawthorn drew further and further away, lapping the German car, to score his second World Championship race victory. A victory not as spectacular as that won at Reims, but nevertheless very well deserved.

Now Hawthorn had to make his plans for the 1955 season. There were distinct advantages in driving for Vanwall; as a member of a British team he would be able to spend more time in England looking after the family business, and as Vanwall competed only in Formula One, he would be able to accept an offer to drive for the works Jaguar team in Sports Car races. Likewise Jaguar competed in only a limited number of races and so Hawthorn would still be able to drive for Ferrari in some Sports Car events. Mike explained the position to the Commendatore and parted from Ferrari on friendly terms, which was just as well in view of later developments . . .

His first race in 1955 was the Sebring 12 Hours in which he shared with American Phil Walters a quasi-works Jaguar entered by Briggs Cunningham. Even this race was a victory marred, for in the closing laps the Jaguar made several pit stops for new plugs and Allen Guiberson, entrant of the second-place Ferrari driven by Phil Hill and Carroll Shelby, protested that his car was leading when the flag fell. The protest was rejected, but it left a nasty taste. And all was far from well at Vanwall. The car was not proving as fast, as reliable or handling as well as Mike had hoped. In the team's first race, the *Daily Express* Trophy at Silverstone, Mike's car was delayed by brake trouble and then he was forced to retire because of a fractured oil pipe; at Monaco his car retired with throttle linkage trouble and the final straw came in the Belgian race at Spa-Francorchamps. Tony Vandervell drove the car from the garage to the course himself and Mike reckoned that the 'Old Man' cooked the clutch. In any case the car only survived nine laps before succumbing to an oil leak. That evening after the race in the bar of the hotel at which the team was staying tempers

John Michael Hawthorn

flared and Vandervell and Hawthorn parted company. There was a drive waiting for him at Maranello, but in 1955 the latest 4-cylinder Ferraris were completely outclassed and his chances of success were little better than at Vanwall. Before his first single-seater Ferrari drive of the season, however, Hawthorn was to be a central figure in a tragic controversy.

At Le Mans he co-drove a works Jaguar with Ivor Bueb and in the early hours of the race thrilled the spectators with a furious duel with Fangio at the wheel of a Mercedes. Lap after lap Hawthorn, in his element with a car that he really enjoyed driving, was cornering in long high-speed power slides, for the D-type despite the road-holding limitations imposed by its rigid rear axle was completely controllable, drawing away from the Mercedes on acceleration on the Mulsanne straight and several times lowering the lap record. Hawthorn was leading with two and a half hours racing over and due to make a pit stop. He passed Macklin's Austin-Healey (a much slower car) shortly before reaching the pits and then signalled that he was pulling into the pits. For some reason the Austin-Healey swerved in front of the Mercedes of Pierre Levegh who was keeping well over to the right to allow team-mate Fangio to lap him. Levegh's Mercedes hit the Austin-Healey, ricocheted into the left-hand bank, exploded in flames and the front of the car in a cascade of burning metal hit the packed spectator enclosure as though it had been strafed by rockets. Eighty-two spectators and Levegh lost their lives.

Whoever may have fired the detonator that triggered off the explosion, the real causes of the Le Mans tragedy were too narrow a road in front of the pits and lack of adequate protection for the spectators, matters that had been dealt with by the following year's race. The enquiry held later completely cleared Hawthorn of all blame. At the time he appeared utterly broken, he blamed himself completely for the accident and vowed that he would never race again. To those close to him at Le Mans it was obvious that unless he could be coaxed out of his near-hysterical state and induced to take the wheel again that evening he probably never would run in another race. 'Lofty' England, now Managing Director of Jaguar, persuaded Hawthorn to carry on driving and he and Bueb completed the race to win a sad, and rather hollow victory after the withdrawal of the Mercedes team.

As a result of the Le Mans disaster many of the year's races were cancelled, and the remaining Grands Prix brought Hawthorn little joy. He was seventh at Zandvoort, was in sixth place at Aintree when overcome by heat and handed his car over to Castellotti, and he retired at Monza. The one bright spot in the season was the Tourist Trophy race, a round in the Sports Car World Championship held on the 7.6-mile Dundrod road circuit in Northern Ireland. Jaguar with one car driven by Hawthorn and young Irish driver Desmond Titterington faced the might of Mercedes. On the billiard-table smooth surfaces of la Sarthe the Jaguar was a match for anything on four wheels, but it was at a severe disadvantage on a difficult, tortuous road course where cornering power was of great importance. Mercedes were expecting a walk-over, but both Mike and his co-driver rose to the occasion, flinging their car through the bends with gay abandon and, with Lofty's consent, going well above the safe rev limit. Twice Hawthorn thrust the big green car into the lead, all the time worrying the silver Mercedes to the point where their pits organisation was disintegrating. He was in second place on the last lap but one when clutch slip caused the engine to over-rev even higher than the driver intended, it seized up and the car spun up a side-road.

Once again Hawthorn found himself facing the problem of sorting out a Formula One drive for the coming year. Anxious to stay a member of the Jaguar team—which would no longer have been possible if he had signed up with

Ferrari—he elected to handle the new BRM in Formula One events. The BRM had first appeared in September 1955 and it was obviously the fastest of the British Grand Prix contenders. Throughout 1956 it was plagued by brake and drive-shaft troubles and persistent failures of the very large inlet valves forced the team to withdraw from racing in mid-season. Hawthorn's Grand Prix season proved even more dismal than in 1955.

The season started well enough, however, for Hawthorn took third place in the Argentine Grand Prix with the BRM-owned Maserati that was fielded while development work continued on the team's own cars. At Sebring he shared a D-type Jaguar with Titterington, but they retired with brake trouble. Then started his catalogue of troubles with the ill-fated BRM. At the car's first race of the season at Goodwood, Hawthorn crashed badly when the transmission locked up and the BRM hurtled end over end into the ploughed infield—Mike was thrown out of the car and lucky indeed to escape with a shaking and a lacerated ankle. At Aintree the brakes failed and the car ran straight on at a corner; during private practice for the *Daily Express* Trophy the bonnet flew off and almost knocked him unconscious and in the race itself the engine failed. The team was unable to start at Monaco because of valve trouble in practice and Mike was now without a drive for the Belgian and French races. He offered his services to Ferrari and Maserati; the latter accepted and he was practising with a car belonging to the Modena team when Ferrari complained bitterly that he should drive for them; to avoid ill-feeling Mike packed his bags and returned home. At Reims he was to drive a Vanwall, but he was at the wheel of the second-place Jaguar in the 12 Hours Sports Car race preceding the Grand Prix, he was too tired to take part in another race and after only a few laps handed his car over to Harry Schell.

BRM returned to racing at the British Grand Prix at

Silverstone, but no one had much confidence that their troubles had been cured. That the car was still the fastest racing, however, was only too obvious and Hawthorn led for the first fourteen laps, only to slow off and retire with oil leaking from the final drive. Team-mate Tony Brooks's crashed when the throttles jammed open, burnt itself out in its own funeral pyre and Brooks who had been thrown from the car escaped with facial injuries. Both drivers had now lost all confidence in the BRM and neither raced again for the team which withdrew from racing until 1957.

Mike was looking for another Formula One drive and for the German Grand Prix he agreed to handle a Ferrari. At the last moment the organisers announced that their insurers would not give Hawthorn the necessary third-party insurance and he could only run if he could provide the necessary cover himself. The reason given was that when he was driving a works Jaguar in the Nürburgring 1000 km race in May he had passed another car on the wrong side of the road in front of the pits. Many other drivers had been guilty of the same pecadillo and on the occasion in question Hawthorn had been badly baulked by a German driver. Ever since the Le Mans crash the German press had been trying to pin the blame on Hawthorn—despite the fact that he had been completely exonerated by the enquiry —and this appeared to be another move in the campaign of hate. Hawthorn did not compete again in Formula One until 1957.

For the 1957 season Hawthorn signed up again with Scuderia Ferrari where his team-mates included his old friend Peter Collins, Luigi Musso and Maurice Trintignant. During 1956–7 Ferrari raced the Lancia V-8 cars which had been presented to him after the Turin team's withdrawal from racing in mid-1955 and although these had been progressively modified, they were no match for the latest Maseratis and Vanwalls. But despite the shortcomings of the cars, Mike was now driving for a team he liked and he had fallen in love with Jean Howarth, his constant companion, to whom he became engaged a year later, and the season was amongst his happiest. That year the star of the Ferrari team was Musso and little success came Mike's way. He retired at Buenos Aires, was eliminated in a multi-car crash at Monaco and trailed home in fourth place at Rouen. At Aintree he was in second place behind Behra's Maserati when the French driver's engine blew up and he punctured a tire on part of the debris—he rejoined the race to finish third. Another sound performance followed at the Nürburgring where he took second place, and he finished sixth at Monza after a pit stop.

Mike remained with Ferrari for the 1958 season and the team was now fielding new V-6 cars which were called the Dino in memory of Enzo Ferrari's son. Early in the year Mike took a third at Buenos Aires and won the minor 100-mile race at Goodwood on Easter Monday, but once the European season proper got under way, the cars showed themselves to be no match for the Vanwalls. Hawthorn was leading at Monaco when his car retired with a fractured fuel pump mounting and, for all his hard driving, the best he could manage at Zandvoort was fifth place. Mike huffed and puffed about the performance of the cars, complaining bitterly to new Ferrari team manager Tavoni (formerly with Maserati) and writing a fusillade of angry letters to Enzo Ferrari. At Spa things began to look up and after setting fastest time in practice, he took second place in the race to the Vanwall of Tony Brooks—Brooks crossed the line struggling to engage a cog in his seized-up gearbox and Mike went by enveloped in a cloud of blue smoke from a burnt piston. Mike again set fastest lap in practice at Reims and took a lead on the first lap that he retained throughout the 258 miles to score his third ever Championship race victory from the Vanwall of Stirling Moss, but all the joy of the victory was lost for Hawthorn by the death of his teammate Musso who crashed while holding second place.

Mike's chances of winning the World Championship had never been better and he and Moss were level-pegging with twenty-three points each. At Silverstone it was Hawthorn's team-mate Peter Collins who led throughout the race, Moss's Vanwall expired in a cloud of white smoke and Hawthorn took second place. He was already seriously considering retiring from racing and what happened at the German Grand Prix made up his mind. Stirling Moss led initially with his Vanwall, but when his car expired out on the circuit the Ferraris of Collins and Hawthorn seemed to be in complete control of the race. But Tony Brooks, in third place with his Vanwall, was determined to make a fight of the race. He closed up on the two Dinos, challenged for the lead and swept in front. The Ferrari drivers fought back, but then in full view of Hawthorn, his close friend Peter Collins lost control at the difficult right-hand bend known as the Pflanzgarten at close to 100 mph, the Ferrari hit the bank and rolled over the hedge. Mike knew that the chances of Collins surviving that accident were slight indeed, but somehow he had to keep racing. He struggled on for another lap until the clutch gave trouble and then pulled into the pits to retire. Collins was flown by helicopter to Bonn hospital where he succumbed to his injuries.

There was now no pleasure left for Hawthorn in motor racing, but he led the World Championship and had to keep on racing until the end of the season. He was still deeply affected by Collins's death at the Portuguese Grand Prix and it was by gritting his teeth and using all his willpower that he managed to turn in second fastest practice time at Oporto. In the race Moss soon went ahead with his Vanwall, but despite ever-deteriorating brakes Mike managed to hold on to second place. He stopped for the brakes to be adjusted and after rejoining the race set fastest lap which was at this time worth a Championship point. Before the end of the race Moss made two mistakes which were to cost him the Championship and ensure that it was won by

John Michael Hawthorn

Hawthorn. The Vanwall pit hung out a sign reading 'HAWT REC,' but for some reason Moss misunderstood this and made no effort to better Hawthorn's time. On the last lap Moss, with third-placeman Lewis-Evans also at the wheel of a Vanwall in his slip-stream, was right behind Hawthorn and about to lap him. Because of brake trouble Hawthorn ran wide at one of the corners and Moss slipped by; at this Mike looked very unhappy because in the heat of the moment he thought that he had been passed by Lewis-Evans—both drivers wore white helmets and were otherwise concealed by the high sides of the Vanwall cockpit. Seeing his change of expression Moss waved Hawthorn in front again and when they completed that lap, Mike started *his* last lap, Moss was shown the chequered flag as winner of the race and Lewis-Evans was flagged off in third place, a lap behind. On his last lap Hawthorn got into difficulties again at the same corner, the Ferrari spun up the escape road and the engine stalled. Mike jumped out of the car and began to push it to re-start it along the footpath against the direction of the race, while Moss had stopped and was watching Mike's efforts. Eventually the Ferrari engine fired, Hawthorn swung around in a circle and completed the lap to take second place. If Moss had not lapped Lewis-Evans shortly before the finish, the Welshman would have taken second place and not Hawthorn. As it was, Hawthorn was told that he would be disqualified for pushing the car against the direction of the race and it was only on Moss's intervention to confirm that Mike had been pushing the car on the footpath and not the circuit as such that he was allowed to keep second place.

Moss retired at the Italian Grand Prix and Brooks snatched the lead from Hawthorn in the closing stages of the race when the Ferrari driver's car was slowed by clutch slip. The position in the World Championship was that Hawthorn had gained forty points from the six races (the maximum number he could count towards his total) and

Moss, who had finished in only five races, had accumulated thirty-two points. If Moss won the remaining round of the Championship at Casablanca and set fastest lap he would win the Championship by the margin of one point *provided* Hawthorn finished lower than second—if he took second place, he would count the six points instead of the four gained in the Argentine and would win the Championship with forty-two points.

Rarely has there been such a needle-match. Moss was all set to beat the opposition into the ground, Brooks's role was to cling on to second place, while in the Ferrari team the tactics were that Phil Hill would drive like the hammers of hell to lead if possible, if not to hold second place, while Hawthorn, driving a steadier race would be allowed to slip by his team-mate in the closing stages of the race. The Vanwall team-leader drove a perfect race to score his nine points, but Brooks's Vanwall blew up its engine, Hill held second place and then eased off to let Mike through to win the Championship.

When Mike finished the first thing he said to team-manager Tavoni was that he was retiring and Casablanca had been his last race. The Italian did not believe him, but yet another tragedy had tinged Hawthorn's victory and tipped the scales beyond the point of no return. The third-string Vanwall driver Stuart Lewis-Evans had crashed badly when his engine seized and had suffered terrible burns. He was flown back to England accompanied by a nurse in the Vickers Viscount which Tony Vandervell had chartered for the race and Mike was a member of the party that had flown out with Vandervell. On the return journey Mike spent most of the flight with Lewis-Evans whose life was quietly ebbing away in a curtained-off part of the aircraft.

Shortly afterwards Hawthorn formally announced his retirement from racing. For Mike, motor racing had never been his life and much of his racing career had been coloured by tragedy and misfortune. Even when he was grinning broadly in the heat of battle or living it up at a post-race party, it always seemed that there was something superficial about his happiness, that real contentment and satisfaction for Hawthorn lay in other pursuits. Now he was determined to enjoy those other things, but once again fate was not on his side. On 22nd January 1959 he lost control of his Jaguar 3.4 saloon on the Guildford By-pass, crossed the central dividing strip and hit the rear of an oncoming lorry. Hawthorn suffered a fractured skull and died almost immediately.

5
The Champion Who Never Was
STIRLING MOSS

Now recognised as one of the greatest drivers of all time and with one of the longest careers at the forefront of Grand Prix racing, Stirling Moss never quite managed to win the World Championship, although he took second place four years running, 1955 to 1958 (defeated in the last of these years by only a single point) and third place three years running, 1959 to 1961. Moss was a far greater Champion than many of the men who gained the title and there can be no better example than Moss of the weakness of the World Championship in failing to distinguish between true Champions and merely successful racing drivers.

Moss was a member of a very rare breed of drivers, completely and intensely dedicated to motor racing to the exclusion of other pursuits and almost unique in the manner in which he used to switch from car to car during the same afternoon. At a typical Silverstone meeting in the early 'fifties, he would drive his Formula Two car, a Cooper '500,' a Jaguar Mk VII saloon and a Jaguar sports car, competing in almost every race of the day and usually winning at least two. It was not until after 1954 that he limited the number of cars he drove and he would then still belong to

Stirling Moss

both Formula One and Sports Car teams, flitting from circuit to circuit and car to car, rather like a leading jockey switches from horse to horse. Only two other drivers sharing this unique versatility come to mind, Roy Salvadori and Jacky Ickx, neither of whom has matched his ability.

When Stirling started his competitions career, he had the great advantage of two parents who were motor racing addicts; both his father and mother had competed in pre-war days and the exploits of his father, dentist Alfred Moss, were particularly well remembered. His sister Pat was dedicated to horses and was something of a juvenile phenomenon at horse-shows, turning in later years to international rallying. Stirling himself was no mean horseman and initially his tastes for riding and racing were keenly balanced but he became a confirmed racing driver soon after acquiring his Cooper 500.

His first competition appearance was at the wheel of a BMW '328,' one of the finest of pre-war sports cars, belonging to his father and then in May 1948 he appeared at Prescott hill climb at the wheel of a JAP-engined Cooper '500.' The diminutive 500 cc class of single-seater racing cars on which the fortunes of Charles and John Cooper were founded had been introduced in post-war days as a relatively cheap means of going motor racing. Initially all the cars competing were home or garage-built 'specials,' but the Coopers and others started to build production cars at first powered by JAP push-rod ohv engines and later by Norton 'double-knocker' (twin-cam) units. The Formula flourished, the Cooper products achieved almost overwhelming popularity and in 1950 the class was given International status as Formula Three. In those days it was the only International class of racing dominated by British cars, in Britain there were races almost every weekend during the season and the close cut-and-thrust struggles between evenly matched cars, whose main differences lay in the varying talents of the engine tuners, spawned a new generation of British drivers, several of whom graduated to Formula One. Foremost amongst these was Stirling Moss, and another almost equally well-known driver who served his apprenticeship in Formula Three was Scuderia Ferrari driver Peter Collins.

At his first outing with the Cooper on the slopes of the Gloucestershire hill belonging to the Bugatti Owners' Club, slim, dark-haired eighteen-year-old Moss was fourth fastest; at Stanmer Park hill climb near Brighton three weeks later he set fastest time and already his reputation was in the making. Stirling's first race with the Cooper came on the short Brough motor-cycle circuit (it was only six-tenths of a mile long) and he won both his heat and the final. During the remainder of 1948 and the next two seasons Moss went from success to success in 500 cc racing, winning at hill climbs and races all over the country, but venturing abroad on occasions. In 1949 he drove a Cooper with a twin-cylinder 1000 cc engine in a Formula Two race at Lake Garda in Italy and finished third behind two V-12 Ferraris, having led one of them for some while.

Such talents could not go unnoticed for long. Despite terribly limited finances which meant running the team on a very hand to mouth basis, John Heath, together with his partner George Abecassis, who together ran a garage business at Walton-on-Thames, had decided to build a team of Formula Two cars which they named HWMs after their garage. These cars were of simple design and construction, were powered by Geoffrey Taylor's 1960 cc Alta engine of pre-war origins and were based on the single car with two-seater body raced by Heath in 1949. The 1950 cars retained two-seater body work as the original intention was that they should be easily convertible to run in sports car races. Both partners wanted to race a car which meant a vacancy for one outsider and the man chosen was Stirling Moss. The big, bulky HWMs contrasted strongly with the Coopers raced by Moss, their handling was completely different and they were silky smooth compared with the almost barbaric vibrations emanating from the single cylinder 500 cc engines. Moss quickly adapted himself to driving 'real' racing cars and during the team's long and often fruitless Continental tours in 1950 he took a second place at Mettet in Belgium and third places at Reims, Bari and Perigueux.

Moss had been pestering all the leading sports manufacturers in Britain to loan him a car to race, but without success, and he was beginning to think that to break into this class of racing was impossible. Then, in September 1950, that doyen of British motoring journalists, Tom Wisdom, lent him his own Jaguar XK120 to drive in the Tourist Trophy race in Northern Ireland. In this first post-war 'TT,' run on the eve of his twenty-first birthday, Stirling controlled the XK, a car not really designed for racing, superbly, setting a new lap record of 77.61 mph on his last lap and winning the race from the much more experienced Peter Whitehead. In that race Stirling won £1400 in prize money and bonuses and it led directly to a contract with Jaguar for the 1951 season.

For 1951 Stirling switched to a Kieft Formula Three car, winning four races during the year and staying with HWM for whom he drove at eighteen different meetings that season. Apart from four victories in minor races at British circuits, he took a second place at Aix-les-Bains in France and thirds at Marseille, Monza and Zandvoort. For Jaguar he was racing the new and beautifully streamlined C-type cars which had a top speed of close to 150 mph. At Le Mans, Stirling's instruction were to 'tiger' with the opposition and pull out as big a lead as possible. After just over eight hours of racing he and co-driver Jack Fairman were heading the field by a comfortable margin and Stirling had set a new lap record of 105.24 mph when a con-rod broke as Moss accelerated out of Arnage. The race was won by team-mates Peter Whitehead and Peter Walker. Later in the year Moss scored his second win in the Tourist Trophy.

Of his 1951 season with HMW Moss has written: 'It was obvious that I could never win even in the most favourable circumstances' (because of the strength of the Ferrari opposition) and went on to say: 'although I was told of the plans to have more cars with better road-holding for 1952, I am afraid that I could see no possibility that they would break through to the point of being a winning force.' * At Dunstable in Bedfordshire the ERA company was building a new Formula Two car of very light construction to be powered by the Bristol engine and Moss concluded that this would be his best bet for the coming year. Unfortunately development was slow, when the ERA did appear it was trouble-ridden and unsuccessful and during the year Moss also appeared at the wheel of both HWM and Connaught cars. In Formula Two racing, which was now also Grand Prix racing, Moss achieved no success at all with any of the cars he drove and as far as this category was concerned his efforts were completely wasted.

In sports car racing Moss fared a little better. At the beginning of the year he drove a Jaguar in the Mille Miglia but went off the road while holding third place. Then came a win with a C-type Jaguar in the Production Sports Car race at Silverstone, but at Monaco he was disqualified after being involved in a multi-car collision which was no fault of his. At Le Mans all three Jaguars fitted with hastily and untested streamlined bodies retired with over heating. In fact Stirling was instrumental in Jaguar making this foolish error, for he had returned from the Mille Miglia, full of tales of the high speed at which the Mercedes, likely to be Jaguar's stiffest opponents at Le Mans, had whistled past his C-type and the new bodies represented a panic attempt to gain extra speed. The following month he scored a fine victory in the Sports Car Grand Prix at Reims with a

* *Design And Behaviour Of The Racing Car* written with Laurence Pomeroy and published by William Kimber in 1963.

C-type. Another car driven by Moss during the year was the V-16 BRM which he handled in the Ulster Trophy, but this too brought no joy and he retired with mechanical troubles.

For 1953 the problem of what to drive in Formula Two raised its ugly head once again and Moss decided, in the absence of a competitive British car, to embark on the ambitious course of having a car built for him. John Cooper, Sports Editor of *Autocar*, designed the car which was built by Ray Martin (the same pair had been responsible for the very successful Kieft '500') and it was largely based on Cooper-Bristol components. The new car featured an Alta engine, completely new suspension and disc front brakes. It was built in haste, it had no proper development and it was a complete failure. Half-way through the season the engine was switched to a standard Cooper chassis. The first car had been built in twelve weeks, the new one was assembled in twelve days and barely had it been completed than Stirling drove it into sixth place in the German Grand Prix. Later in the season he finished third at les Sables d'Olonne in France and won a race at the Crystal Palace circuit in London, but on balance 1953 was another wasted year in Formula Two.

Moss switched back to Coopers for Formula Three in 1953–4, but in sports car racing he continued to drive Jaguars. He retired again in the Mille Miglia, a race that was destined never to be won by a British car, finished second at Le Mans co-driving with Peter Walker after setting the pace in the early hours of the race and partnered by Peter Whitehead won the 12 Hours race at Reims. In the Tourist Trophy race he fought for the lead with the Aston Martin of Peter Collins and Pat Griffiths, but on this circuit the Jaguars were a tremendous handful and the very abrasive surface resulted in gearbox trouble; when Moss realised, near the end of the race, that his gearbox was beginning to break up, rather than risk another lap he stopped short of the finishing line and when the winner crossed the line, nursed his Jaguar into fourth place to gain three points in the Sports Car Championship. Intelligence in the heat of the battle was always a strong Moss characteristic, as was the desire to finish, however far down the field, rather than retire.

Until the name of Mike Hawthorn hit the headlines in 1952, Stirling Moss had been the 'boy wonder' of British motor racing, but now he had a rival, a rival who was achieving far greater success. Not that Hawthorn was a better driver (he was not) but because he had signed up to drive for Ferrari, who built the world's fastest cars, while Moss, patriotic to the point of obsession, had persisted in driving uncompetitive British cars and spurned advances from Commendatore Ferrari. At the end of 1953 Moss still cut a very youthful figure, dedicated to motor racing, bubbling with enthusiasm, modestly confident, perhaps still slightly gauche in what was essentially a man's world and, happily, without that slightly superior air that characterised his later racing days. But now the crunch had come, not only was there no competitive British car for Moss to drive in the 2500 cc Formula One races of 1954 onwards, but there was no car, period. The days of patriotism were, of necessity, over. Moss's manager, Ken Gregory, made approaches to Mercedes-Benz who were known to be about to re-enter racing, but at this stage they were not interested in signing up British talent. Moss decided that he would have to buy a foreign car and, with financial assistance from BP, ordered £5000 worth of Maserati 250F. This was to prove the turning point in Moss's career.

Only four days after taking delivery of his car, he took fourth place at Bordeaux and was holding second place in the *Daily Express* Trophy race at Silverstone when the rear axle of the 250F, its Achilles' heel, let him down. A victory followed at Aintree and at the Belgian Grand Prix, against the might of the works Ferrari and Maserati teams, he took third place. The name 'Moss' was news again. At the British race he was asked by the Maserati factory to drive his hardest on the understanding that they would foot the bill if anything broke and he was holding a superb second place behind Gonzalez's Ferrari when the rear axle let him down again. And this was not through over-driving, for he had kept the Maserati well within its rev limits and throughout the race he had driven with consistency, precision and confidence. After the Silverstone race he was invited to join the works Maserati team and at the wheel of his own car, painted red, but retaining a green nose-band, he led the Italian Grand Prix at Monza from Fangio's Mercedes until loss of oil pressure caused him to stop. In typical, determined Moss fashion he pushed his car across the line into tenth place.

In 1954 Moss enjoyed his last—and successful—season of Formula Three racing and drove again for the Jaguar team. At Le Mans he was at the wheel of one of the new D-type Jaguars with beautifully streamlined appearance dominated by a single, large, tail-fin. That year's Le Mans race went to Ferrari by a narrow margin from a Jaguar driven by Tony Rolt and Duncan Hamilton, but Stirling Moss went out of the race in dramatic fashion after only eight hours when his brakes failed on the Mulsanne straight and he took to the escape road at a horrific, nerve-shattering 160 mph. Moss retired in the Reims race when he and co-driver Walker are leading by a substantial margin and he was out of the picture in the Tourist Trophy because of mechanical trouble.

Although they had rejected the offer of his services twelve months' previously, Moss was now in demand at Mercedes and on 9th December 1954 he signed a contract with them to drive for the German team in all the major Grands Prix and sports car races. He reserved the right to drive other cars when not needed by Mercedes and in fact retained his Maserati which he drove to a number of victories in minor races, but entered it in various World Championship events for other drivers, including Lance Macklin, John Fitch and Peter Walker. When Moss joined Mercedes, he was already a vastly experienced Grand Prix driver, certainly one of the top six racing at the time, but at Stuttgart he served an apprenticeship in racing all over again with maestro Juan Fangio. Race after race, driving in Fangio's wheel-tracks, Moss gave his own very considerable skill and ability a final polish that was to help raise him to the level of the master from whom he was learning. It, however, also became apparent during the year that Moss was the world's greatest sports car driver and in the field of long-distance endurance racing there were few lessons that anyone could teach him.

With the exception of two races in which Mercedes plans went completely awry, the team dominated both Grands Prix and sports car racing in 1955. The first race of the season, the Argentine Grand Prix, was running in enervatingly hot conditions that badly affected all the competitors except two local drivers, Fangio and Roberto Mieres. When Moss stopped with his car out on the circuit because of fuel vapor lock, he decided to relax in the shade while the car cooled down. There he was resting quietly, when up came an ambulance to whip him off for treatment despite his vociferous protests! After an interpreter had intervened, Moss was eventually released to return to the pits where he took over Hans Herrmann's car to finish fourth. The Argentine Grand Prix was an exceptional race by any standards and normal Mercedes team tactics were given little chance to operate. In the normal way Mercedes team manager, the great Alfred Neubauer, gave his drivers no specific instructions, but Fangio was a substantially better driver than Moss—Stirling admitted this readily—and in the early part of the race would pull out a considerable lead. When Fangio was half a minute ahead of the field, he would be signalled to ease off and then Moss would gradually close up to take station behind him. The expected pattern emerged in the team's next race, the Buenos Aires City Grand Prix, and Fangio and Moss took the first two places.

Stirling's next race for the Mercedes team was the Mille Miglia, the results of which made history and provided one of the most stirring motor racing stories ever. In this race Stirling was passengered by Denis Jenkinson, Continental Correspondent of *Motor Sport*, and after an exhaustive and exhausting series of runs over the 1000-mile course, they compiled an elaborate roll of notes listing all the difficult bends and corners and from which by a series of hand signals 'Jenks' was able to inform Moss with details of the road ahead. The system worked perfectly and Moss won the race at record speed, the only win by an English driver in its history, the first victory by other than an Italian car since 1931 (when another great driver, Caracciola won with a Mercedes) and he beat team-mate Fangio into second place. Denis Jenkinson's account of this race, first published in the June 1955 issue of *Motor Sport*, is one of the greatest ever pieces of motor racing writing.

At Monaco all the Mercedes retired, but Moss took the expected second place to Fangio in the Belgian Grand Prix. Then came Le Mans, that terrible 24 Hours race in which Levegh's Mercedes crashed and disintegrated into the spectator enclosure where over eighty persons were killed. The other Mercedes were withdrawn when the car shared by Fangio and Moss had a comfortable two-lap lead. The repercussions of the Le Mans incident were enormous, many races were cancelled and Mercedes ran in only six more events that season before withdrawing from both Grand Prix and sports car racing. The Dutch went ahead with their Grand Prix only a week after the Le Mans tragedy and again Moss finished second behind the maestro. Then at the British race at Aintree the tables were turned and Stirling Moss took the chequered flag ahead of Fangio, having led for most of the race. Moss has admitted that Fangio was the vastly better driver and yet 'Moss and Fangio seemed to be dicing in earnest trusting each other not to make a mistake,' in the words of Gregor Grant, so did Moss beat the World Champion or was he allowed to win? Motor racing experts have often pondered over the outcome of this particular race, but, again Gregor Grant's opinion makes interesting reading: 'It has been said—and, reiterated by Moss himself—that Juan Manuel Fangio could have won, but preferred to give his young team-mate the chance to score his first major GP success. This may well be true but in my opinion Stirling Moss *had* to drive with all he knew to secure his victory. The slightest falling off would have seen the Champion of the World in front. Moss certainly had to earn his keep and, on his showing at Aintree is not very far behind Fangio in general driving skill.' *

Subsequently in 1955 Moss finished second to Fangio in the Swedish sports car Grand Prix and retired in the Italian Grand Prix, but he did score two fine sports car victories. After being chased for the whole race by the D-type Jaguar of Hawthorn and Titterington, Moss and American co-driver John Fitch won the last Tourist Trophy to be held on the difficult and dangerous Dundrod road circuit. In October he was partnered in the Targa Florio by newcomer to the Mercedes team Peter Collins. The Sicilian race, over a 44.7 mile circuit made up of roads that by British standards are little better than country lanes, the edges of the road thickly thronged by spectators who surge on to the course and only shuffle back at the approach of a car, is one of the most difficult in the racing calendar. Moss and Collins won the race at record speed—despite Moss colliding with a wall and dropping the car over a three-foot bank into a field. This off-course excursion cost about twelve minutes while Moss spun the wheels and boiled away the radiator water in his frantic efforts to regain the road.

Out of six Championship Formula One races during the

* *Autosport,* 22nd July 1953.

year, Fangio had won four and Moss one and they took the first two places in the Drivers' Championship. Even though the team had withdrawn from Le Mans, it won three out of four Sports Car Championship races entered and dominated the Championship results. Moss had driven or co-driven in all these three races and could fairly claim to be the world's best sports car driver.

Stirling still nursed a strong desire to drive a British Formula One car and before making any firm plans for 1956, tried out all three British cars, Connaught, BRM and Vanwall, but was still left with the definite impression that the Maserati was the better bet for defeating Fangio (driving for Ferrari), his principal rival in 1956. To help him resolve the problem, Stirling, his father and his manager Ken Gregory entertained seventeen journalists to dinner at the Royal Automobile Club. When the meal was over, Moss told the assembled company that he thought that the Maserati team had the best chance of winning the World Championship in 1956 and that he had been offered the chance of returning to the team as number one driver. He recounted his tests with the British cars, but added that he thought that he could achieve faster times with Maserati. Which team, he asked those present, did they think he should join? Nine journalists voted in favour of Maserati and not long afterwards Stirling signed up again with the Maserati team.

The wisdom of Stirling's choice reveals itself in the results of the 1956 season. World Champion Fangio, fellow-Ferrari driver Peter Collins and Moss were all closely matched in the Championship, each won two victories on their own, but Fangio had the advantage of being able to take over the cars of team-mates who were well placed and this gave him enough points to beat Moss into second place. At Monaco Stirling led throughout in one of the finest races of his career, handling his red Maserati with precision, smoothness and consistent lap speeds. It was through good fortune, which only too rarely shone on Moss during his career, that he scored his second Championship race victory of the season at Monza. The Ferraris were plagued by tire troubles and Moss built up a good lead, only to run out of fuel on the course. Private Maserati owner Luigi Piotti, seeing the stricken works car, quickly summed up the situation and shunted Moss's car back to the pits so that it could take on extra fuel. Moss rejoined the race to win from Juan Fangio who had taken over Peter Collins's Ferrari. On the day of the race it was thought that the fuel consumption of the Maserati had proved unexpectedly heavy, but the following day the car was taken out again for test purposes, fuel was poured into the tank and ran straight through because of a split in the bottom! Although he co-drove the winning car in the Buenos Aires race at the beginning of the year, only limited success came Moss's way in sports car racing in 1956 and he crashed in the Mille Miglia because of the atrocious handling of his new Maserati.

Back in May 1956 Stirling had driven a British Vanwall to victory in the *Daily Express* Trophy race at Silverstone and he had been very impressed, although not at that stage regarding the car as a serious World Championship contender. Now with a further season's racing experience and development behind it the Vanwall was a very different and much improved prospect. At long last Stirling thought that he had found a really competitive British car and much to Tony Vandervell's delight agreed to lead the Vanwall team in 1957. Although the 'Old Man' still tended to meddle too much in the detail workings of the team instead of leaving team manager David Yorke and the mechanics to get on with the job, the Vanwall organisation was a closely-knit, friendly team that struck a typically British compromise between the Teutonic efficiency of Mercedes and the frenetic chaos of Maserati. The Vanwalls had rather too many silly niggling faults at the beginning of 1957 that should have been cured at least a year or so before, but by the middle of the season most of these had been cured.

For Moss the first six months of the year were far from auspicious. He set a new lap record at Siracusa in Sicily, but lost the lead after a pit stop and finished third. Throttle linkage trouble eliminated him at Goodwood. Precisely what happened at Moss's next race is something about which he has been decidedly cagey. He led at Monaco for three laps, but on the next lap went straight on into the barricades at the chicane, scattering poles all over the track and causing a multiple pile-up which also eliminated the Lancia-Ferraris of Collins and Hawthorn. There was no Dutch or Belgian race in 1957 and Moss missed both the French Grand Prix at Rouen and the Reims Grand Prix because of a sinus infection.

The motor racing circus next appeared at the dull, flat characterless Aintree circuit, over-shadowed by the smoke and grime of Liverpool and running round the soot-flecked green of the famous steeplechase course. The race was the European Grand Prix and it was to prove one of the most important in the history of British motor racing and Moss's own career. Moss soon took the lead in this race, but then his car developed an engine misfire, it looked as though British chances of victory were lost, and the usual Italian domination would re-assert itself. However, Moss's teammate Tony Brooks, still not fully recovered from a bad crash at Le Mans, was flagged in and Moss rejoined the race with Brooks's car in what was clearly a win-or-bust effort.

Moss swept by Fangio's Maserati, closed up on and passed Musso's Lancia-Ferrari and then began to chase after Peter Collins with another Maranello entry. By lap 47 of this 90-lap race he was in fourth place behind another Vanwall driven by Stuart Lewis-Evans and just as he was about to overtake his team-mate, the engine of the leading Maserati driven by Jean Behra blew up, depositing bits and pieces all over the track; Hawthorn, in second place with a Lancia-Ferrari, punctured a tire on the debris and to the delight of the very patriotic crowd Moss was back in the lead. Although Lewis-Evans stopped out on the circuit with throttle linkage trouble, Moss was now completely unchallenged and even had time to make a precautionary refuelling stop to take on extra fuel. The Aintree victory was one of the most important in Moss's career. It was the first victory by a British car in a major Grand Prix since Segrave's win with a Sunbeam in the 1923 French Grand Prix and it represented the turning point in British Grand Prix fortunes.

Although the Vanwalls proved a terrible handful in their next race, the German Grand Prix at the Nürburgring, because of suspension deficiencies, Moss went on to win two further 1957 Championship races for Vanwall: the Pescara Grand Prix over a difficult 15.9-mile road circuit that combined long straights with tortuous mountain sections and the Italian race at Monza in which Moss defeated Fangio in an epic duel, out-driving the Argentinian in one of the most exciting fights seen at the Monza circuit. For the third year in succession Stirling took second place in the Drivers' Championship, with 25 points to Fangio's 40.

Relations at Vanwall could not have been happier and all three drivers, Moss, Brooks and Lewis-Evans, stayed with the team for 1958. Up until the 1958 season entrants could choose their own fuel and Vanwall used a brew containing a high percentage of alcohol for internal engine cooling. For 1958, however, 130-octane aviation fuel was compulsory and the conversion work necessary to the Vanwall engines meant that the team had to miss the first race of the season, the Argentinian Grand Prix. So Moss was free to look for a drive elsewhere for this race and he agreed to handle Rob Walker's 2-litre Cooper-Climax. The rear-engined dark blue Cooper was nothing more than a Formula Two with an enlarged engine and in Grand Prix racing at this time no one took the Coopers very seriously. The Argentine race proved very hard on tires and while the Ferrari drivers reckoned on stopping for a wheel-change, Moss and the Walker team realised that he could not, because the Cooper was fitted with bolt-on wheels which would take too long to change. So Moss was forced to drive a canny race, conserving his tires, and as the faster cars stopped at the pits as expected, he came through to lead the race and score his first victory of the season, despite strong efforts by Musso of the Ferrari team to catch him in the closing laps of the race. At the finish the Cooper had the canvas showing through on one tire!

By 1958 the Vanwall design was rather long in the tooth, it was not the easiest of cars to convert to run on petrol, adherence to rev limits was critical and the engines generally were rather unreliable. Moss scored victories with his Vanwall at Zandvoort, Oporto and Casablanca and took a second place at Reims, but retired with engine trouble at Monaco, Spa (where it was his own fault because he missed a gear and the revs soared past the critical limit) and Silverstone, with magneto failure at the Nürburgring, and gearbox trouble at Monza. He was pipped for the World Championship by Mike Hawthorn by only a single point and was unlucky indeed to be beaten, for his driving throughout the year had been superb and with a little more engine reliability he would have had the Championship in the bag. Moss was never one to cry over spilt milk, however, and would cheerfully have carried on with Vanwall for another season if Tony Vandervell had not sprung the surprise announcement in January 1959 that he was withdrawing from racing because of ill-health. For the 1959 season Stirling agreed to drive for Rob Walker who proposed fielding both the usual Cooper-Climax, now with full 2500 cc engine, and a BRM-powered Cooper. But Stirling also made arrangements with Sir Alfred Owen for a front-engined BRM to be made available to the British Racing Partnership and at some races during the year he elected to drive this sickly yellow-green-painted car. This was a move which did not please the BRM personnel for they felt that it revealed Sir Alfred's lack of confidence in them. The BRM-powered Cooper proved hopelessly unsuccessful and because Cooper refused to supply Walker with the usual Cooper gearbox for the Climax-powered cars, he was forced to order special gearboxes designed by Italian Valeiro Colotti. The gears were not machined in exact accordance with Colotti's drawings and the Walker Coopers were plagued by gearbox trouble throughout the year.

At the beginning of the season Moss scored victories in the New Zealand Grand Prix and in the Formula One race at Goodwood, but he retired at Aintree, Monaco and Zandvoort and could already see the chances of victory in the World Championship slipping out of his grasp. He had driven a works BRM in the *Daily Express* Trophy race at Silverstone, but on only the fifth lap the brakes failed completely and he was lucky indeed not to have a serious accident. Nevertheless Stirling decided to drive the British Racing Partnership BRM in the French Grand Prix at Reims; he held second place, despite the loss of the use of his clutch, until he spun on melted tar and the engine stalled. With no clutch he had no hope of re-starting the car himself, so he had the car pushed by marshalls and drove round to the pits to retire, knowing that he would be disqualified for receiving outside assistance. A second place with the BRM followed in the British race at Aintree, but at Avus he drove the Cooper, retiring on only the second lap with transmission trouble. In this race the BRM, driven by Hans Herrmann, was completely destroyed when the brakes failed and Moss drove Coopers for the rest of 1959.

Now at last the season began to go Moss's way and he completely dominated the Portuguese Grand Prix to win by over a lap from Masten Gregory's works car. At Monza he drove one of the finest races of his career, out-foxing the Ferrari team. It was a circuit on which it was expected that the power of the Ferraris would bring them victory and it was anticipated that all the faster cars would have to stop for new rear tires. Moss's Cooper was fitted with knock-on rear hubs instead of the usual bolt-on wheels, apparently, to facilitate the wheel-changes. In the race Moss contented himself with sitting on the tail of race-leader Phil Hill, letting the Ferrari driver set the pace and do all the work, while he cornered gently and avoided hard acceleration. When Hill stopped for new rear tires, Moss took the lead and instead of making the anticipated pit stop, drove on and on to run through the race on the original tires which he had so carefully conserved in the opening stages of the race. The outcome of the World Championship was not settled until the United States race in December where Stirling retired with mechanical trouble and the Championship went to Jack Brabham with Moss in third place behind Tony Brooks.

During 1958–59 Stirling had driven Aston Martin DBR1 cars in Sports Car Championship events and with some spectacular results. In 1958 he had set a new lap record in the Targa Florio before his car retired with final drive trouble, he won the Nürburgring 1000 Kilometres race with Jack Brabham as co-driver and sharing a car with Tony Brooks scored another victory in the Tourist Trophy at Goodwood. Moss brought Aston Martin their third successive victory in the Nürburgring 1000 Kilometres race in 1959, and it was a truly remarkable drive; Moss led during his spell at the wheel, but team-mate Jack Fairman spun on the wet track and rejoined the race in fourth place. Moss brought the Aston back through into the lead, handed the car over to Fairman for another short spell during which he again lost ground which Moss made up to win by forty-one seconds from the pursuing Ferrari of Gendebien and Hill. Moss also co-drove the winning car in the Tourist Trophy race.

For 1960 Rob Walker bought one of the new rear-engined

Lotus 18 cars, a car that was very much simpler and much more effective than previous Formula One cars from the Lotus stable. At the beginning of the year Moss finished third in the Argentine race with the Cooper, but by Monaco he was at the wheel of the Lotus and scored a fine victory. He took fourth place at Zandvoort after a pit stop for a wheel-change, but then disaster struck in practice for the Belgian Grand Prix when the nearside rear wheel came off the Lotus while it was travelling at around 100 mph and Stirling crashed badly, suffering broken ribs, a fractured nose and leg injuries. Moss did not race again until the Portuguese Grand Prix in August where he dropped to sixth place after a pit stop for new plugs; he had risen to fifth place when his engine cut out altogether and he was disqualified for pushing his car against the direction of the race in his efforts to re-start it. Brabham now had the Championship in the bag, but Stirling collected two more Formula One wins before the end of the season, in the Gold Cup race at Oulton Park and in the United States Grand Prix at Watkins Glen. For 1960 Stirling had transferred his allegiance in Formula Two from Cooper-Borgward cars to a Rob Walker-entered Porsche and with the German car he won four races.

In 1961 the Rob Walker team faced an additional handicap. Like all the British teams, they had to struggle on with the old 4-cylinder Climax engine, but in addition, because of oil contract difficulties, Lotus were unable to supply the latest 21 model and Moss continued to race the older, square-shaped 18. On most circuits even Moss was completely outpaced by the Ferraris, but in two races he was able to demonstrate effectively that there was no substitute for skill. At Monaco he drove one of the greatest races of his career, displaying a mastery of car and circuit that no other driver could match; lapping with great precision and holding off the Ferrari drivers by his superior ability in lapping slower cars, keeping a good eye on his mirror so that in the closing stages of the race, when Ginther's Ferrari was really close, he could ensure that he was maintaining a big enough gap, and at the chequered flag he was just 3.6 seconds ahead of the first of the Maranello entries.

It was impossible for Moss to pull it over the Ferraris again in the races that followed at Zandvoort, Spa, Reims and Aintree, but yet again at the Nürburgring he achieved the near-impossible. In the German race Moss had two aces in his hand; he knew the difficult 14.2-mile circuit intimately, having won the 1000 kilometres race there three years in succession, in 1958–9 with Aston Martins and in 1960 with a Maserati; secondly Moss had an advantage as far as tires were concerned—on the morning of the race, rain had threatened, but the sun was shining before the start of the Grand Prix and the Dunlop technicians warned competitors not to run in the dry on the new wet-weather tires. The Ferrari team took Dunlop's advice and changed to the normal covers, but from experience in a race at Solitude, the Lotus drivers knew that the tires were safe in the dry and Moss took a gamble by starting on the wet-weather covers. Moss took an immediate lead and began to draw away from the Ferrari opposition; and when rain began to fall in the closing stages of the race, he had the German Grand Prix in the bag, for the Ferraris started to slither and slide and fall even further behind. At the fall of the chequered flag Moss was twenty seconds ahead of the Ferrari of von Trips, scoring what was on paper a highly improbable victory. Moss also scored a number of minor victories during the year, including three wins in Inter-continental Formula races with Cooper cars and a win in the Gold Cup race at Oulton Park with the revolutionary four-wheel-drive Ferguson.

Early in 1962 Moss won the New Zealand Grand Prix and the Lady Wigram Trophy race, another New Zealand event. He had now been at the forefront of Grand Prix racing for eight successive seasons, but his brilliant career was destined to come to an abrupt and untimely end. At the wheel of a Rob Walker Lotus loaned to the UDT-Laystall team at the Easter Goodwood meeting, Moss was delayed by mechanical trouble, but rejoined the race, intent on beating the lap record. As he caught Graham Hill's BRM on the fast and difficult stretch before the bend known as St Mary's his Lotus took to the grass, shot past Hill and continued at undiminished speed into the grass bank. Moss, trapped in the car, was severly injured and although he made a full recovery, he never again raced. What caused that accident remains a mystery.

6
Australian Champion
JACK BRABHAM
1959-60, 1966

PERSISTENCE IS PROBABLY the word that comes closest to summing up the secret of Jack Brabham's long career of Grand Prix wins. Persistence in learning from his mistakes, persistence in gaining in experience and improving his speed and style until he won his first two World Championships at the wheel of Cooper cars; persistence in his determination to retire, but still carrying to win another World Championship at the wheel of cars bearing his own name—Brabham is still the only man to have achieved that feat—and scoring Grand Prix wins right up until his last season of racing in 1970. Brabham was the first antipodean driver to break into Grand Prix racing with success, but only the first of many, and his early press-on style of driving, hurling his car into corners and scrabbling round with the tail hanging well and truly out both brought him a reputation that stayed with him even when his driving was much more refined and was a fine testimony to the inherent safe handling characteristics of rear-engine Coopers.

Jack Brabham was born at Hurstville, ten miles to the south of Sydney on the 2nd April 1926. His father ran a greengrocery business, but was a keen motorist which did much to encourage Jack's later interest in the sport. There were three trucks belonging to the business and driving these round and round the yard, Jack was initiated into the problems of controlling a motor vehicle. Long before he was old enough to hold a driving license, his father used to allow him to drive the truck back from market and he was soon a very proficient and able driver. At technical college Jack studied practical engineering with the emphasis on metalwork, woodwork and technical drawing and his main sporting interests were tennis and swimming. He left school at fifteen—Jack's inclinations always tended towards the practical rather than the academic—and after working for a very short while in an engineering shop, took a job at a garage. It was while working there that with the help of his father he acquired his first and long awaited motor-cycle, a 350 cc Velocette.

At the age of eighteen Jack joined the Royal Australian Air Force and received his initial training as a flight mechanic at Adelaide. He was discharged from the Air Force in 1946 and now faced the problem of finding a job. Instead of going out to work, Jack decided to let the work come to him and with the full co-operation of the family, his uncle, who was a builder, erected a workshop for him in the grounds of his grandfather's house in Sydney. Soon afterwards Jack went to a couple of midget car races in Sydney in which a friend was competing. Jack was beginning to get interested in racing, but at this stage his interest was more on the mechanical side of things and he decided with his friend, Johnny Schonberg, to build a new car for Schonberg to race. After a season's racing, Schonberg's wife persuaded him to give up the sport and so Jack decided to have a crack himself. Jack soon proved that he was a competent dirt-track driver and took part in the sport with great success for nearly six years. Eventually, at Adelaide, where he was competing in the South Australian Championship, his engine threw a rod, certainly not the only mechanical misfortune he had suffered, but one of the worst because the engine was completely destroyed. He decided that he had had enough of this form of racing.

In 1951 Jack had started competing with midget cars in hill climbs and won the Australian Hill Climb Championship that year. That same year he had married Betty Beresford whom he had known for about six years. Jack's marriage did not stop him racing simply because Betty was almost as involved in the sport as he was, she had been helping him in the engineering shop, had cleaned and polished the midget and she knew exactly what sort of future she was taking on! Jack and Betty have three sons, Geoffrey, Gary and David, and now the eldest, Geoffrey is following in his famous father's footsteps and has competed with success in Formula Ford races in Australia.

Jack's first contact with the Cooper Car Company came when he bought a Mark V Cooper (the second car of the marque he owned) which he raced with an 1100 cc JAP engine. From the 1100 cc Cooper he graduated to a Cooper-Bristol, bought cheaply because its owner committed suicide before it reached Australia, and, with financial assistance from the Redex fuel additive company, this was later raced as the 'Redex Special.' During 1953–4 Jack raced the Cooper-Bristol with great success, crossing the Tasman Sea to compete in the New Zealand Grand Prix in early 1954 and 1955. In 1955 he decided to come to England to race, but thinking that his Cooper-Bristol would not be competitive, he sold it to Australian Stan Jones and bought Peter Whitehead's Cooper-Alta. From his first race with his new mount, Jack realised that he made a terrible blunder and that the Alta engine was hopelessly deficient in both power and reliability. The chassis was the same as that of the Bristol-powered cars, so he bought a Bristol engine and raced the car in that form.

It was while racing the Cooper-Bristol that Jack met John Cooper and was given a trial at Goodwood with the new rear-engined Cooper-Climax sports car. Jack was tremendously impressed with the new Cooper and shortly afterwards when he started at Cooper's Surbiton premises, he was given consent to build his own rear-engined Cooper which he fitted with the Bristol engine so that it could run in Formula One events. His first race with his new and unpainted car was the British Grand Prix at Aintree, the race in which Mercedes-Benz took the first four places—and Jack trailed round at the tail of the field, having started the race without the use of the clutch, until he eventually retired with overheating problems. At Snetterton in August he battled with a far from well Stirling Moss who beat him for third place behind the two leading Vanwalls and he then took the Cooper back to Australia where he drove it to victory in the Australian Grand Prix.

Jack sold the Cooper in Australia and returned to Britain in 1956 to race the ex-Owen Organisation Maserati 250F which he had just bought. In his autobiography, *When The Flag Drops* (William Kimber & Co Ltd, 1971) Jack comments: 'It was in such a bad condition that I could have spent all the year repairing it.' Jack should know, but it must be remembered that although this particular 250F had been used for extensive development testing in connection with the new BRM that appeared in 1955, it had been driven into third place in the Argentine Grand Prix by Mike Hawthorn at the beginning of the year, and 250Fs would survive race after race without a great deal of attention. Jack only raced the 250F a few times, never seeming really happy at the wheel, but his main concern in 1956 was driving works rear-engined Cooper sports cars with which he achieved many successes, including a second place to Castellotti's Osca in the Imola Grand Prix. During the latter part of the year Jack also handled one of the new rear-engined Formula Two Cooper single-seaters.

Over the winter of 1956–7 Jack returned home, competing in races in both Australia and New Zealand. He returned to

Europe in the spring, driving works cars and also for Rob Walker who was racing in collaboration with the Cooper team. After running at Siracusa and Goodwood, he was entered with a 2-litre Cooper at Monaco; the engine was a special enlarged version of the familiar 4-cylinder unit which had been paid for by Rob Walker. In practice Jack crashed the Cooper badly near the Casino, but the engine was transferred to a Rob Walker-owned chassis that was to be driven by Les Leston. Jack worked his way up to third place in the race, but only five laps from the finish the engine cut out completely. With that dogged determination for which he was to become renowned, he pushed the car all the way from the Station hairpin to the finish to take sixth place. At Le Mans he co-drove an 1100 cc Cooper sports with Ian Raby and they finished thirteenth overall and third in their class. The Coopers ran in a number of Formula One races in 1957, without much in the way of success, but with his car in Formula Two trim Jack won a total of five races and finished second in two others. He also took a second place at Goodwood with a Tojeiro-Jaguar belonging to John Ogier who ran the Essex Racing Team. Jack's last race of the year was at Brands Hatch on Boxing Day and he drove Rob Walker's 2-litre Cooper-Climax to victory in the Formule Libre race.

Jack then flew to New Zealand to compete in the New Zealand Grand Prix which he won at his fifth attempt. In 1958 Cooper tackled a full season of Grand Prix racing for the first time with Jack and Roy Salvadori as works drivers, as in 1957, and with the added impetus that Stirling Moss had already won the Argentine race with a 2-litre Cooper belonging to Rob Walker. Although Salvadori achieved some good places in Formula One during that year, Jack was largely out of luck and his successes were limited to a second place behind Hawthorn's Ferrari at Goodwood, a fourth at Monaco and a sixth place at Reims. In Formula Two he was rather more successful, winning two races and finishing second in two others. He also shared the winning Aston Martin with Stirling Moss in the Nürburgring 1000 kilometres race, but Stirling did the lion's share of the driving and while he was at the wheel Jack lost a lot of ground that Moss subsequently made up.

Over the winter of 1958-9 Jack returned home again and still driving Coopers finished second to Stirling Moss in both the Australian and New Zealand Grands Prix. He also finished second to Ron Flockhart in the Lady Wigram Trophy race and third in the race at Teretonga Park. Jack returned to Europe in 1959 to lead the Cooper team in which he was now partnered by New Zealander Bruce McLaren, and now drove cars powered by Coventry-Climax engines of a full 2500 cc. The latest Cooper was a much improved car, with far superior handling to its predecessors as well as greatly increased performance. The Surbiton team's main opponents were the front-engined Ferraris and, at long last, Brabham had a car to match these on all but the very fastest circuits. On the Cooper's debut with the new engine Brabham scored a fine victory in the *Daily Express* Trophy race at Silverstone and went on to score another victory at Monaco. At Zandvoort his car was slowed by gearbox trouble and he had to settle for second place behind Joakim Bonnier's BRM, the only win scored by a Bourne car in a Championship race since the make had first raced in 1950.

In two of their next three races the Coopers could not match the speed of the Ferraris. In the French Grand Prix at Reims Jack was beaten into third place by a brace of the Maranello cars. Despite finishing the race with a bald front tire, Jack won the British race at Aintree from Stirling Moss's BRM and another Cooper driven by team-mate McLaren. The German Grand Prix was held on the horrific Avus track at Berlin with its lethal, steeply banked North turn. Most drivers hated the circuit and it was never used again for an important race. All the Coopers except that driven by Maurice Trintignant retired in this race and

Ferraris took the first three places. In the Portuguese race at Lisbon Jack crashed his Cooper, almost certainly the result of loss of concentration after seeing a small child run across the track, and he finished third in the Italian Grand Prix at Monza. The outcome of the World Championship was not known until the United States Grand Prix at Sebring in December and Jack, Stirling Moss and Ferrari driver Tony Brooks could all win it. Moss seared away into the distance at the start of the race, but retired, and Jack seemed all set for victory when his car ran out of fuel on the last lap, coasting to a halt five hundred yards before the finishing line. Jack's career seemed dotted with instances of this sort and once again he pushed the car to the finish, crossing the line in fourth place. Nevertheless Brabham won the World Championship with 31 points to the 27 gained by Tony Brooks.

Cooper sent two works cars out for Jack and Bruce McLaren to drive in the 1960 Tasman series; Brabham and McLaren took the first two places in the New Zealand Grand Prix and Jack also won the Lady Wigram Trophy race. The drivers were involved in quite a lot of flying around at the beginning of 1960 because the Argentine Grand Prix had been restored to the calendar after an interval of two years. Jack was out of luck in South America and retired in both this race and the Buenos Aires City Grand Prix. He then travelled to New Zealand where he won the Tasman race at Longford, flew home to Australia to compete in the Philip Island race and then to Siracusa for a Formula Two race in which he retired. He went on to win the Formula Two Brussels Grand Prix, the Pau Grand Prix and with the latest and even better Formula One Cooper fitted for the first time with coil spring suspension finished second to Innes Ireland's Lokis in the *Daily Express* Trophy race at Silverstone.

The first Championship race of the European season was at Monaco where Brabham spun on a wet track and hit a wall and was disqualified for receiving 'help' from marshalls who were trying to clear the car off the road. Jack was another driver who disliked Spa because of the high speeds attained, for these meant that any accident was likely to be a serious one. He won the Belgian Grand Prix there in 1960 and there followed a whole string of victories that ensured his second World Championship victory. Even on a really fast circuit like Reims the Coopers could now match the straight-line speed of the Ferraris and after a battle with Phil Hill at the wheel of one of the Maranello cars Jack scored another victory in the French race. Other wins followed at Silverstone (where Jack was passed by Graham Hill who spun off shortly before the end of the race) and the Portuguese race at Oporto. The British teams boycotted the Italian race because it was held on the combined road circuit and banked track at Monza which they considered to be dangerous (but it seems doubtful whether Cooper would have given it a miss if the Championship were not in the bag) and Jack's last race under the 2500 cc Grand Prix Formula was the United States Grand Prix at Riverside Raceway in which he finished fourth after two pit stops to extinguish fuel fires.

Brabham stayed with the Cooper team for the 1961 season, but he was well advanced with plans to start his own racing company. Already he had his own tuning business run by Ron Tauranac and the first car built by the new company known as Motor Racing Developments was the MRD Formula Junior car which made its debut at Goodwood in August 1961. In the meanwhile Jack was struggling in Formula One with Coopers powered by the old 4-cylinder 1500 cc engine, but his only successes were wins in the Brussels Grand Prix, a non-Championship race, and the Aintree '200.' The new Cooper with the V-8 Coventry-Climax engine made its debut in the German Grand Prix at the beginning of August. After setting second fastest time in practice, he went off the road on the first lap and 'by 7 pm that evening Brabham had still not removed his crash helmet . . . a sure sign that the Australian was upset with someone.' He retired with the V-8 in both the Italian and United States races.

Cooper's—and Brabham's—best efforts of the season was at Indianapolis where he drove a car with the engine stretched to 2.7 litres and, because the wheelbase did not comply with Indy's minimum length rule, allowed to run as a special concession. Jack drove a steady race to take ninth place and it was this performance that encouraged other British constructors to have a go at the banked track in later years. Only two other successes came Jack's way in 1961, a win in the New Zealand Grand Prix and second place in September in the Gold Cup race at Oulton Park with one of the 4-cylinder cars.

While work was progressing on Brabham's new Grand Prix car, he drove a Cooper in the Tasman races, winning the Hudson Trophy at Levin and the Lakeside race, and then acquired a Lotus Formula One car for the European season. Jack did not have much in the way of success with the new car, but finished second in the 2000 Guineas race at Mallory Park and fifth in the British Grand Prix. The new Brabham Grand Prix car, which was largely the work of Ron Tauranac, appeared at the German Grand Prix. There was always some resentment at Coopers that Jack should have gained so much knowledge at the Surbiton works and then gone off and applied it to his own cars. Jack had always 'mechanicked' his cars himself and his technical knowledge was such that he was in a far stronger position than most drivers when he started his own business. But the new Brabham was a conventional enough car, powered by the usual V-8 Coventry Climax engine, and finished in a distinctive turquoise. The first season was very much one of trial and error and Jack retired his new car at the Nürburgring, finished third in the Gold Cup race at Oulton Park, missed the Italian Grand Prix, took fourth place at

Watkins Glen and rounded the season off with a second place in the non-Championship Mexican race.

When Porsche withdrew from Grand Prix racing at the end of 1962, Californian Dan Gurney was free to drive for the Brabham team which regularly entered two cars during the 1963 season. Jack was so impressed with Dan's driving that not for the first—or the last time—he seriously considered retiring himself and concentrating on the administrative and management side of the team's business. Jack's own successes in 1963 were limited to a second place in the Mexican race and fourth places at Reims, Monza and Watkins Glen. In 1964 Gurney would have won the Belgian race but for running out of petrol just before the finish, but scored victories at both Rouen, scene of the French race, and Mexico City. Jack was still taking a back seat and his score was limited to third places at Spa and Rouen and a fourth in the British race. But he did win the non-Championship Aintree '200' and *Daily Express* Trophy races. In other categories of racing he was as active as ever, scoring four Formula Two victories, and running at Indianapolis, where he retired with split fuel tanks. In all these races Jack was, of course, at the wheel of his own cars.

Gurney failed to win a single Formula One race for the Brabham team in 1965 and Jack's best performances were a third at Watkins Glen, a fourth at Spa and a fifth place at the Nürburgring. One of the team's problems had been lack of engine reliability and during the year Brabham clinched two deals that were to change the team's fortunes completely for the 1966 season when the new 3000 cc Grand Prix Formula came into force. For Formula One racing the team used the V-8 Repco engine built in Australia and with its origins in (but no actual components from) an Oldsmobile engine design. The 1966 Brabhams proved the epitome of reliability and Jack, partnered by Denis Hulme who had driven in a few Grands Prix in 1965, made a comeback that was to lead to his third World Championship. In

Formula Two racing the Brabham team used Honda twin overhead camshaft engines that were considerably more powerful than the Cosworth units fitted to rival cars. During the 1966 season Jack Brabham won ten Formula two races, teammate Hulme two and of the remaining three held that year, two were won by Jochen Rindt with a Cosworth-powered Brabham and one by Jean-Pierre Beltoise with a Matra.

The new Brabham Grand Prix car was ready at the start of the season and Jack himself drove the first car in the South African Grand Prix, not in 1966 a round in the Championship, held as usual on New Year's day. Right from the start the Brabham combination set the pace and would certainly have won but for a seized fuel injection pump. Jack won his first Formula One race since early 1961 when he scored an easy victory in the *Daily Express* Trophy race at Silverstone in May, but it was not until July that the Brabham team found its form in Championship races. At Monaco Jack felt ill and retired with a seized gearbox and in the next round at Spa he was a poor fourth. Then the wins started to roll in. Jack won the French Grand Prix at Reims from the Ferrari of Mike Parkes and team-mate Hulme took third place. Another first for Jack followed at Brands Hatch with Denny Hulme in second place and he won the wet German Grand Prix from John Surtees's Cooper. This was Brabham's first victory in the German Grand Prix and he regarded it as one of the most satisfying wins in his career.

Jack now led the World Championship with 39 points and his nearest rival was Graham Hill with 17. Another success, albeit of a less important nature, followed later in August when Jack and Denny took the first two places in the Gold Cup race at Oulton Park. Although Jack led the Italian race for four laps, he retired early because of an oil leak. Despite this failure, it was a happy race for Brabham, for the retirement of his nearest challengers in the Championship ensured that he could not now be caught and the

Championship was in the bag. Another retirement followed, but in the Mexican race at the end of the season Jack and Denny took second and third places behind Surtees's Cooper-Maserati. When the final points were calculated, Jack was fourteen points ahead of his nearest rival in the Championship, with 42 to the 28 gained by Surtees. At the end of the year Jack was awarded the OBE which gave rise to the classic tale, given much press publicity at the time, of how his car refused to start after the presentation ceremony at Buckingham Palace and he eventually left, still dressed in tails, but with a liberal coating of grease.

The Brabham domination of Grand Prix racing continued for another season with Jack taking a couple of victories and the simple, unsophisticated single cam per bank Repco-Brabhams performing with clockwork regularity while their faster rivals were plagued by mechanical problems. In the South African Grand Prix Jack's car was suffering from engine trouble, but he staggered on to finish sixth and win a single Championship point. His first Formula One victory of the year came in the Spring Cup race at Oulton Park and he took second place in the *Daily Express* Trophy race at Silverstone. At Monaco his car retired on the first lap with engine trouble, but he made up for this with a fine second place behind Clark's new Lotus at Zandvoort, retired again with engine trouble at Spa, won the French Grand Prix on the Bugatti circuit at Le Mans from team-mate Hulme and finished fourth in the British race. Hulme was the victor at the Nüburgring, but Jack took second place, less than a minute behind; he finished second again to Surtees's Honda at Monza and won the Gold Cup race the following weekend. He rounded the season off with a fifth place at Watkins Glen and a second at Mexico City to finish second in the Championship with forty-six points, five less than team-mate Hulme. For Jack, life had certainly begun *again* at forty!

Once again at the end of 1967 Jack was considering retiring, but he realised that if the Brabham team was to field two cars, it was essential for economic reasons that he should drive one and he reconciled himself to carrying on in 1968. Denis Hulme had decided not to renew his contract with Brabham and had teamed up with Bruce McLaren, so the search was on for another driver. Jack had been impressed by Jochen Rindt's driving with Winkelmann Racing Team Formula Two Brabhams and he engaged the young Austrian for the 1968 season. That year the Brabhams were powered by new twin cam per bank versions of the Repco engine, but unfortunately they proved hopelessly unreliable. From Jack's point of view the season was completely unproductive. He ran in eleven of the twelve Championship races during the year, but finished in only one, the very wet German race in which he took fifth place.

After this disastrous season Jack was all set to retire again, but changed his mind when he learned that Jochen was not staying with the team, but had decided to sign up with Lotus. To replace the Austrian Brabham signed up young Belgian driver Jacky Ickx and in 1969 the team enjoyed a fair run of successes with cars powered by Ford engines. Jack's first success of the year came in the wet *Daily Express* Trophy race in which he scored his first win since the 1967 Gold Cup race. He failed to finish in a Championship race until Zandvoort in June in which he took sixth place, but then crashed during a testing accident at Silverstone and suffered a broken ankle which kept him out of the French, British and German races. Jack returned to Grand Prix racing at Monza where he retired early in the race, but he took a second place at Mosport, a fourth at Watkins Glen and a third at Mexico City. Jacky Ickx won the German and Canadian races and took second place in the Drivers' Championship.

In the latter part of 1969 Jack had been trying to persuade Jochen Rindt to rejoin the team and on the understanding that he would be returning to Brabham, Jack decided definitely that he would be retiring. Eventually at the Canadian Grand Prix Jochen told Jack that he had decided to stay with Lotus and Brabham found that once more he would have to reverse his decision and carry on racing. It was later arranged that the second Brabham would be driven by young German driver Rolf Stommelen with finance provided by outside sponsors. In 1970 Jack also agreed to drive Matra Prototypes, which seemed an odd decision at the time and seems just as odd in retrospect. One theory was that Jack was interested in building up a good relationship with Matra with a view to using the French team's V-12 engines in Brabham Grand Prix cars, but Jack's complete withdrawal from Motor Racing Developments on his retirement demolished that idea. Although he drove the Matras at most rounds in the Sports Car Championship, success eluded the team and Jack's best performance was a fifth place and Prototype class win with Beltoise in the Monza 1000 km race.

The 1970 Grand Prix season started in fine style for the forty-five-year old veteran, now in his twenty-third season of racing. In the South African Grand Prix he scored a fine victory, leading home former team-mate Hulme's McLaren. In the Spanish Grand Prix he retired with engine trouble, but not before he had set fastest lap over the Jarama circuit. Jack certainly should have won the Monaco race, but for a terrific spurt by Rindt in the closing stages of the race which brought him right through to sit on Jack's tail on the last lap and under pressure he misjudged the Gasworks hairpin and thumped the straw bales, rejoining the race to finish second. He retired at Spa and at Zandvoort in unofficial practice crashed at the wheel of Stommelen's car when a tire punctured and over-turned; in the race he finished a hopeless eleventh after two pit stops to change punctured tires. A third place followed at the French Grand Prix at Clermont-Ferrand, but in Jack's next race at Brands Hatch he suffered a bitter disappointment. After a fierce

Jack Brabham

battle with Jochen Rindt, he took the lead and steadily drew away from the Lotus driver, only to run out of fuel on the last lap and coast across the line into second place. Periodically cars do run out of fuel for inexplicable reasons and there was no good reason on this occasion because the tanks had been topped up brim-full just before the start.

Although most drivers dislike Hockenheim, this was one of Jack's favourite courses; the circuit was the scene of the German Grand Prix in 1970, but his car did not last long and retired early in the race with an oil leak. Another disappointment followed in the Austrian Grand Prix, the first to be held at the new and very scenic Österreichring close to the old Zeltweg circuit. He was holding fifth place when his radiator was holed by a stone flung up by Galli's Ferrari, lost three laps in the pits and rejoined the race to finish in thirteenth place. At Monza Jack was dicing with Cevert's March, trying to outbrake him at the Parabolica curve when the engine cut out altogether, he hit a patch of oil and slid unceremoniously into the guard-rail. In the remaining three rounds of the Championship Jack achieved no success at all.

Now Jack finally announced his retirement from racing. On 29th November 1970 he was present at Brands Hatch with Betty at a special 'Homage to Jack Brabham' meeting and lowered the flag for a 20-lap race for Brabham cars only which was won by Alistair Walker's Formula Two car. Jack disposed of his interest in Motor Racing Developments to Ron Tauranac who in turn sold the business to Bernard Ecclestone after only one unsuccessful season and both Brabham and Tauranac returned to Australia. Tauranac later returned to Europe and is now involved in a motorcycle racing project. Jack's main concern is his Ford dealership in Bankstown, only a short drive from his home alongside the Georges river in the suburbs of Sydney. He also has his own fairly small aviation business, a 350-acre farm in Victoria and spends a lot of his leisure time fishing with his younger sons. Nowadays he rarely goes to motor races, but his fertile mind is still very active and he is becoming increasingly interested in powerboat racing and gliding. It seems that after so many years in which he was totally dedicated to the sport of motor racing, Jack Brabham has succeeded in making an almost complete break and is looking for fresh fields to conquer.

7

Yankee Champion
PHIL HILL
1961

THERE HAS ONLY been the one American World Champion, Californian Phil Hill who won the title in 1961, almost by default through the death of team-mate Wolfgang von Trips in that year's Italian Grand Prix. It was a sad and very hollow victory for Hill, who raced because he loved racing and never nurtured any ambitions to win the Championship. Hill was one of three very successful American drivers to break into European racing and he joined Scuderia Ferrari in 1956. Dan Gurney joined the Ferrari team in 1959, but stayed only the one season before moving on to BRM, Porsche and Brabham and then finally set up his own All-American Racers team to run the Eagle V-12 car in 1966. Although no American has yet emulated Jimmy Murphy's victory with a Duesenberg in the 1921 French Grand Prix, that of an American driver at the wheel of an American car winning a major European Grand Prix, Gurney has come closest to it with his victory with an Eagle at Spa in 1967. The Eagle was not, however, an all-American car, for although it was American-inspired and financed, it was built in Britain, had a British-developed engine and a British gearbox. The third of the triumvirate to break into European racing was Richie Ginther, a friend of Phil Hill, who joined the Ferrari team for 1960.

Born at Santa Monica, California in 1928 to the postmaster and his musician wife, Philip T. Hill, junior, at the age of seven astounded and dismayed his relatives by calmly reeling off the technical details of car after car. When Phil related the story in later years, he reckoned that he had known the specifications of some 300 to 400 cars built since the First World War. In his boyhood days Phil never knew what career he wanted to follow, but all he was interested in were cars. As a teenager he had his own elderly automobile on which he spent hours of painstaking labour. His parents regarded it as a phase through which he would pass and were anxious that he should pursue his studies. He was sent to the University of Southern California where he read business studies, but the subject completely bored him and he left without any qualifications after what he regarded as two completely pointless years. He drifted from job to job, building up a collection of miscellaneous cars on which he still worked as hard as he could in his spare time. Then he took a job as a mechanic in a Los Angeles garage. The proprietor was the owner of a midget racing car and eventually when the regular driver failed to turn up at a meeting, the mechanic was given his big chance. Phil qualified as a starter and ran in this and two other midget races. In his third race at San Bernadino he scraped the fence and another competitor's car and decided 'the hell with this,' midget racing was not for him and he never raced one of these cars again.

In 1949, by the time he had reached his twenty-first birthday, Phil had scraped together enough money to buy a European sports car, an MG 'TC' which he progressively modified and fitted with a supercharger. Phil raced the MG, but without any real ambitions of becoming a racing driver because, 'I had a terrific inferiority complex because I wasn't really anything. So it really seemed to me that it was

Phil Hill

the car that won—not me!' The same year he went to work for a large importer of British cars and in 1950 was sent on training courses to Jaguar and MG, returning with a great deal more mechanical knowledge and a new Jaguar XK120. Phil raced the Jaguar regularly, but he soon realised that it was no match for the latest Allards and Cunninghams that were beginning to dominate sports car racing on the West coast of America and traded it in for a supercharged 1937 Alfa Romeo 8o-2900B, an elderly car of tremendous performance (its maximum speed was close to 130 mph).

Hill raced the Alfa throughout 1951, but it was a sad year for him because of the death of both his parents, his mother after a long illness and his father a couple of months later from a heart attack. The same year he had an operation for sinus trouble, but it was still not completely cured and continued to bother him during his later racing days. By 1952 the Alfa was fifteen years old and proving rather less than reliable, so he part-exchanged with Ferrari concessionaire Luigi Chinetti for a 2.6-litre Maranello car. As well as running his own Ferrari, Hill drove for wealthy entrants. In 1953 he raced a new 3-litre V-12 Ferrari and made his first racing trip to Europe—to compete at Le Mans with Richie Ginther at the wheel of an Osca—the car retired with differential trouble. That autumn he drove a new 4.1-liter Ferrari for Allen Guiberson in the Carrera Panamericana road race—the second time he had competed in this event —and took Richie Ginther as passenger. On the second stage of the race he crashed badly, for, in his own words: 'We had just topped a steep rise and we were into a mean, curling right-hand turn before we even knew it was there. Our brakes had practically faded away and in a split second we had gone off the edge. Thank God it wasn't one of those sheer drops where you'd fall thousands of feet before you'd even touch the side of the mountain, but it was bad enough. We went end over end down a pretty steep drop for about a hundred feet. Neither Richie nor I were hurt, but we sure got out of that car fast.' Hill later discovered that local peasants had removed the corner sign simply for the fun of watching drivers trying to negotiate a difficult corner of which they had no warning!

In 1954 Hill was suffering from ulcer trouble. His doctors warned him that his real problem was his anxiety about racing and that unless he gave up the sport, it was likely that the ulcer would perforate and he would die from an internal hemorrhage. He ran in the Buenos Aires 100 kilometres race at the beginning of the season and then for ten months gave up racing altogether. He tried to divert his mind from racing by restoring a 1931 Pierce-Arrow car with his brother Jerry and he worked as studio adviser on the film *Such Men Are Dangerous* based on the novel *The Racer* by Hans Ruesch. But Phil knew that racing was now too deeply in his veins for him ever to be able to give it up and returned to competition work in November 1954. In the Carrera Panamericana Mexico race he drove Guiberson's new 4.5-litre Ferrari and although he could not match the speed of the works 4.9-litre car driven by Umberto Maglioli, he finished second.

Throughout 1955 Phil drove Ferraris for private entrants, mainly Monza 4-cylinder cars for Guiberson and George Tilp and as a result of Chinetti's influence appeared at the wheel of a Ferrari at Le Mans—but retired with engine overheating. In America he scored victories at Elkhart Lake, Pebble Beach and Nassau and, co-driving with Carroll Shelby, finished second in the Sebring 12 Hours race in a disputed result in which victory was eventually awarded to the D-type Jaguar of Hawthorn and Walters. Throughout 1955 Hill was still in a nervous, tense state, never relaxing, constantly dosing himself with tranquilisers and placing reliance on the theory that tenseness in racing was self-provoked so as to sharpen the reactions and judgment. It was a theory that he gradually rejected as he became more

Phil Hill

and more experienced and, as a result, more and more relaxed.

Luigi Chinetti was a great influence on Hill's racing career, he had supplied him with Ferraris at very favourable rates, he had secured his Le Mans entries and now he used his influence with Enzo Ferrari to gain him a works Ferrari drive in the Buenos Aires 1000 kilometres race. Co-driving with Belgian Olivier Gendebien, he drove a fine race, taking second place to the Maserati of Stirling Moss and Carlos Menditeguy. The result was an invitation to join Scuderia Ferrari for the European sports car season; Hill was now on his way to International fame. He retired at Sebring, finished third co-driving with Alfonso de Portago in the Nürburgring 1000 kilometres race, led Moss and Castellotti in the Rouen Grand Prix until engine trouble intervened, causing him to fall back to sixth place at the finish, won the Swedish Grand Prix with Maurice Trintignant (a driver for whose ability he had immense respect), finished second at Oporto with Tilp's private Ferrari and won the Messina Night Race. After the Messina race Hill was involved in a punch-up with a group of Italian thugs who hit him over the head with a board and tried to burn his face with a cigarette because he was supposed to have pushed their 'friend's' car off the road. Phil was only saved by the timely intervention of a friend waving a pistol!

In 1956 Phil had been promised a drive in a Grand Prix Ferrari, but this never materialised and although he was invited to rejoin the works team in 1957, he was now slightly disillusioned. Still no Formula One drive came in 1957 which was a poor year from Phil's point of view and his successes were limited to a second place with Wolfgang Seidel in the Reims 12 Hours race, a second place with Peter Collins in the Swedish Grand Prix and a win with Collins in the Venezuelan Grand Prix, a race that in 1957 was a round in the Sports Car World Championship. At

Sebring his Ferrari had refused to restart after a pit stop and he missed a drive at Le Mans because his Ferrari retired with piston trouble only a few laps after the start with Peter Collins at the wheel. At the beginning of the year he had carried out all the preliminary runs and testing at Bonneville salt flats with the streamlined MG that Stirling Moss was to use for record-breaking. Hill said that he found the experience of driving this car terrifying, especially on one occasion when engine fumes were sucked into the ventless cockpit—'I just held my breath for about the longest thirty seconds of my life until I could get the thing stopped from something over 200 mph.'

By the end of 1957 Hill's confidence in himself had greatly increased and his fears that he had not been allowed to race a Formula One Ferrari because the Commendatore did not rate his driving very highly were partly dispelled early in 1958 when he was nominated to share one of the new V-6 Ferrari Dinos with Wolfgang von Trips in the Buenos Aires City Grand Prix. Von Trips was to drive in the first heat and Hill in the second, but unfortunately the young German pranged the car during his turn at the wheel and Hill missed his chance. In sports car racing he was continuing to do well; he had started the season co-driving with Collins to victory in the Buenos Aires 1000 kilometres race and with this same co-driver another victory with the 3-litre V-12 'Testa Rossa' car followed at Sebring. He was lying second in the Targa Florio when he crashed, hardly surprising as he was completely new to the almost impossibly difficult Little Madonie circuit in Sicily, but got the car back on the road, changed the wheel and limped to the Ferrari service depot at Bivio Polizzi in the mountains for repairs; despite this crash Hill and Collins finished fourth. At the Nürburgring Phil shared a car with Luigi Musso and finished a none too satisfactory fourth, but the following month he scored his finest victory to date. Co-driving with Olivier Gendebien, he scored a win at Le Mans, a race in which he was particularly keen to score a victory. Hill's sports car successes were no flash in the pan and time was to show that along with Gendebien, Moss, Siffert and Rodriguez he was one of the really great sports car drivers of the post-war years.

Phil Hill had been promised a drive in the Formula Two Ferrari in the Coupe de Vitesse at Reims, the accompanying race to the French Grand Prix, but in fact the car was driven there by Collins. Anxious not to be deprived of yet another single-seater drive, he arranged to handle Joakim Bonnier's elderly Maserati in the Grand Prix, finishing in a respectable seventh place. At last it seemed that Ferrari had got the message and Phil was entered in the Formula Two category of the German Grand Prix with the 1500 cc V-6 car. He led the class comfortably until he hit a patch of oil, skidded off the course and during his excursion through the undergrowth tore away the oil breather pipe running under the car; for the remainder of the race he was spraying his back tires with his own oil mist, but he carried on to finish ninth overall and fifth in the class.

It was not until the Italian Grand Prix in September 1958 that Phil was given a Formula One drive proper by Ferrari. Hill made a brilliant start, swept into the lead at the fall of the flag and led until the seventh lap when a tire threw a tread and necessitated a pit stop. Later in the race he was forced to stop again for a wheel change, but he finished third, after being slowed down by the Ferrari pit to prevent him from passing Hawthorn, and set a new lap record, the first 200 kph race lap at the Monza circuit. Then came Casablanca, the race in which it was Hill's job to break up the opposition if possible and ensure that Hawthorn finished second, thereby winning the World Championship. In the early laps he battled with Moss's leading Vanwall, disappearing up an escape road when his drum brakes proved unable to match the discs of the British car, thundering back to hold second place and easing off in the closing stages of the race to let Hawthorn through to second place.

With the deaths of Musso and Collins and the retirement of Hawthorn, Phil was a much-needed regular member of the Ferrari Grand Prix team in 1959. In 1958 Ferrari's greatest opponent had been the front-engined Vanwall, now it was the rear-engined Cooper and it was only on the very fastest circuits that Ferrari power came into its own. His first race of the season was the *Daily Express* Trophy race at Silverstone, a circuit with which he had difficulty in coming to grips, and he finished a none-too-happy fourth. At Monaco he was fifth after a pit stop to change two wheels buckled by contact with curb—Phil had never raced at a tortuous circuit like Monaco before—and he finished sixth at Zandvoort. The French Grand Prix at Reims was run in excessively hot conditions and poor Phil was badly affected by the heat; he was over-shooting at the two hairpin bends, going sideways and misjudging his braking all the way round the circuit, his concentration and judgment completely shattered by the weather conditions. Even so he managed to keep going to the finish to take second place behind teammate Tony Brooks. Ferrari missed the British race and later in the season Phil took third place in the German Grand Prix run on the high-speed, dangerous Avus circuit in Berlin, was eliminated in the Portuguese race when namesake Graham spun right in front of him, took second place in the Italian race and retired with mechanical bothers in the first United States Formula One Grand Prix at Sebring.

1959 had not proved one of Hill's more successful sports car seasons. At Sebring he had shared the winning 'Testa Rossa' after his own car had retired, but his car retired in the Targa Florio and he and co-driver Gendebien were trounced by Stirling Moss's Aston Martin at the Nürburgring, trailing home in second place. All the works Ferraris retired at Le Mans and in the final round in the Sports Car Championship, the Tourist Trophy at Goodwood, Hill's Ferrari had succumbed to valve trouble after only one lap.

By 1960 the front-engined Ferraris were completely outclassed by the Coopers, despite very hard driving by Hill and team-mates von Trips and Mairesse. In the Argentine Grand Prix Phil finished a hopeless eighth, but things looked up a little at Monaco where he finished third after one of the hardest drives in his career; his driving, especially when a rain shower turned the oil-coated circuit into a skating rink, was forceful and spectacular. Hill retired at Zandvoort, but after suffering a minor fire out on the circuit he finished fourth at Spa. In the French race at Reims he tried desperately to use the power of his Dino to get past Brabham's Cooper, the nose of the Ferrari was buckled from contact with the tail of the British car and Jack Brabham wrote in his memoirs: 'I had passed Phil on the straight and was on the left-hand side of the circuit in the braking area, and just before turning right across the track to take the right-hander I fortunately looked in my rear-view mirror. I could hardly believe my eyes. There was the Ferrari coming down the inside with all four wheels locked and not a hope of stopping . . . I guarantee he was going 50–60 mph faster than I was. He went straight up the escape road as though he were going right into Reims.' Phil rejoined the race and carried on, but later retired with transmission trouble. At Silverstone Hill was a poor sixth, but he was eliminated in the Portuguese race by what amounted to a lapse of concentration. Despite the lose of use of his clutch, he had worked his Dino up to second place, but while struggling to make a clutchless gear-change, he collided with the curb and buckled a wheel. Obviously he had to stop at the pits for a wheelchange and the team manager told him to cover one more lap and then stop before the finish and push the car over the line. When he stopped, he was told by the officials to move on but his efforts to push-start the car proved abortive and he was forced to abandon it out on the circuit.

Because the British teams refused to compete on the combined road and banked track circuit at Monza, the Ferraris were completely unopposed in the Italian Grand Prix and Phil led the race throughout to win at 132.07 mph, and he set a new lap record of 136.74 mph. This was Phil's first World Championship race win—it was so typical of his career that it should be such a hollow victory—and the first by an American driver in a major European Grand Prix for thirty-seven years. In sports car racing in 1960 Phil's best performances were a second place with von Trips in the Targa Florio and a turn at the wheel of the third-place car at the Nürburgring (his own car had blown up its engine).

By 1961 and the introduction of the new 1500 cc Grand Prix Formula the picture in Formula One had changed completely and in that year the Ferrari team, well prepared with new rear-engined V-6 cars that had been thoroughly tested the previous year, dominated the scene, while the British teams, caught with their pants down, were struggling with cars powered by outdated 4-cylinder engines of very modest power output. At Phil's first Formula One race of the year, the Monaco Grand Prix, his driving did not exactly shine. Stirling Moss took the lead with his outdated Lotus and Phil trailed badly in second place. Ginther, in third place, caught up his team-mate and in the next phase of the race, in the words of Denis Jenkinson, 'Phil Hill was certainly no match (for Moss) . . . It had been obvious for some time that though Ginther was setting the Ferrari pace from third position, he was being held up by Hill, for whereas Hill was looking hot and breathless, Ginther was looking cool and calculating, chewing his gum and driving with a very set expression on his face.' Eventually Richie forced his way past Hill who finished a none-too-happy third.

At Zandvoort, Hill finished second behind team-mate von Trips, but it was his turn to win at Spa-Francorchamps where the Maranello cars took the first four places. The

Ferrari attack disintegrated at Reims into confusion and shambles. Both Ginther and von Trips retired and Hill collided with Moss's spinning Lotus; after great difficulty in inducing his car to fire again, Hill rejoined the race to finish ninth. The winner was novice driver Giancarlo Baghetti at the wheel of a semi-private Ferrari. In the rain-soaked British race Phil finished second and he was third at the Nürburgring where the Ferrari team was again soundly trounced by Moss's elderly Lotus and inspired driving. Before the Italian Grand Prix von Trips led the Championship with thirty-three points to the twenty-nine of the American driver. Clearly the young German was all set to clinch the Championship at Monza, but at this circuit Ferrari plans went disastrously awry. Poor 'Taffy' von Trips was killed in a second-lap collision with Clark's Lotus which cost the lives of fourteen spectators, Ferrari had made a 'grand-slam' entry of six cars at this race and of the remaining five, four retired leaving Hill lapping alone at the front of the field. He went on to win the race and what must have been the unhappiest Championship victory in the series.

It was ironic that Phil was one of the few drivers to whom the World Championship did not mean a great deal and had said of it: 'I don't want to win it terrifically badly. The fact that some people seem to think I have a chance—well, I wish they didn't. The point is I function best when I'm doing something better than expected of me. It's an absurd situation, but that's the way it is.'

In sports car racing Hill, again partnered by Gendebien, scored a fine victory at Sebring. In the Targa Florio and at the Nürburgring Phil crashed, but at Le Mans, still at the wheel of a front-engined 'Testa Rossa' car, he scored his second victory at the Sarthe circuit, again co-driving with Gendebien.

It was in 1962 that Hill's career began its slow and rather sad decline. After a year of ascendancy, the V-6 Ferraris proved no match for the latest British V-8 cars, Phil never managed to win another Grand Prix and at some circuits that year his lap times in practice were slower than in 1961. As the season progressed and Ferrari development seemed to regress, Phil appeared to lose interest in racing and at times he trailed round at the back of the field, apparently completely apathetic as to the outcome of the race. Things did not go too badly at the start of the season, with a third in the Aintree '200' race, another third at Zandvoort, a second at Monaco—his best performance of the season—and third again at Spa, but there was little joy in the rest of the season's racing. Ferrari missed the French race because of industrial trouble and only a single car for Hill was fielded at Aintree. It was hopelessly uncompetitive, Phil trailed round in thirteenth place and eventually retired with distributor trouble. He was twenty-nine seconds slower in practice at the Nürburgring in 1962 than he had been the previous year, held third place on the first lap, but dropped further and further back, stopping at the pits to complain about the car and eventually getting so fed up that he retired. Another hopeless performance followed at the Italian Grand Prix where Hill took eleventh place. In 1961 Ferrari had missed the American race because the Championship was in the bag, but in 1962 he missed it because there was no chance of success.

Ferrari was, however, still a power to be reckoned with in what was now known as the category for Grand Touring Prototypes. At Sebring Hill and Gendebien drove the new Ferrari 250 GTO Grand Touring car into second place. Phil crashed in practice for the Targa Florio and non-started in the race, but then came two fine victories, both co-driving with Gendebien. They won both the Nürburgring 1000 kilometres race with the new rear-engined 246/SP car and at Le Mans with the faithful 'Testa Rossa,' but in this race powered by a larger 4-litre engine—this was Phil's third victory at the Sarthe circuit and Gendebien's fourth.

As the 1962 season progressed, so relations at Maranello

had been increasingly strained and both Phil Hill and teammate Giancarlo Baghetti left the Ferrari team to drive the new ATS V-8 cars. The ATS was the work of Carlo Chiti, the very talented engineer who with the team manager and other Ferrari staff had left Maranello at the end of the previous year. Development work on the ATS was slow, the team was constantly short of money and when the cars eventually appeared they looked scruffy and ill-prepared and they were hopelessly unreliable. The 1963 season proved a hopeless waste of Hill's very considerable talents. On the new cars' debut at Spa, he retired with transmission trouble. A week later he drove the new Aston Martin 215 Prototype at Le Mans with Lucien Bianchi, but the car retired early in the race with rear axle failure. At Zandvoort Hill's ATS was eliminated by a broken rear stub axle (a rather frightening failure to experience) and the V-8 Italian cars did not run again until the Monza race in September where Hill at last finished in eleventh place. Hill's final appearance with the ATS was in the United States Grand Prix where he retired early in the race with oil pump failure.

ATS withdrew from racing at the end of the season and it looked as though Phil would be without any Grand Prix drive in 1964. At the Snetterton meeting in March he appeared at the wheel of one of the BRMs belonging to the private Scuderia Centro-Sud and drove this into fourth place, but by the Aintree meeting the following month he had been signed as number two in the Cooper team to replace Tim Mayer (brother of Teddy Mayer, now McLaren joint managing director) who had been killed during the Tasman series. Throughout the season Hill had a miserable time at the wheel of a car that was usually inferior to that of team-mate McLaren, his best performance was a sixth place in the British Grand Prix and his season culminated with a crash in the Austrian race when his ill-handling car went out of his control, hit the straw bales and burst into flames. He was 'rested' for the Italian race, but returned to the team for the United States Grand Prix. In two-seater racing Hill enjoyed a fine, albeit not conspicuously successful season, driving with great elan the immensely fast, but as yet unreliable Ford GT40s and Carroll Shelby's Cobras which were thundering, ill-handling brutes, but tremendous fun to master. His best performance of the year was in the Daytona 2000 Kilometres race in which he co-drove the winning Ferrari with Pedro Rodriguez.

After 1964 Phil did not again drive for a Formula One team, but continued to race Prototypes. In 1965 he stayed with the Ford team and also raced McLarens, but for the following season changed his allegience, joining the Chaparral team. Driving the Texas-built cars, Hill scored a victory with Joakim Bonnier in the 1966 Nürburgring 1000 kilometres race, won the Laguna Seca Can-Am race and finished second at Mosport Park. The following year Phil's only success was a win with Mike Spence at the wheel of the latest Chaparral coupé, its appearance dominated by the high, rear-mounted aerofoil, in the B.O.A.C. '500' race, the last victory in his career.

Hill's constant anxiety always revealed itself in his quick movements, his rapid speech, his restlessness which never allowed him to relax and these were weaknesses which he never completely succeeded in mastering during his racing career. He was a man of many interests, especially devoted to music and with a vast collection of records and stereophonic tapes. He said: 'I like all music except lousy music,' but he had many other interests including architecture and medicine and read widely. At different times he had played the piano, alto sax, guitar and drums. But above all he was devoted to motor racing. He was never a great driver, but was always a great enthusiast.

8
The Man Who Rowed
GRAHAM HILL
1962, 1968

TWICE-WINNER OF the the World Championship Graham Hill is probably the most famous racing driver in the history of the sport; his toothy, mischievous smile, the suggestive curve of his moustache, the quick repartee under the glare of studio lighting have become as quickly recognisable trademarks on the screens of millions of television viewers as the facial features of any leading screen actor. Yet Hill has not been groomed for fame in the way that many another famous face has been moulded and promoted. From his earliest television appearances Hill has responded with a natural charm that is both engaging and provocative, his public success was instantaneous and from a producer's point of view he became an almost essential appendage, a guarantee of success, for any programme vaguely connected with motoring.

As a racing driver Hill was a late-comer to a sport that was rapidly becoming a young man's monopoly; he was twenty-five when he drove in his first race, thirty-three when he won his first World Championship and now, eleven years later he is competing in his sixteenth successive Grand Prix season and against men most of whom were still at school when he entered Formula One. At Monaco in 1973 he celebrated his 150th Grand Prix appearance. Graham Hill was never a great driver, at his best he was fast, consistent and reliable and for four successive seasons, while he drove the 1500 cc V-8 BRMs, he was at the forefront of racing, winning the Drivers' Championship in 1962 and finishing second in the three seasons that followed.

In 1968 Graham Hill drove with skill and courage to win the Drivers' Championship for a second time, but the following year his performances declined sadly and his racing year culminated in his terrible accident at Watkins Glen. Few men have fought harder to recover from injuries and Hill's return to racing, in March 1970, was spectacularly quick. Yet Graham has never recovered the dash and sparkle that characterised his driving of earlier days. At the wheel of Rob Walker's Lotus cars in 1970 and then in 1971–2 driving works Brabhams, Hill has trailed round hopelessly at the tail of the field in race after race and since his accident has scored only one Formula One victory, in the 1971 *Daily Express* Trophy race at Silverstone. Yet, despite his failures, despite the wishes of many of his supporters that he should retire while his fine reputation remains untarnished, Hill has carried on racing. 'I love racing,' said Hill in an interview with the *Daily Express*, 'and as long as I enjoy it, I shall continue to race.' It is an argument with which it is difficult to quarrel.

Born at Hampstead on 15th February 1929, Graham Hill spent almost all his youth in the London area. By the outbreak of the Second World War the Hill family had moved to Hendon. Hill senior had volunteered for the Royal Air Force and Graham, younger brother Brian and their mother stayed in London throughout the 'blitz.' In 1946 at the age of sixteen Hill was apprenticed to instrument makers S. Smith & Sons and was sent to the company's college at Cheltenham. Every weekend Graham would cycle the hundred miles to London to see his girl-friend and then cycle back again. This resulted in a weekend that was all exercise and no fun and so he bought a 1936 Velocette motor-cycle. Returning home from a weekend in London he collided with an unlit stationary car and spent three months in hospital recovering from a broken left thigh. To replace the Velocette, Graham bought a Matchless motor-cycle which he ran in a number of scrambles—racing on a rough, muddy circuit—and on his return to work at the main Smith factory at Cricklewood took up rowing.

Because of his apprenticeship, Graham's call-up for his National Service was deferred until he was twenty-one. For his two-year stint he joined the Navy, spending much of the time as a petty officer aboard a cruiser, and was discharged in June 1952. Graham had joined the London Rowing Club during a period of his National Service when he was posted at Chatham barracks and he continued to row after his return to Smith's. Although courting Bette at this time (who also rowed), his rowing was almost all-consuming and he was out on the water every evening of the week and also on both Saturdays and Sundays. The insignia of the London Rowing Club, adopted by Graham for his helmet when he took up motor racing, has become one of the best known racing 'trade-marks.'

Graham's first car was a 1934 Morris Eight tourer which he bought in 1953, but towards the end of the year the Morris was written off in an accident caused by another motorist pulling out of a side road without looking where he was going. By this time Graham was an incurable motor racing addict. Although he has never really explained how racing came to exercise such a sudden and powerful grip on him, Hill's first brush with the sport came when a work-mate suggested that he should try a Formula Three Cooper belonging to a racing driver's school at Brands Hatch. Graham drove this venerable JAP-powered car for four laps at five shillings a lap and stepped out convinced that motor racing was the sport for him. Unable to afford his own competition car and with little prospects of ever being able to buy one,

Graham decided that the best way of getting involved in the sport was by helping on the mechanical side.

While still working at Smith's, Hill spent his spare time helping the man who ran the racing driver's school and then for another man who had two Formula Three cars which were kept in a barn near Westerham in Kent and ran them under the grand title of Premier Motor Racing Club. Graham received no payment for working on the cars, but had left Smith's, signed up with the Labour Exchange from whom he received 'dole' for a short while and travelled to Westerham and back each day by Green Line coach. It was a pretty hopeless way of trying to enter motor racing, a course of despair followed by many a young man that ended up in a lot of hard work, full advantage of the situation taken by the owner of the cars and nothing but frustration for the would-be racing driver. However, Graham was allowed to drive the Cooper-JAP in a race at Brands Hatch in April 1954 and he finished fourth. Not long afterwards he drove the same owner's Kieft-Norton at Brands Hatch, but retired with engine trouble. It was at this race meeting that Graham first encountered Colin Chapman who at this time was racing his sensational streamlined Mk 8 car.

Graham persuaded Chapman that he could be of assistance at Lotus and was offered a pound a day in return for his services. Later he worked as mechanic for Dickie Steed who raced a private Coventry-Climax-engined Mk 8 Lotus and as unpaid mechanic to Dan Margulies who had an ex-works C-type Jaguar previously raced by Duncan Hamilton. Hill accompanied Margulies on a trip to North Africa in early 1955, writing a report of the Agadir race for the British magazine *Autosport*, and drove this car himself in a race at Castle Combe. Margulies then took the car on a Continental tour with Graham as mechanic; the highlight of the tour was the Sardinia Trophy race, an Italian road event in the best traditions, in which Graham rode as passenger, later writing in his report for *Autosport:* 'The race was over a distance of 249.8 miles, traversing much of the famous Mediterranean island, and constituting something of a "pocket" Mille Miglia, with enthusiastic spectators packing every village and lining the roads. The course varied from fast undulating roads over plainland, to distinctly mountainous sections, with many bumps, brows and blind bends to catch the unwary . . . Margulies was able to get his C-type up to 140 mph on some of the better roads, but the bumpy surfaces, plus a gusty cross-wind, made this race distinctly exciting!' Margulies and Hill finished third. In June Hill co-drove with Margulies in the Messina Night race, but the owner spun the car into a wall.

Graham then returned by train to England for his marriage to Bette! He now took a job on a full-time basis with Lotus at their tiny Hornsey works. It was at Lotus that he had his first opportunity to go motor racing on anything like a serious basis. Chapman allowed Graham to build his own Ford-powered Lotus Eleven on the understanding that the car remained Chapman's property and that Chapman would receive all prize and starting money. In his autobiography, *Life At The Limit* (William Kimber & Co. Ltd., 1969), Graham recounts how this bright yellow-painted car was entered in the *Autosport* Championship and that when he goes to address motoring clubs there is always someone with a good memory who reminds him of his race with the Eleven at Brands Hatch in 1956. According to Graham's version of the story, he spun four times, but in this writer's memory it was more like six and in *Autosport,* Gregor Grant wrote: 'Hill was everywhere, but on the circuit proper, and it was no shock—even to him—that the stewards gave him the black flag, and disqualified him for repeated revolutions!' This was a classic example of an inexperienced driver trying too hard, both at the start and, later, in his efforts to make up for his mistakes. Certainly Graham learned a lot from that race and never again repeated such a reprehensible performance!

Nevertheless Graham had been driving the Lotus fast enough and steady enough to be in second place in his class before the final round of the Championship, a three-hour race at Oulton Park, and Colin Chapman was sufficiently impressed by Hill's efforts to turn up at the Cheshire circuit to manage the Lotus pit. Unfortunately Graham retired after a minor collision, a spin, a broken fan pulley and, finally, con-rod bolt failure. Racing with Hill in those days was anything but uneventful!

By 1957 Colin Chapman had decided that Graham was far too useful on the mechanical side to be allowed to race and this was not a decision that pleased Hill at all. He left Lotus to work as a mechanic on a freelance basis and scrounged whatever drives he could. During 1957 Hill handled a wide range of different machinery including various Lotus Elevens, and old A-series Connaught Formula Two car, an Aston Martin DB3S, Tojeiro-Jaguar and the Willment-Climax. John Willment was planning his own Formula Two car and invited Hill to join him on the project. When Hill told Chapman of this latest development, he was invited to drive for Lotus! Although this was exactly what Graham had wanted, it was too late, for he was already committed to Willment. The new Willment was, however, never completed, but an important development was the offer of a works Cooper Formula Two car for the *Daily Express* Trophy race at Silverstone in September 1957—Graham spun on a patch of oil and finished at the tail of the field. A direct result of this drive for Cooper was an invitation to sign up with Lotus for the last couple of races in 1957 and for the 1958 season.

For two seasons Graham remained with Team Lotus, driving both sports cars and single-seaters. In the early part of 1958 the team fielded the Formula Two cars that had appeared the previous year with 2-litre Climax engines, but were no match for the rear-engined Coopers and, later in the year, the new 16 model, still front-engined, but of very small frontal area; the new model was a complete failure because of overheating and transmission problems and Graham had to suffer two very unsuccessful seasons. His Grand Prix debut was at Monaco in 1958 and he scraped in as a qualifier with a place on the back row of the grid. With three-quarters of the race run, he was holding fourth place when a rear wheel came off the Lotus. Later in the season little success came Graham's way, although he did manage a fifth place in the Italian Grand Prix, despite several pit stops for extra water and running out of fuel on the last lap, and he also scored a victory in the 1500 cc Sports Car race at the May Silverstone meeting with a Lotus 15.

The 1959 season followed much the same unhappy pattern. At Monaco Hill retired when his car caught fire and at Zandvoort he lost his rear brakes completely, but carried on to finish seventh. He retired again at Reims, finished ninth at Aintree (but won the Sports Car race held the same day) and retired in the German Grand Prix held that year at Avus. He spun on fuel from his own leaking tank in the Portuguese race at Lisbon and was rammed by Phil Hill's Ferrari—both cars were eliminated. He took a good second place in the Kentish '100' Formula Two race at Brands Hatch at the end of August and in his final race for Lotus, the Italian Grand Prix, retired with transmission trouble.

After two seasons of driving hopelessly unreliable cars Graham decided that the time had come to make a break and when he was offered a drive by the BRM team, he accepted without hesitation. At the time it looked as though Hill might well be jumping from the frying pan into the fire because BRM's record of unreliability was almost as bad as that of Lotus. Since the first 2500 cc BRMs had appeared at the end of the 1955 season, they had won only one Championship race, the 1959 Dutch Grand Prix in which Joakim

Bonnier had driven one of the Bourne cars to victory. Both Lotus and BRM were building rear-engined cars for 1960, a direct result of the enormous run of successes scored by the rival Coopers, which had pioneered rear location of the engine. For his first race, the Argentine Grand Prix, he was given a front-engined car, but he retired with engine trouble. The new rear-engined car was ready by the start of the European season, but initially it both handled badly and was hopelessly unreliable. Hill finished fifth at Goodwood, crashed at Monaco, but then his fortunes improved and he took a third place at Zandvoort, his best Championship performance to date.

Both Graham and the BRM were a rapidly improving combination, however, and in the Belgian Grand Prix at Spa-Francorchamps, Hill was in second place and chasing race-leader Brabham when his engine blew up. Hill had difficulty in engaging the gears at the start of the French Grand Prix at Reims and his stationary BRM was struck at the start by Trintignant's Cooper which tore off a wheel. The British race at Silverstone started almost as badly for Graham, for he stalled on the grid and this time was rammed by Tony Brooks's Cooper. Fortunately the BRM was undamaged and after a push-start Graham joined the race almost thirty seconds in arrears. This was the start of one of Graham's best and unluckiest drives. By the twentieth lap he had risen to sixth place, ten laps later he was fourth and by lap thirty-eight he was in second place, only five seconds behind race-leader Brabham. Gradually Graham closed the gap, on lap fifty-four he swept by into the lead and, driving with great skill and polish, he succeeded in keeping the Australian at bay. As the race progressed, however, the BRM's single rear transmission brake was getting hotter and hotter and only six laps from the finish as Hill was lapping two slower cars under braking, he misjudged his braking power and spun into the ditch and out of the race. As Graham stepped out of his car, he was almost in tears.

In 1960 the German Grand Prix was held as a Formula Two race, the British teams boycotted the Italian Grand Prix which was held at Monza on the combined road and banked track circuit because they considered that the banking was dangerous and Graham appeared in only two more Formula One races before the existing 2500 cc Grand Prix Formula came to an end. In the Gold Cup race at Oulton Park he finished third and he suffered yet another retirement in the United States Grand Prix held at Riverside Raceway in California. During the year he also drove works Porsche Formula Two and sports cars, but his only successes were a class win and third place overall with Bonnier in the Buenos Aires 1000 kilometres race at the beginning of the year and a fourth place and class win with a Carrera Grand Touring car in the Tourist Trophy run at Goodwood in August.

Graham Hill remained with the Bourne team for 1961, but like all the British teams BRM were under a severe handicap. The British constructors had opposed the introduction of the new 1500 cc Grand Prix Formula of 1961 onwards and optimistically believing that their view would prevail had delayed the start of development work on engines to suit the new Formula. Throughout 1961 the British teams, including BRM, were forced to rely on the old 4-cylinder Coventry-Climax engines which dated back to 1957 and in the face of powerful Ferrari opposition little success came their way.

At the beginning of the year the BRM team competed in the Tasman races in New Zealand and Australia, but these were largely Cooper-dominated and Graham's best performances were a third in the New Zealand Grand Prix and second place to team-mate Dan Gurney at Ballarat. With the 4-cylinder BRMs Hill could only manage an eighth place in the Dutch Grand Prix and a sixth in the French race at Reims. The new V-8 BRM was due to make its debut in the Italian Grand Prix at Monza, but it caught fire in practice and Graham drove an older car in the race, retiring with valve trouble. In the last race of the season, the United States Grand Prix at Watkins Glen, Graham was still at the wheel of a 4-cylinder car and after a pit stop finished fifth. During 1961 Hill also drove a Jaguar saloon and one of the new E-types for John Coombs in British races and made a couple of appearances at the wheel of Porsche sports cars.

In 1962 BRM missed the Tasman series so as to concentrate on development testing of the new V-8 which would be facing opposition not only from Ferrari, but also from Lotus, Cooper, Lola and, later in the year, Jack Brabham's new car, all of which were powered by the rival V-8 Coventry-Climax unit. Graham's first race with the new BRM was the Brussels Grand Prix run on the Heysel circuit with the results decided on the aggregate of three heats. Despite severe back pains (a direct legacy of his motor-cycle crash) Hill won the first heat, but at the start of the second the starter motor failed and the car was push-started; Hill was then black-flagged and disqualified. Although the French version of the regulations did not permit push-starts, the British translation did and naturally it was this copy of the regulations that the BRM team was using. It was an unfortunate mix-up and a bad start to what was to prove otherwise Graham's finest year and the best in BRM's history.

At the Easter Goodwood meeting Hill scored his first ever Formula One victory with the BRM, but it was a victory marred by Stirling Moss's bad crash. Moss, two laps behind after a couple of pit stops, was trying to make up lost ground and was passing Hill at the moment of his crash. Another and sensational victory followed in the *Daily Express* Trophy race at Silverstone. After holding fourth place Hill moved up to second spot behind race-leader Clark with the latest Lotus. In the early part of 1962 the BRM was fitted with stub exhausts which were angled upwards. During the race the V-8 lost five of its eight exhausts at different places round the track and the engine was sounding flatter and flatter. Rain had begun to fall and despite his exhaust problems, Graham made up a seventeen-second deficit on the leader in the last six laps. As the two cars entered Woodcote, the last corner before the finish, Graham tried to pass Clark on the inside, failed and then hurled the BRM in a cloud of spray round the outside of the Lotus, crossing the line sideways, but slightly ahead of his rival. To the onlooker the manoeuvre looked lethal and one could only trust that Graham knew what he was doing!

With two Formula One wins to their credit, Hill and BRM travelled to Zandvoort, scene of the year's first Championship race, with great confidence, confidence that was not misplaced, for Graham led from lap eleven to the finish to score BRM's second-ever Championship race victory and second in the Dutch Grand Prix. Hill led at Monaco, but retired with engine trouble, finished second to Clark at Spa and retired again in the French race at Rouen. A fourth place followed in the British Grand Prix at Aintree, but then BRM power re-asserted itself and Graham won at the Nürburgring and Monza, finished second again to Clark at Watkins Glen and rounded off the season with yet another victory in the South African Grand Prix at East London. With four victories and two second places Graham won the Drivers' Championship with forty-two points to the thirty of Jim Clark. At the beginning of the year BRM chief Sir Alfred Owen had warned the team that he would withdraw from racing unless substantial success was gained during the year and the whole BRM organisation had responded magnificently.

During the years of the 1500 cc Formula (it came to an end in 1965) Graham Hill was at the peak of his ability. Without doubt the greatest driver of the time was Jim Clark, but Clark's Lotus cars tended to be less reliable than the BRMs and Hill, ready to pounce, often sat on Clark's tail and moved up into the lead when the Lotus faltered. This pattern repeated itself in 1963 when Hill took the first of three successive second places in the Championship. At the beginning of the year he drove the front-engined Ferguson four-wheel-drive car in a number of Tasman races, without success apart from a second place to Surtees's Lola in the Lakeside race.

He returned to Europe to drive BRMs to victory in the Lombank Trophy at Snetterton and the Aintree '200' races, but retired with mechanical troubles in both the Formula One race at the Easter Goodwood meeting and in the *Daily Express* Trophy at Silverstone. At Monaco Graham led initially, but Clark overtook him only to spin off because of a seized-up gearbox and the BRM driver won what was to prove to be the first of five victories at Monaco. At Spa he held second place behind Clark until his gearbox broke. Then came a lighter interlude, driving at Le Mans with team-mate Richie Ginther the experimental Rover-BRM gas-turbine car. The car did not compete in the race as such, but was given the number 00 and competed on its own for a special prize for gas-turbines for which it had to cover at least 3600 kilometres in the twenty-four hours (an average of about 93 mph). This rather ungainly-looking coupé ran magnificently, and the distance covered of 4172 kilometres put it ahead on the road of the seventh-place AC Cobra of Peter Bolton and Ninian Sanderson.

In the Dutch Grand Prix Hill again trailed Clark's Lotus until overheating necessitated a pit stop for extra water and he retired with engine trouble before the end of the race. The 25 monocoque Grand Prix Lotus had been the sensation of the 1962 season and at the 1963 French Grand Prix at Reims the BRM team introduced their own monocoque car. This was rather different in design from the Lotus and featured tubular frames front and rear. Unfortunately the new car handled far from well and on its debut the best that Graham could manage was third place. Another third place with the older car followed in the British race at Silverstone and Hill retired at both the Nürburgring and

Monza. He led the United States race from start to finish to win from team-mate Ginther, finished fourth at Mexico City and rounded off the season with a third place in the South African race at East London.

In 1964 Hill was pipped for the World Championship by the narrowest of margins and in circumstances that did not reflect a great deal of credit to the Ferrari team. After competing in the Tasman races at the wheel of a Brabham, Graham began his European season with the latest and much-improved monocoque BRM at Snetterton in March. In very heavy rain the car went out of control, mounted the bank, a wheel was torn off and the BRM continued on to return to the track leaving the driver shaken and surprised, but unhurt. Another retirement followed at the Easter Goodwood meeting where a broken distributor rotor arm was the trouble and he was beaten into second place in both the Aintree '200' race and the *Daily Express* Trophy at Silverstone by Jack Brabham at the wheel of one of his own cars.

At Monaco Graham scored his second successive victory on this circuit, but it was to prove one of only two victories scored by Hill during the year. He took a fourth at Zandvoort after a pit stop to cool an overheating fuel pump, he was fifth at Spa after running out of fuel, second to Gurney's Brabham in the French race, second to Clark by a narrow margin in the British Grand Prix at Brands Hatch and second again to Clark at the Nürburgring. Hill retired in the Austrian race held on the very bumpy Zelweg circuit and at Monza he never even left the starting grid because the clutch thrust mechanism jammed in the 'out' position. At Watkins Glen BRM fortunes improved and Hill won the race for the second year in succession after the retirement of Clark and Gurney.

With one race to go the World Championship was still undecided. Hill led with thirty-nine points, but it was possible for both Surtees with thirty-four and Clark with thirty to beat him. Clark could only win the Championship if he finished first and Hill finished lower than third. If Hill finished in the first three, he could substitute the points gained for the three points earned for fourth place at Zandvoort. Graham started the race badly, upset by the fact that the elastic of his goggles had broken on the grid and he had tied the two ends together only seconds before the flag fell. At the end of the first lap he was in tenth place, but he gradually worked up to third place ahead of Ferrari driver Lorenzo Bandini, a position in which he would be content to finish, as it was good enough to ensure victory in the Championship. Then Bandini started to worry the BRM driver, trying to overtake him at the hairpin where there was clearly no room to get by. Graham was shaking his fist warningly at the Italian, but Bandini was taking no notice. Bandini tried again to get past, the two cars collided and one of the Ferrari's wheels buckled the BRM's exhausts. Both cars spun off and Surtees's Ferrari went by into third place. It would be harsh and perhaps rather unfair to suggest that Bandini had deliberately chanced his arm in pushing the BRM off, but, at the least, it was a risky manoeuvre and one that Bandini knew could do nothing but benefit his team-mate. Race-leader Clark retired, Surtees finished second to Gurney's Brabham and won the Championship by one point and unlucky Hill rejoined the race after two pit stops to finish eleventh.

There had been no South African Grand Prix in 1964 because it had been postponed a few days until 1st January so that it became the first race of 1965. The year 1965 proved an almost complete Clark benefit, but as in 1963 Graham was usually there, keeping close contact with the Lotus and ready to move up into the lead should anything break on Clark's car. In the South African race Graham finished third, he took a second to Clark at Goodwood and retired in the *Daily Express* Trophy at Silverstone. Neither Clark nor Dan Gurney competed at Monaco because of Indianapolis and so life should have been rather easier for the BRM team-leader. He was comfortably in the lead when he came upon Bob Anderson's Brabham with the gearbox jammed in first crawling through the chicane and had no alternative but to take to the escape road. He pushed the car back to the track, rejoined the race in fifth place and started on a furious chase of the leaders. He soon caught team-mate Stewart who had spun at another part of the course, moved up into third place on Brabham's retirement and closed up on the leading Ferraris of Surtees and Bandini. On lap fifty-three, just after half-distance, Hill took second place from 'Big John' on the descent from Casino Square and eleven laps later passed Bandini into the lead. At the chequered flag he was four seconds ahead of the Italian after one of the most determined races in his career, it was a victory that could not have been better deserved and it was Hill's Monaco 'hat-trick.'

In the next two races poor Graham did not fare so well and was over-shadowed by young team-mate Stewart who finished second to Clark in both the Belgian race at Spa and the French race at Clermont-Ferrand. The Belgian race was run in the wet and Graham reckoned that his car was not set up for these conditions and attributes his fifth place to handling problems. At Clermont he went off the road in practice, suffered a bad shaking and was very off-form in the race; again he trailed badly to finish a poor fifth. The press-on Hill style re-asserted itself in the British race at Silverstone where he finished a close second to Clark despite brake trouble and it was second again to Clark at the Nürburgring. But for a slight mistake on the last lap but one Hill would have won the Italian race; after taking to the rough, loose surfacing at the edge of the track he dropped to second place behind team-mate Stewart. Hill's second Championship win of the season came at Watkins Glen, again only after race-leader Clark had retired early on and again a 'hat-trick' for Hill who has made a habit of persistently winning some races and always failing to win others—he has never succeeded in winning the British Grand Prix. Despite retiring in Mexico Graham again finished second to Clark in the Championship with 40 points to the Lotus driver's 54.

The change to the new 3000 cc Grand Prix Formula brought with it a change in fortunes for Hill as far as Formula One racing was concerned. For most of the season Hill and Stewart were forced to drive the 1965 car with engines enlarged to 2000 cc, the form in which they competed in the Tasman races at the beginning of the year, while Tony Rudd tried to turn the complicated new H-16 car into a race-worthy proposition. The Tasman races were largely a Jackie Stewart benefit, but Hill scored wins in the New Zealand and Australian Grands Prix. After taking a third place at Monaco, Hill flew out to Indianapolis where both he and Stewart drove Ford-powered Lolas for John Mecom. In the closing stages of the race, on a very slippery, oil-coated track, Steward, Hill and Jim Clark with a Lotus were holding the first three places. Atrocious luck for Stewart when his oil scavenge pump failed in the closing laps meant good luck for Hill who then assumed the lead and won the race from Clark by a margin of just over forty seconds.

During the remainder of the year little success came Graham's way, although he did pick up a number of good places in Grands Prix by sheer persistency, plugging on with his underpowered BRM as hard as possible and finishing high up the field through the retirement of faster cars. At Spa he was one of the many drivers to go off the course on the first rain-soaked lap and although his car was undamaged and could have continued, he stayed instead to help release team-mate Stewart from his shattered BRM. Shortly afterwards Hill drove a 7-litre Ford at Le Mans—his last appearance at the Sarthe circuit until his victory drive in 1972—but retired when the front suspension collapsed. His Formula One record during the remainder of 1966 season consisted of a third at the British Grand Prix, a second in the Dutch, a fourth at the Nürburgring and retirements in the season's other races.

Graham Hill's relationship with BRM was so close and of such long standing that he had never considered leaving the team until he received an approach from Henry Taylor, Competitions Manager of Ford, who tried to interest him in rejoining the Lotus team. BRM could offer little prospect of an immediate improvement in their fortunes, for there were no signs that the H-16 was going to be any more reliable in 1967 and, in fact at the end of that year BRM abandoned it altogether in favour of a new V-12 design. So Hill rejoined Lotus as joint number one driver with Jim Clark, while Mike Spence who had been number two in the Lotus team in 1965 joined BRM.

The big carrot dangled by Ford and Lotus had been the new V-8 Cosworth engine financed by Ford. This was not ready to race until the Dutch Grand Prix in June and at the first two races of the season Hill and Clark had to drive the old 1965 Lotus 33 cars with 2-litre engines. Hill retired in the South African race at the start of the year, but soon displayed at Monaco that the 2-litre car in the right hands was still fairly competitive on the more tortuous courses and came home second despite a slipping clutch and broken chassis. At Indianapolis he drove a Ford-powered Lotus, but after he had been delayed at the start by trouble with the external starter and was trailing badly in the race because of a very rough engine, the race was abandoned because of rain and restarted the following day. Overnight the cars were impounded and Hill was forced to re-start with the engine as rough as ever and survived only a few laps before it failed altogether.

Hill returned to Europe to drive the new Ford-powered Lotus 49 on its debut at the Dutch Grand Prix. From the moment the cars first turned a wheel in practice at Zandvoort, it was clear that they were the most competitive 3000 cc cars to be built and despite possible early teething troubles they would be soon dominating the Grand Prix scene. Although Clark drove one of the new cars to victory in the Dutch race, a remarkable success for both Chapman and engine designer Duckworth—as it is almost a motor racing tradition that only Grand Prix Mercedes have won on their race debut—they had their fair share of troubles during 1967 and it seems mere bad luck that it was almost inevitably Graham's car that failed and Jimmy's that made it to the finish.

On the cars' debut at Zandvoort, Hill led initially, but retired with engine trouble and subsequently retired at Spa and the Bugatti circuit at Le Mans, scene of the French Grand Prix. More bad luck followed at Silverstone; in practice Hill was travelling at low speed when the car veered into the retaining wall and wrote itself off. Another car was assembled overnight, but first Hill was delayed by a bolt falling out of the rear suspension while he was leading the race and later the engine broke. At the Nürburgring the rear suspension broke, at the first Canadian race at Mosport Hill spun on the streaming wet track and rejoined the race to finish fourth, engine failure again caused Hill's retirement at Monza, he was second at Watkins Glen and finally retired at Mexico City with drive-shaft trouble. All in all a dismal catalogue of mechanical troubles that must have made Graham wonder whether he had done the right thing in rejoining Lotus!

The 1968 South African Grand Prix was the last race in which the Lotus Formula One cars appeared in the team's traditional green and yellow livery. In subsequent races the cars ran under the banner of Gold Leaf Team Lotus and in red, white and gold colours. At the South African race the 49s of Clark and Hill took the first two places, but a bare three months later Clark was dead, killed in a Formula Two crash at Hockenheim. One of the terrible, but at the same time inevitable aspects of a dangerous sport like motor racing is that however distraught team-members and drivers are at the time of tragedy, whatever scars it leaves, the sport has to go on. It was a terrible ordeal for Hill, Chapman and Lotus to carry on racing after Clark's death, but it is a brutal conclusion that but for Clark's death, he and not Hill would almost certainly have won the 1968 Championship. And but for Stewart's wrist injury which caused the Scot to miss two of the year's races, Graham's chances of success in 1968 would have been even further reduced.

The main European season started well for Graham in 1968 and, in Stewart's absence, he won both the Spanish race at Jarama and at Monaco for the fourth time. Retirements followed at Spa, Zandvoort, Rouen and Brands Hatch —in three of these races Hill was eliminated by transmission trouble and he was leading in the British race at the time of his retirement. Hill gained second place in the rain-soaked and mist-enveloped German race, he lost a wheel at Monza, finished fourth at St Jovite, scene of the Canadian race, after a pit stop because of suspension trouble, and took another second place to Stewart at Watkins Glen. When he arrived at Mexico City for the last round of the 1968 Championship, Graham led by three points, and could still be beaten by Stewart and Hulme. Hill drove a perfect race, battling with Stewart and Siffert in the opening laps, and after these drives had run into trouble went on to win the race and his second World Championship.

During 1968 Graham Hill had been joined in the Lotus team by up and coming Formula Two driver Jack Oliver, a driver of great promise, but not one who at any stage in the season challenged the position of Hill as Lotus team-leader. It was a very different situation the following year when Colin Chapman engaged Jochen Rindt as joint number one driver with Hill. Jochen was increasingly becoming a force to reckon with in Grand Prix racing, he was lapping faster and faster, his driving was becoming more and more polished and it seemed that Hill had a subconscious resentment of the young Austrian whose driving powers were waxing while his waned. In the early part of the season the two Lotus drivers battled with each other as though they were deadly rivals and not team-mates and Colin Chapman's preoccupation with the new 63 four-wheel-drive car, a model which neither of his drivers liked, resulted in less preparation work on the conventional cars. For much of 1969 Gold Leaf Team Lotus was not a happy team, there was too much of an atmosphere, too much last-minute work on the cars on the morning of the race and at least one race lost because of the rivalry between the drivers. The season was also marred for the team by bad crashes, involving both drivers in the Spanish Grand Prix and culminating in Hill's disastrous accident at Watkins Glen at the end of the season.

The year started well enough for Graham with a second place to Stewart in the South African Grand Prix, but then both Hill and Rindt crashed at Montjuich Park because of aerofoil failures. Hill was lucky enough to step from the shattered wreckage of his car unhurt, but when Rindt crashed, he suffered injuries bad enough to keep him out of the Monaco race. It was as a direct result of these accidents that a ban was imposed on aerofoils at Monaco. The race through the streets of the principality was to prove Graham's only Championship race win of the season and, to date, the last in his career. Conserving his car in the early stages of this race which is so hard on the cars' transmissions, he moved up into the lead to score his fifth win at Monaco after the retirement of Amon's Ferrari and Stewart's Matra. Little success came Hill's way during the rest of the 1969 season. At Zandvoort Hill and Rindt battled furiously for the lead, while a relaxed Stewart, holding a comfortable third place, watched them with amusement. Almost inevitably mechanical trouble intervened, Rindt retired, Hill stopped at the pits and finished well down the field, and Stewart won the race.

By the Watkins Glen race in October the only success

achieved by Hill since his Monaco win was a fourth place in the German race and now his disappointing and largely fruitless season came to an abrupt end. Unhappy with the handling of his car, Hill was holding on to a steady fifth place when he spun on a patch of oil and stalled. Hill undid his seat belts, pushed the car to re-start it and clambered back in. It was impossible for Hill to do his seat belts up again himself (this was always done for him by a mechanic), but he was not too worried as he had noticed that the rear tires were bald and he intended stopping at the pits for a wheel-change. He never reached the pits because a tire deflated on the straight, the Lotus, out of control, hit the bank, threw Hill out and rolled over.

Graham Hill had broken his right knee and badly dislocated the left. At the time it seemed unlikely that he would ever race again, but Hill is a man of iron-willed determination, it was through the greatest determination that he became a successful racing driver and through determination that he fought for recovery from his latest accident. In January 1970 he was still wheelchair-bound, but a bare two months later made a wonderful come-back at the South African Grand Prix. That year Graham drove Lotus cars for Rob Walker and although as the season progressed, so his stamina, strength and confidence gradually improved, it was a season of complete failure. For much of the year Hill had to make do with Walker's old and outdated 49C car and even when the team took delivery of the latest 72 model in August, it was far from right and the remainder of the season was spent sorting it out.

At the end of 1970 Rob Walker decided to throw in his lot with John Surtees's new team and once again Graham was looking for a Formula One drive. He signed up as number one in the Brabham team, but both that year and in 1972, when the team was run by his friend Bernard Ecclestone, Hill spent most races trailing round at the back of the field, led by many of the younger drivers who were just breaking into Formula One racing. Hill's only success in Formula One in 1971 came in the *Daily Express* Trophy race at Silverstone after both Jackie Stewart and Ronnie Peterson had crashed.

One race in 1972 went a long way towards consoling him for the many disappointments of recent years. Hill has rarely driven sports cars—his most recent success had been a second place at Le Mans in 1964—but in 1972 he received an invitation to handle a works Matra at Le Mans. After the withdrawal of the works Ferrari team the strong entry of French-built cars were almost unopposed and Hill, co-driving with Henri Pescarolo, came through to win the race after team-mates Cevert and Ganley had lost the lead because of a long pit stop. In 1972 Graham Hill ran his own Formula Two team and at the wheel of his Brabham Formula Two car he scored an unexpected win in the Lottery Grand Prix at Monza and took fifth places at Imola and Hockenheim.

The success of this Formula Two team encouraged Graham to press on with the formation of his own Grand Prix team for the coming year. On the strength of his reputation and fame, rather than his present ability, Hill was able to work out a lucrative sponsorship deal with the W. D. & H. O. Wills division of the Imperial Tobacco Company. Hill's team, managed by Alain de Cadenet, bought a Shadow car (a model designed by Tony Southgate who was formerly with BRM) and this was painted in the colours of Wills Embassy cigarettes and entered as the Embassy-Shadow. For much of the season the new car was plagued by 'teething' problems and when it did run well, Hill was not able to lap fast enough to achieve any success. Nevertheless Hill's Embassy Racing team has ambitious plans for the future; it will be fielding two cars in 1974 and these may well be of the team's own design.

Throughout his career Hill has been tirelessly supported by his wife Bette, a great character herself and almost as inseparable a part of the motor racing scene as her husband. Much of Graham's pleasure in life is relaxing with his wife and three children at their country house in Kent, and he has succeeded in retaining many interests outside motor racing. He flies his own private aircraft (like many other drivers), is addicted to shooting and enjoys a round of golf. When he eventually decides that the time has come to hang up his crash helmet, he will still have plenty to keep himself occupied.

9
The Greatest Champion of Them All?
JIM CLARK
1963, 1965

IT IS EASY enough to distinguish between a run-of-the-mill Grand Prix driver and a true champion by their records of successes, their style, their degree of precision, whether they have the restraint to drive within their limits, whether indeed they know the limits of their ability, their ability to fight when the odds are against them and their lap times on roughly comparable cars. To distinguish between a man who has won the World Championship and a truly great driver one can use the same yardsticks, but one must always take into account that some drivers of enormous potential and largely unstrained resources have died before attaining greatness. By these standards the truly great drivers of the post-war era have been Juan Manuel Fangio, Stirling Moss and Jim Clark. Alberto Ascari was a border-line case, Jochen Rindt died before he could attain greatness and Jackie Stewart is well on his way towards it. To attempt to distinguish between the greatest drivers is to stray into the realms of conjecture and this writer will content himself with the expression of his personal opinion and not attempt to justify it: Jim Clark was the greatest British driver in the

Farina at Goodwood in 1950 with his 4CLT 'San Remo' Maserati.
(*Photo:* Guy Griffiths)

Dottore Giuseppe Farina, first World Champion, after his victory in the 1950 British Grand Prix at Silverstone.
(*Photo:* Guy Griffiths)

Fangio hurls his Alfetta round Silverstone in the 1951 British Grand Prix in futile pursuit of Gonzalez's Ferrari. (*Photo:* Guy Griffiths)

In practice at Aintree in 1957, Fangio gets two wheels on the grass. (*Photo:* T. C. March)

Juan Manuel Fangio, the greatest Argentinian driver, at the wheel of his Alfa Romeo. (*Photo:* Guy Griffiths)

One of Ascari's finest drives was in the 1954 Mille Miglia in which he scored a magnificent victory at the wheel of a Lancia. (*Photo:* Publifoto)

At Silverstone in 1949 Ascari won the *Daily Express* Trophy race with this Ferrari. (*Photo:* Guy Griffiths)

A happy man—Ascari, at the peak of his fame, at Silverstone in 1953. (*Photo:* Guy Griffiths)

Mike Hawthorn completely dominated the 1958 French Grand Prix with this Dino Ferrari, winning the race and setting the fastest lap. (*Photo:* Edward Eves)

Mike Hawthorn with his Cooper-Bristol in the 1952 *Daily Express* Trophy race at Silverstone. (*Photo:* Guy Griffiths)

Hawthorn at the wheel of the winning Ferrari after the 1953 *Daily Express* Trophy race. (*Photo:* Guy Griffiths)

At the start of a long and brilliant career—Stirling Moss at the wheel of his first Cooper 500 at Prescott Hill Climb in 1948. (*Photo:* Guy Griffiths)

Tactically one of Moss's finest races was the 1959 Italian Grand Prix in which he defeated the works Ferrari team. Here he leads Phil Hill's Ferrari. (*Photo:* Motor Sport)

In 1960 Jack Brabham and the Cooper-Climax dominated Formula One racing. Here they are seen at Silverstone in the British Grand Prix. (*Photo:* T. C. March)

When Brabham retired at the end of 1970 he had won three World Championships. (*Photo:* Nigel Snowdon)

Brabham at Zandvoort in 1966 where he scored his third Grand Prix victory of the season. (*Photo:* Nigel Snowdon)

In 1963 Phil Hill drove the new Italian A.T.S. cars which proved completely unsuccessful. Here Hill is seen at Spa where he retired with gearbox trouble. (*Photo:* David Phipps)

Yankee Champion—Phil Hill who won the 1961 Championship at the wheel of a Ferrari. (*Photo:* David Phipps)

In 1964 Hill signed up as number two in the Cooper team. He is seen above at Monaco. (*Photo:* David Phipps)

Graham Hill signed up to drive for B.R.M. in 1960. That year the team raced new rear-engined cars and Hill is seen in the Oulton Park Gold Cup race. (*Photo:* T. C. March)

Champion on the decline—during 1971–2 Hill drove for Brabham. His sole Formula One victory in 1971 was in the *Daily Express* Trophy race. (*Photo:* Diana Burnett)

After the accident—Hill, still chair-bound at the 1970 Racing Car Show.
(*Photo:* Nigel Snowdon)

Jim Clark, Champion of the World, 1963 and 1965.
(*Photo:* Nigel Snowdon)

Jim Clark's first Formula One season with Lotus was in 1960. The nose of his car patched after a practice crash, he took third place in that year's Portuguese race. (*Photo:* David Phipps)

In 1967 the brilliant new Lotus 49 with Ford engine appeared and Jim Clark drove it to victory on its race debut at Zandvoort. (*Photo:* Nigel Snowdon)

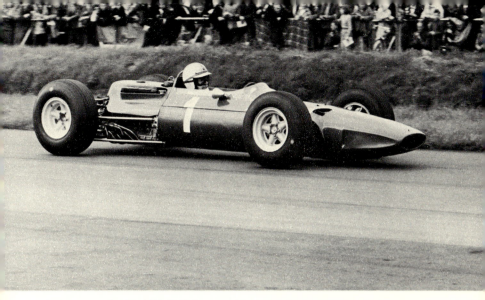

Surtees seen in the 1965 British race with his flat-12 Ferrari. He finished third. (*Photo:* T. C. March)

John Surtees proudly displays his new TS7 car at his Edenbridge works in 1970. (*Photo:* Nigel Snowdon)

John Surtees, in his happiest, perhaps more relaxed days with the Ferrari team. (*Photo:* Nigel Snowdon)

Denny Hulme drove Brabham cars to score his World Championship victory in 1967. He is seen here at La Source hairpin in the Belgian Grand Prix. (*Photo: Nigel Snowdon*)

At the 1971 German race are Eoin Young, McLaren director Phil Kerr, Hulme and Teddy Mayer. (*Photo: Nigel Snowdon*)

Shortly after the start of the 1971 Monaco race, Hulme heads Beltoise and Hill. (*Photo: Nigel Snowdon*)

Jackie Stewart's second Championship race victory came at Monaco in 1966. (*Photo:* Nigel Snowdon)

Jackie Stewart, Helen and the kids with the Tyrrell at the 1971 London Motor show. (*Photo:* Nigel Snowdon)

In the 1971 French Grand Prix, Stewart and the Tyrrell ran away from the rest of the field to score their third Grand Prix win of the season. (*Photo:* Nigel Snowdon)

Rindt with his Cooper-Maserati at Stavelot corner in the 1966 Belgian Grand Prix. (*Photo:* Nigel Snowdon)

A World Champion in Action: (centre) Jochen at Monaco, 1970, with the old Lotus 49C—he won the race after Brabham's last lap mistake and (below) at Clermont-Ferrand with the new Lotus 72. (*Photos:* Nigel Snowdon)

The matured Rindt in later days when he was driving for Gold Leaf Team Lotus. (*Photo:* Nigel Snowdon)

Emerson Fittipaldi, World Champion driver in only his second full season of Grand Prix racing. (*Photo:* Nigel Snowdon)

Brazilian Emerson Fittipaldi with the old 49C Lotus which he drove into eighth place in the 1970 British Grand Prix. (Photo: Nigel Snowdon)

Fittipaldi scored the first of his run of Grand Prix victories with the John Player Special at Jarama in 1972. (Photo: Nigel Snowdon)

Jim Clark

history of motor racing and the greatest of all during the post-war years.

But what made Clark great? The answer lies partly in fact, his racing record, partly in the interpretation of his qualities. Certainly Clark possessed superb reactions, excellent judgment, the ability like a rider to become one with his mount and the ability to learn quickly from experience—essential qualities of any successful driver—but Clark's ability went much further. With experience came increased confidence and with that confidence he learned to overcome fears that the car might break, something about which all but the most stoic of drivers worry, and the ability to control the race from start to finish. Clark would streak into the lead at the start of the race, build up a comfortable lead and then adjust his pace so as to maintain a good distance between himself and the following cars. Like Fangio, Clark always seemed to be completely relaxed, but with Jimmy the calm was more than a facade and he was a wonderfully controlled person. He had an almost complete understanding of his own abilities, always drove within his own limits and although he would drive really hard when the pressure was on, his style was so smooth, so precise, so consistent that he was a rather disappointing driver for the ordinary spectator to watch. Jim Clark was the nearest approach so far seen to the perfect racing driver.

Jim Clark was born in 1937 at Kilmaddy in Fifeshire. His father, James Clark senior, had five children, four girls and Jimmy, and farmed in a big way. Jimmy was educated at Loretto public school near Edinburgh and on leaving school took over the management of Edington Mains, a 1250-acre farm in Berwickshire where his family had moved. Clark was soon dividing his attentions between crop-raising and cattle-fattening in the week and competing in motor sporting events at the weekend. He had acquired a Sunbeam Mk III saloon, a fast near-100 mph saloon, but on the heavy side and with rather primitive handling. He ran this in a number of club events, but it was another motoring enthusiast, Ian Scott Watson, who encouraged him to take his motor sport more seriously. Besides competing in rallies and sprints with the Sunbeam, he also drove the two-stroke DKW and Porsche belonging to Scott Watson and the next step on the ladder to fame came in 1958 at the wheel of a D-type Jaguar belonging to the Border Reivers, a private Scottish team run by Jock McBain. This pale green Jaguar had previously belonged to a Jaguar dealer who had entered it for Henry Taylor, later Ford Competitions Manager.

On his first outing with the 170 mph Jaguar at Full Sutton, a circuit at an American Air Force base near York, Clark achieved the distinction of being the first British driver to lap a British circuit at over 100 mph at the wheel of a sports car. Shortly afterwards he competed abroad at Spa-Francorchamps, the very fast Belgian circuit. Some drivers love Spa, others loathe it and Clark was in the latter category, taking an instant dislike to its fast, open bends dotted with trees, a dislike heightened by the fact that Archie Scott-Brown, a brilliant driver apparently not at all handicapped by having an unformed right hand, crashed his Lister-Jaguar while leading Clark's race and died in the ensuing inferno. In 1959 he raced a faster, lighter Lister-Jaguar and a pre-production Lotus Elite coupé. At Le Mans the Elite ran as a works Lotus entry and with John Whitmore as Clark's co-driver took tenth place overall and second in its class. Success after success followed in 1959 with these two very competitive cars and at the Tourist Trophy race at Goodwood in September Clark was invited to co-drive an Ecurie Ecosse Tojeiro-Jaguar with Masten Gregory, the sports car driver who had always been Clark's hero and six years later was destined to share the winning Ferrari at Le Mans with Jochen Rindt. The car was in seventh place when Gregory lost control and hit a bank.

At the end of 1959 the Aston Martin team withdrew from sports car racing and the Border Reivers team bought one of the ex-works Sports Car Championship-winning DBR1/3-litre cars for Jimmy to drive. Then came the invitation to drive a Gemini Formula Junior car at the Boxing Day Brands Hatch meeting, it was not much of a car and it retired in its race, but it was Clark's first ever race with a single-seater. Early in the new year Clark was given trials for both the Aston Martin Formula One team and by Lotus. He signed up to drive for Aston Martin in Grand Prix racing, but in fact never appeared for the David Brown team as the season had barely started before it withdrew altogether, and for Lotus in Formula Two and Formula Junior racing.

During 1960 Clark and the new rear-engined Lotus 18 proved an almost unbeatable combination in Formula Junior racing and scored eight wins and two second places. At Le Mans Clark co-drove the Aston Martin with Roy Salvadori into a fine third place behind a brace of works Ferraris. But already his career had taken another step forward. John Surtees was unable to drive a Formula One Lotus in the Dutch Grand Prix three weeks before Le Mans as intended and the car was offered to Clark who drove a smooth, unruffled race, moving up to fifth place before retiring with gearbox failure. At Spa he again appeared at the wheel of a Formula One Lotus, but although Clark took a very satisfactory fifth place, it was a tragic race for Team Lotus, as one of their regular drivers, Alan Stacey, was hit in the face by a bird, crashed and was killed.

It is a sad fact that when 'promotion' comes for a racing driver, it is often after a tragedy and following Stacey's death, Clark joined the Lotus Formula One team on a regular basis. In the French race at Reims he again finished fifth, was last in the British Grand Prix after a pit stop and retired in the Guards Trophy race at Brands Hatch. In 1960 the German Grand Prix was a Formula Two race in which Lotus did not compete and Jimmy's next outing with a Formula One car was in the Portuguese race at Aporto. In practice he tried rather too hard, the car went into a vicious slide and crumpled its nose against the straw bales. The car appeared in the race with a hastily patched nose cone, but Jimmy, apparently not at all upset by the incident, drove a beautiful race to finish third, beaten only by the Coopers of Jack Brabham and Bruce McLaren. At the end of August Clark won the Kentish '100' Formula Two race at Brands Hatch and in September he was second in the Formula One Lombank Trophy race at Snetterton. The season ended with two crashes. In the Oulton Park Gold Cup race Brian Naylor at the wheel of his JBW-Maserati moved across on to his normal line at Lodge corner just as Clark was about to lap him and inevitably the cars collided. The second accident was in the United States Grand Prix at Riverside Raceway when he and team-mate Surtees collided.

Although at an objective level Clark knew that he could not blame himself for either accident, they worried him and he thought that with greater anticipation they could have been avoided. When Chapman wanted to renew his contract with Clark for the coming year, Jimmy thought hard before deciding to accept. He was now a fully committed, professional racing driver; in three short seasons of serious racing he had become a fully-fledged works driver, a meteoric career that was a few years later to be matched by fellow-Scot Jackie Stewart.

In 1961 Clark's efforts were marred by underpowered cars, the same fate as that suffered by all the drivers of British cars and a direct result of the delay in commencing engine development work for the 1500 cc Grand Prix Formula that came into force that year. At the beginning of the year he competed with a Lotus 18 in three Tasman races but his only success was second place in the Levin International race. The new 1961 Lotus was not ready at the start of the European season and Clark and team-mate Innes Ireland continued to drive the old 1960 18 cars. At Pau, in the absence of Ferrari opposition, Clark led from the end of the first lap—despite the fact that he was still putting on his gloves when Raymond Roche dropped the flag for the start —and stayed in front until the end of the race, ninety-nine laps later. This was Clark's sole victory of 1961 until Team Lotus travelled out to compete in South Africa at the end of the year. The World Championship races were dominated by the Ferraris of Phil Hill, Wolfgang von Trips and Richie Ginther, but the British drivers, headed by Moss and Clark, worried them to the limit of their cars' endurance. At Monaco Clark appeared at the wheel of the new Lotus 21, but finished tenth after a long pit stop shortly after the start of the race. He pipped Ginther's Ferrari for third place at Zandvoort, finished twelfth at Spa after a pit stop, and in that historic French Grand Prix, in which all the works Ferraris ran into trouble and the victor was the quasi-private Ferrari of Giancarlo Baghetti he took another third place. Clark retired in the British race, but turned in another fine drive at the Nürburgring albeit overshadowed by Moss's brilliant victory, to finish fourth behind two works Ferraris.

September proved to be one of the most terrible months in Clark's life. On the tenth of that month Clark drove his Lotus 21 in the Italian Grand Prix. As the pack approached the Parabolica curve on the second lap Clark pulled out of the slip-stream of von Trips's Ferrari to pass it, but the young German had not been keeping a close enough eye on his mirrors, moved into the path of the Lotus and the two cars collided. While Clark's Lotus spun harmlessly on to the grass, there was a more terrible fate in store for von Trips. His car spun up the banking and launched itself against the wire netting against which many spectators were leaning. Fourteen onlookers were killed and, perhaps mercifully, von Trips who had been flung out of his car died without recovering consciousness. The race developed into an almost funereal procession, von Trips had been leading the World Championship and Phil Hill's victory gave him a very hollow crown.

Jimmy was devastated by this accident, which again was

no fault of his, but had pulled himself together sufficiently to drive a Lotus at Zeltweg the following weekend. At the end of the year Team Lotus fielded a team of cars in the non-Championship South African races and Clark scored victories in the Rand, Natal and South African Grands Prix in December and on New Year's day finished second to team-mate Trevor Taylor in the Cape Grand Prix.

For the first time, Jim Clark was in 1962 a likely contender for victory in the Drivers' Championship. The uncompetitive 4-cylinder 1961 cars had been abandoned and Team Lotus was entering new cars with the now fully developed and fully competitive V-8 Coventry-Climax engines. At first the team fielded the 24 cars, conventional rear-engined cars with space-frame chassis developed from that of the 1961 21 model, but early in the season at Zandvoort Colin Chapman introduced his 25 model with monocoque chassis that was destined to revolutionise racing car design. At the beginning of the year Clark scored wins in the Lombank Trophy at Snetterton and in the Aintree '200' race and was narrowly beaten by Hill in the *Daily Express* Trophy race. The team then ran in the first round of the Championship at Zandvoort. Jimmy was leading the race and all set to win his first ever Championship race when his ZF gearbox failed and he was eventually classified ninth.

Jimmy's next drive was another that brought him no success, but it was among the most memorable in his career. At the Nürburgring 1000 kilometres race there appeared a brand-new sports Lotus, the diminutive 23 model which was little more than a Formula Junior chassis, a 1500 cc twin-cam engine which was the prototype of that used in the production Elan and a streamlined glass-fibre body. The car was entered in the name of the Essex Racing Team, but it was handled by works Lotus drivers Clark and Trevor Taylor and fully supported by technical staff from the works. Despite the presence of a strong contingent of works Ferrari and Porsche entries, Clark with the tiny Lotus took the lead on the first lap and began to draw further and further away from the rest of the field so that by the end of lap eight he had a lead of two minutes. Gradually the more powerful cars began to overhaul the little green car, and only four laps later at the Kesselchen, twelve kilometres from the start, Clark, overcome by fumes from a broken exhaust, went off the road after one of the most impressive drives in his career.

A week later Jimmy was back at the wheel of the monocoque Grand Prix car at Monaco and lost second place when the engine failed. Although the season was beginning to look as dismal as the previous year, his luck now began to change. At Spa-Francorchamps, the circuit for which Clark had formed such a strong dislike, he scored his first Championship race win and the first of four successive wins on this, one of the most difficult of European circuits. Retirements followed at Reims, the French Grand Prix at Rouen and at Solitude, but another success followed in the British race at Aintree. He led the race from the first lap to the finish, set fastest lap and was now only a point behind Graham Hill in the Championship.

At the German Grand Prix Clark stalled his engine at the start, but began a furious chase through the field, rose to fourth place and was menacing the leaders when his engine began to run rough because of fuel starvation. He was unable to improve further on his position and had to settle for fourth place at the finish. He won the Gold Cup race at Oulton Park, retired with engine trouble at Monza in the Italian Grand Prix and scored his third Championship win of the season at Watkins Glen. Jimmy was now nine points behind Hill in the World Championship, but still with a slight chance of defeating the BRM driver—if he won the South African race and Hill scored no points, Clark would have been the winner on the basis of the number of wins gained during the year. Clark's car refused to fire at the non-Championship Mexican Grand Prix, he was disqualified for receiving a push-start, but then took over Trevor Taylor's Lotus to win the race. At East London in the South African race Clark led initially, but retired, Hill won the race and the Championship and Jimmy was in second place still with 30 points to Hill's 42.

Now the careers of both Jim Clark and Colin Chapman were getting into top gear. After the Watkins Glen race in 1962 Jimmy had tested the Lotus 25 at Indianapolis, a dummy run prior to the appearance there the following year of a Ford V-8-powered Lotus. In addition to being fully involved in the development programme for the twin-cam Ford Cortina, he was still driving Lotus 23 sports cars occasionally. And, most important of all, there was still the Formula One programme; the Lotus 25 was largely unchanged from 1962, but the Climax engine now featured fuel injection and was generally more reliable.

After a break of three months Jimmy was back at the wheel in March 1963 at Snetterton where his Lotus 25 was beaten into second place in the Lombank Trophy race by Graham Hill's BRM, a week later he won a sports car race at Oulton Park with the Lotus 23 and in the following two weekends he won the Pau and Imola Grands Prix. At Aintree in the '200' race he took third place and at Silverstone in May he revenged himself for his defeat by Hill the previous year in the *Daily Express* Trophy race by winning from Bruce McLaren and team-mate Trevor Taylor. The season started in earnest at Monaco on 26th May and Clark was leading the race when the gearbox seized, enforcng his retirement. Four days later he drove a Lotus-Ford at Indianapolis. Clark handled the Lotus magnificently and led the race, but there were a great number of accidents and these resulted in the Lotus team being out-manoeuvred. While the yellow danger flags were flying Parnelli Jones made his pit stops and eventually took the lead to beat Clark into second place.

Only two days later Clark was driving a Lotus 23 at Mos-

Jim Clark

port Park in Canada, then it was back to Europe again for the Belgian Grand Prix. Jimmy led the race throughout to score the first of four successive Championship wins. Despite an altercation with the Dutch police, at Zandvoort Clark displayed that invincibility that was soon to be so familiar. He set fastest lap in practice, led the race from start to finish, lapped the entire field, set a new lap record and became the first man ever to record an over-100 mph lap in a race at the Zandvoort circuit. A week later he made it a hat-trick on the fast Reims circuit, scene of the French Grand Prix where the race pattern was almost identical; Clark was fastest in practice, led throughout and set a new lap record. In the British race at Silverstone he again was the winner, but the victory was not *quite* so easy—he did not take the lead until lap four and John Surtees (Ferrari) set fastest lap!

Next came the non-Championship Solitude race, but here luck was not on Jimmy's side. A transmission 'doughnut' sheared on the start-line and Clark joined the race late to finish eighth. Although in later years Clark became weary of flying from meeting to meeting, competing in race after race, in 1963 he was still cramming as many events into his crowded itinerary as possible. On 4th August he drove in the German Grand Prix, but his Lotus was slowed by an engine misfire and he finished second behind John Surtees's Ferrari. Then he flew back to England to compete at Brands Hatch the following day. His mount was a monstrous Ford Galaxie belonging to Alan Brown and he drove it to a fine victory ahead of Graham Hill's 3.8-litre Jaguar. Next came the Swedish Grand Prix at Karlskoga which he won with a Grand Prix Lotus and the Milwaukee '200' race in which he gained some consolation for his Indianapolis defeat by winning with his Lotus 29-Ford. At the beginning of September he drove in another non-Championship Grand Prix, the Austrian race on the bumpy Zeltweg circuit, but here he retired with a fractured oil pipe.

Clark now led the World Championship by a margin of

twenty-two points and almost had the Championship in the bag. In the Italian Grand Prix at Monza there was a tremendous battle in the opening laps between Clark, Surtees (Ferrari), Hill (BRM) and Gurney (Brabham). Both Surtees and Hill retired and Clark gradually drew away from the American Brabham driver to become the first Scotsman to win the Drivers' Championship. A fortnight later he won both the Formula One Gold Cup race at Oulton Park with a Lotus 25 and the sports car race with a 23. As soon as these races were over he flew to the States to drive his Indianapolis car in the Trenton State Fair race the following day, but retired with mechanical trouble. In the United States Grand Prix at Watkins Glen he lost a lap and a half in the pits because of battery trouble, but rejoined the race to finish third and added lustre to his Championship crown by winning both of the last two rounds in the Championship at Mexico City and Kyalami. His final Championship score was 54 points (the maximum possible) compared with the 29 of second-place man Graham Hill.

For 1964 Clark's programme followed the same familiar, but very successful pattern. He drove Lotus Cortinas in a number of races with considerable success, he handled the Grand Prix 25 and its later development, the 33, his season included Indianapolis and he also appeared at the wheel of Lotus 32 Formula Two cars and the new, but largely unsuccessful Lotus 30 Group 7 sports cars with 4.7-litre Ford V-8 engines. Once again the season started in March with a Formula One race at Snetterton where he retired, but he won the Formula One race at Goodwood at the end of the month. Shortly afterwards he scored his third win at Pau, now a 1000 cc Formula Two race, but he retired in the Formula One Aintree '200.' Another victory followed in the Formula Two Eifelrennen at the Nürburgring, another retirement in the Formula One *Daily Express* Trophy race at Silverstone.

The first Championship race of the season was Monaco on

10th May. This was a race in which Graham Hill always seemed to do well, winning in it on a total of five occasions, but although Clark led the race several times, he never managed to score a victory there. The 1964 race followed the usual Clark pattern. He was fastest in practice, soon built up a commanding lead which he increased even after the rear anti-roll bar broke. Chapman eventually called him into the pits for the remains of the bar to be cut away and he rejoined the race in third place only to retire with engine trouble on the last lap. Under Monaco race regulations he had still covered sufficient distance to be classified fourth. A Formula Two win at Mallory Park followed, he was second in the Formula Two race at the Crystal Palace and then scored a typical Clark win at Zandvoort. He took the lead on the first lap, lapped everyone except second-place man Surtees and set a new lap record.

In 1964 the Lotus team again competed at Indianapolis, but it was a race that he disliked and commented on one occasion that it would be, 'fine without the Americans,' a remark aimed at all the ballyhoo, parading and fuss that surrounds the Independence day classic. The race proved another disappointment for both Lotus and Clark and Jimmy bitterly regretted all the weary flying that had been necessary to cross the Atlantic for qualifying and then back again for European races. He had qualified for pole position on the grid, but the race was stopped after a multi-car crash costing the lives of two drivers. It was restarted, Clark who had been holding first place led away, but then a tire deflated and the car crawled into the infield with collapsed suspension. Jim returned to Europe to run in the Belgian Grand Prix; he won, but it was not one of his best races. He had to fight hard with Graham Hill in the opening laps and he crossed the line in first place only after race-leaders Gurney, Hill and McLaren had run out of fuel, and Clark himself ran out of fuel at Stavelot corner on his slowing-down lap. He retired with engine trouble in the French Grand Prix at Rouen, but enjoyed himself immensely at the wheel of Patrick Lindsey's ERA which he tried out in practice (the ERA was running in an historic event the same day). Denis Jenkinson wrote in *Motor Sport*: 'Clark went faster than anyone has ever driven an ERA, in only four laps, but, after all, Clark is not World Champion for nothing . . . Clark really enjoyed the experience, never having driven anything like an ERA before, but felt that it could go a lot faster round circuits if this and that were altered. He began to to suggest various things, but I had to stop him for he was converting the 1936 ERA into a modern GP car and the whole point of vintage and historic car racing is that the owners and drivers enjoy living in the past . . .'

By the British Grand Prix at Brands Hatch the Lotus-Climax had found its old form and Clark took pole position on the grid, set a new lap record and won the race, but he was chased hard all the way by Graham Hill and his BRM. Shortly afterwards he won the rain-soaked Formula One race at Solitude, but he retired with engine trouble in the German Grand Prix. Apart from a win in the Formula Two race at Brands Hatch on the day after the German Grand Prix, luck was not on Jimmy's side during the remainder of the 1964 season and he achieved little success. In the Mediterranean Grand Prix at Enna in Sicily he was beaten into second place by Jo Siffert who always went fantastically well on this high-speed circuit where bravado often proved a greater asset than skill and experience. Like the cars of so many other competitors, Clark's Lotus shook itself to bits in the Austrian Grand Prix, a Championship race at the bumpy Zeltweg circuit, and he finally retired with driveshaft failure. In the remaining three Championship races Clark retired with mechanical troubles, although in fact at Mexico City he was classified fifth on the basis of the distance covered. There are lots of ifs in motor racing, but if Clark's car had proved rather more reliable in these last three rounds, he would have undoubtedly have won the Championship and not finished third, for he was battling for the lead at Monza and leading at both Watkins Glen and Mexico City when trouble struck.

The 1965 season was to prove the finest in Jim Clark's career and the invincibility with which he dominated racing quashed once and for all any doubts as to his true greatness. Throughout the year he was at the peak of his form, never once did he exceed his own limits in his efforts to gain victory, every Grand Prix he won he controlled with apparent effortlessness from the fall of the flag and his only mistake was in the Race of Champions at Brands Hatch in March where he went off the track while chasing Dan Gurney's Brabham and hit a grass bank.

After a magnificent victory in the South African Grand Prix (one magazine wrote, 'A disappointing race in some ways—Clark was much too fast for the opposition'), Jimmy flew to New Zealand to compete in the Tasman races with a works Lotus. At the wheel of his Lotus 32, he scored five wins out of seven races entered. Then back to Britain for the Race of Champions referred to above and this was followed by a win in the Syracuse Grand Prix. A third in the Formula Two race at Snetterton, a win in the Goodwood Formula One race and another at the Formula Two Pau Grand Prix followed.

Because of Lotus's commitment to run at Indianapolis and the team's concentration on this race, possibly at the expense of Formula One, Clark felt bound to compete in the 500-Miles race, despite his antipathy and despite the fact that because of a clash of dates it meant missing the Monaco Grand Prix. Starting from the front row of the rolling start, Clark went straight into the lead, was passed by A J Foyt, went ahead again, after the first pit stops was a lap ahead of the rest of the field and won the race at record speed, having led for 190 of the 200 laps. Naturally Clark was delighted by this victory, but he now could settle down to the racing that he loved, Formula One, and the pursuit of his second World Championship.

In 1965 the Coventry-Climax concern had introduced a new and more powerful 32-valve version of the familiar V-8 engine. These engines were available only in very limited numbers and were allotted one per team. The BRM chassis and the Lotus 33 were very closely matched, but the new engine gave Clark just that 'edge' he needed to ensure success without anxiety about his car. He led from start to finish in both the Belgian Grand Prix (his fourth successive win at Spa) and in the French race which was held at Clermont-Ferrand for the first time. In both these races he was followed home by Jackie Stewart, newcomer to the BRM team, to make it a one-two finish for Scotland. Three more victories followed at Silverstone, Zandvoort (his third successive win at this circuit) and the Nürburgring and although he won at the last two circuits with consummate ease, the British race was not free from anxiety. In the closing stages of the race his oil pressure fell disastrously and despite the fact the Hill's BRM was closing rapidly, he kept a cool head, driving the car on the ignition switch and coasting through the corners to reduce oil surge. At the chequered flag he was just over three seconds ahead of the BRM driver.

Now Clark was undisputed Champion, regardless of what happened in the remaining three rounds in the Championship. In fact his only Formula One finish during the remainder of the season was at Enna in the Mediterranean Grand Prix where he was again beaten into second place by Jo Siffert with his Brabham. At Monza he battled for the lead with the BRMs until fuel pump trouble caused his retirement and he was eliminated by engine failure at both Watkins Glen and Mexico City. For Jimmy, his triumph was completed when he was made a freeman of the village of

Jim Clark

Duns, not where he was born, but the area in which he had spent most of his life, and from then on he always had himself billed in American race programmes as 'Jim Clark, Duns, Scotland.'

The end of the 1965 season marked the end of a great era and, in fact, the end of Jim Clark's great run of successes. For 1966 the new 3000 cc Grand Prix Formula came into force, but Coventry-Climax had decided to withdraw from racing and although Ford stepped into the breach and provided the finance for Duckworth's Cosworth concern to build a new 3-litre V-8 engine, this was not ready until 1967. In 1966 Lotus had to make do with the old 33 cars powered by the 2-litre Tasman version of the Climax engine and the new 43 car which was powered by the heavy, complex and largely unreliable H-16 BRM. Even when the new V-8 Ford engine made its appearance, it suffered from teething troubles and in its first season failed to achieve the degree of success anticipated.

At the beginning of the 1966 season Jim Clark drove the 39 model with 2.5-litre Climax engine in the Tasman races, but it was no match for the 2-litre BRMs driven by Hill and Stewart and Jimmy's only win was in the Warwick Farm race. At Monaco he was left on the line when the gearbox jammed, but eventually freed it and made up a lot of lost ground only to retire with suspension failure. Even at Indianapolis things did not go according to plan. On an oil-soaked track he spun twice, but to the astonishment of 'Indy' afficiandos succeeded in collecting everything without striking the retaining wall, and later in the race was misled by his pit into thinking he was leading the race when in fact he was lying second behind Graham Hill's Lola. At Spa he accidentally over-revved his engine and retired on the first lap and during practice for the French race he was hit in the eye by a bird and as a result had to be posted as a non-starter. Things looked up a little at the British race at

Brands Hatch where he was well up with the leaders until forced to make a pit stop for brake fluid; he finished fourth and gained his first Championship points of the year. A third place followed at Zandvoort where he battled for the lead with Jack Brabham before stopping to take on extra water and at the German race held on a very wet track he made a mistake, such a very rare occurrence in his career, and went off the road.

In all these races Jimmy had been at the wheel of his 1965 car with 2-litre engine, while most of the opposition apart from the BRM team had full 3-litre units. By the Italian Grand Prix at Monza Team Lotus had taken delivery of its H-16 BRM engine. Clark made a bad start and was fighting his way back through the field when the transmission failed. At Watkins Glen luck favoured Clark in what was otherwise an unsuccessful season. He took the lead with his H-16-powered car and while everyone, including himself, expected this very unreliable engine to break, it carried on to the finish with surprising reliability to give him his one and only Championship race victory of the season. In the ninth and final round of the Championship at Mexico City the transmission failed yet again.

Throughout 1966 Jimmy had been pursuing another interest with almost the same vigour that he put into motor racing. Some years previously he had completed his initial flying tuition, but now he was realising that there were considerable advantages in flying himself from race to race. He had ordered a new Piper aircraft, but this had disappeared while being ferried across the Atlantic and instead settled for buying Colin Chapman's Piper Twin Comanche. As the years went by, so his income from racing had increased and now he was facing the inevitable tax problems. Eventually, over the winter of 1966–7, he decided with some reluctance that he would have to live outside Britain and, because he had many friends there, he decided to settle in Paris.

Once again the start of the season followed its usual pattern. He had now been joined in the Lotus team by Graham Hill as joint number one driver, but for the first two races of the year they were still forced to use the old 2-litre and H-16-powered cars. In the South African race, now held at Kyalami, both drivers retired. Jimmy then flew to New Zealand for the Tasman races in which he competed with a 2-litre Climax-powered Lotus 33. Despite opposition from BRM team he enjoyed a good run of success, winning four races and finishing second in the other three entered. In April he drove the new Lotus 48 Formula Two car in three races, finishing fourth at Pau, winning at Barcelona which was very much a driver's circuit and retiring at the Nürburgring. Later in the year he won other Formula Two races at Zolder, Jarama and Keimola. 1967 was to prove Jimmy's last race at Monaco, but he was still out of luck. At the wheel of a 2-litre Climax-powered car, he spun and restarted at the tail of the field, but climbed back through the field to battle for fourth place with Bruce McLaren, only to spin again and retire. Nor did the Indianapolis race bring him any better luck, and at the wheel of his new Lotus 38 he retired with engine trouble.

When the brilliant new Ford-powered Lotus 49 made its debut at the Dutch Grand Prix it seemed as though Grand Prix racing was about to embark on another era of Clark and Lotus domination. Although the new car displayed staggering speed during 1967 and Clark drove with all his old brilliance, because of a series of minor mechanical troubles of a 'teething' nature, he scored only four Grand Prix wins during the year. On the car's debut at Zandvoort Hill led initially, but after his retirement with camshaft drive failure, Jimmy came through to take the lead and score a brilliant first-race victory for the new car. At Spa Jimmy led, but stopped twice at the pits because of spark plug trouble and eventually finished sixth. Both of the Lotus 49s retired in the

French Grand Prix held on the Bugatti circuit at Le Mans. Clark scored a fine victory at Silverstone after a troublefree race, but retired with suspension trouble at the Nürburgring, with rainsoaked electrics in the first Canadian Grand Prix at Mosport, and took third place in the Italian Grand Prix after two pit stops. A fine victory followed at Watkins Glen where the 49s took the first two places and Clark rounded off the season with a win at Mexico City. In the Championship he finished third with 41 points to the 51 of Brabham driver Denis Hulme who won only two races, but took three second places and three thirds.

Then 1968, an initial victory in the South African Grand Prix, four wins in the Tasman series with a Lotus and Hockenheim, 7th April 1968 when in the first heat of the Formula Two race his Lotus 48 went out of control on a gentle rght-hand bend that could be taken flat-out, disappeared sideways off the track and into the trees and one of the greatest drivers motor racing has ever known was dead. It seemed incredible that Clark should have lost his life driving a Formula Two car in an unimportant race and as Graham Hill later said, 'Of one thing I am sure—it wasn't Jmmy's fault at Hockenhem.'

Clark's death was totally unexpected and although Grand Prix racing—or any form of motor racing—can never be completely safe, it was passing through a period in which few drivers lost their lives. With the change to rear-engined cars in 1959, motor racing had become a little safer. Since then six Grand Prix drivers had been killed. Harry Schell had been killed with a Cooper at Silverstone in 1960; in the 1960 Belgian Grand Prix, Alan Stacey died in freak circumstances because he was hit in the face by a bird, in the same race Chris Bristow died because he allowed himself to be lured into over-stepping his ability in a dice with Willy Mairesse; the following year Wolfgang von Trips lost his life at Monza when he collided with Clark's Lotus; in 1964

Dutchman Carol Godin de Beaufort crashed his Porsche at the Nürburgring and suffered fatal injuries; Lorenzo Bandini died of terrible burns after crashing his Ferrari at Monaco in 1967. It seemed beyond the bounds of credulity that Jim Clark should add his name to that sad list. It still does.

10

Champion on Two Wheels and Four
JOHN SURTEES
1964

SURTEES HAS BEEN unique amongst Champions, the only man to win World Championships with both cars and motorcycles, but like Hawthorn, he won the Drivers' Championship by the margin of only a single point. Surtees's most inspiring season of motor racing was in fact a year in which he failed to finish in the first three of Championship points, 1962 when as a comparative newcomer to the Grand Prix scene, he and the new Lola-Climax displayed an immense potential, undoubted major contenders for Grand Prix success the following season, a season that for them never was because Bowmaker-Yeoman, the entrants of the Lola, withdrew from racing. Rather like Chris Amon, who despite his very great ability, has never won a Championship Grand Prix, Surtees's career has been more notable for the number of uncompetitive cars he has raced than for its successes. After his narrow Championship win with Ferrari cars, there followed a season when the Maranello cars proved uncompetitive, a broken year in whch he left Ferrari after an argument (and could well have won the Championship if he had stayed with the team), two seasons of struggling with the Honda and a final year of disappointment with

John Surtees

BRM before he started racing his own Formula One cars.

On 11th February 1934, Surtees was born at Tatsfield in Surrey straight into the world of motor sport. His father was a professional racing motor-cyclist who won the British sidecar Championship in 1937, 1938 and 1939 and his mother, almost as equally keen a motor-cycling enthusiast, used to ride as passenger in motor-cycle trials. That John should spend a life dedicated to motor sport in one form or another was inevitable and it was a foregone conclusion that he would take up motor-cycling competitively. Surtees senior ran a motor-cycle dealers at Forest Hill in South London and had an agency for Vincent-HRD, the fastest production motor-cycles of their time. When John left school at the age of sixteen, he spent five years apprenticed to Vincent Engineering; he was trained in all the different departments at their Stevenage works and received a thorough general engineering training.

At the age of fourteen John started to ride as a sidecar passenger in motor-cycle races, in 1951 he won his first race as a solo rider at Brands Hatch, and at a time when Geoff Duke was the star of British motor-cycle racing, while Mike Hawthorn and Stirling Moss were challenging the established stars of motor racing, John Surtees was doing the same thing on two wheels. In 1955 he became a member of the works Norton team and the following year, riding MV Augusta works machines, won his first World Championship. Persistent mechanical trouble resulted in a year of failure in 1957, but during 1958 and 1959 Surtees and the Augustas won every Grand Prix entered and he took the World Championship in both the 350 and 500 cc classes. In all John won seven World Championship titles during his motor-cycle racing career.

By 1959 John was thinking in terms of making the switch from two wheels to four, but he was anxious to proceed cautiously. Several motor racing team managers were interested in engaging his talents at the wheel of their cars and he was given tests in 1959 in both Tony Vandervell's latest Vanwall and by Reg Parnell in the Aston Martin DBR1. Both teams made him offers, but both he declined. The still very youthful looking, but already slightly balding Surtees had decided to make a cautious entry into motor racing. For 1960 he bought his own 1500 cc Cooper-Climax Formula Two car which on his debut he drove into second place behind Innes Ireland's works Lotus in the British Empire Trophy race at Oulton Park in April. Surtees did, however, agree to drive Cooper-BMC Formula Junior cars for Ken Tyrrell and he took second place to Jim Clark at the *Daily Express* meeting at Silverstone in May. So impressed was Colin Chapman by Surtees's performances that he invited him to join the works Lotus team and John agreed to drive for Chapman whenever his motor-cycling commitments permitted, a decision that conflicted with his earlier caution. John's first drive for the team was in the *Daily Express* Trophy race at Silverstone, but he retired in both this race and at Monaco. He did not race for Lotus again until the British Grand Prix at Silverstone where he took a fine second place.

A week later Surtees drove Rob Walker's Formula Two Porsche, the only one of these cars in private hands, in the Solitude Grand Prix, but the gear-change, never good on these cars at the best of times, was playing up and he eventually missed a gear and spun off. John returned to the Lotus team to run in the Silver City Trophy race at Brands Hatch on August Bank Holiday Monday, but here he was plagued by clutch slip and a misfiring engine and finished a poor sixth. John's best drive of the season was in the Portuguese Grand Prix later in August and at the wheel of his Lotus he built up a ten-second lead over Brabham's Cooper, only to retire when fuel leaking from the front-mounted tank dripped on to the pedals and his foot sliding off the slippery brake pedal resulted in an excursion into the straw bales and his exit from the race with a split radiator. The remainder

John Surtees

of John's season was equally disappointing; in the Formula Two race at Brands Hatch on 27th August John's Lotus collided, ironically enough, with another Lotus driven by Geoff Duke, he retired with engine trouble at Snetterton, retired with fuel pump failure at Oulton Park and in the last race of the season, the United States Grand Prix, he collided with team-mate Jim Clark before retiring with mechanical trouble.

With the World Championship under his belt in two different classes in 1960, Surtees decided to retire from motor-cycle racing and concentrate on dicing on four wheels. For this season, the first of 1500 cc Grand Prix racing, John signed up to drive for Yeoman Credit, a private team run by a finance company, but with very well prepared cars, as competitive as any of the British entries in 1961 when racing was Ferrari-dominated, and with their own special-bodied version of the Cooper which was aero-dynamically more efficient than that of the works cars. Apart from Stirling Moss, no driver handling British Grand Prix cars did really well in 1961, but throughout the season Surtees drove with great skill and ability and achieved a fair degree of success.

He started the season well with third place overall and first in the Formula One category of the Lombank Trophy race at Snetterton in March (the first two cars home were so-called Inter-continental Formula 2500 cc cars) and he won the Formula One race at Goodwood on Easter Monday. At the *Daily Express* Trophy race at Silverstone in May, another Inter-continental Formula event, he appeared at the wheel of the latest rear-engined Vanwall on its one and only race outing. In heavy rain Surtees handled the powerful Vanwall car with skill, holding third place until he spun, rejoined the race in thirteenth spot and climbed back through the field to finish fifth. In June he drove a brilliant race at Spa, lacking the speed with his Cooper to stay with the four much more powerful Ferraris, but battling with Hill's BRM until it retired and taking a very satisfactory fifth place. He took a good second place with his Cooper in the Inter-continental British Empire Trophy race at Silverstone in July and finished fifth in the German Grand Prix in August.

In 1962 the team became known as the Bowmaker-Yeoman Racing Organisation and fielded the very competitive and very promising Lola Grand Prix cars designed by Eric Broadley. The team was managed by Reg Parnell and the cars were driven by Surtees and Roy Salvadori. Throughout this season Surtees and the Lola went magnificently. In the *Daily Express* Trophy race at Silverstone in May John finished third, he crashed at Zandvoort because of a broken wishbone, but then took fourth place at Monaco, won the 2000 Guineas race at Mallory Park and was fifth at Spa. In the non-Championship Reims Grand Prix on 1st July he built up a twenty-second lead, but then his engine developed a misfire at high revs, necessitating a pit stop and he eventually retired with a broken valve spring. It was much the same story in the French Grand Prix at Rouen the following weekend; Rouen is a particularly difficult circuit and Surtees, driving like a veteran, was only a second behind Hill's BRM when fuel starvation forced a pit stop and he rejoined the race to finish fifth. At Aintree in the British Grand Prix he took a fine second place and another second followed at the Nürburgring where his driving combined great determination and notable calmness. Engine trouble eliminated Surtees in the remaining three Championship races and the only consolation was a third place in the non-Championship Rand Grand Prix in December.

At the end of the season the Bowmaker-Yeoman team made the sad announcement that they were withdrawing from racing, all the sadder because the Lola appeared to be on the verge of achieving substantial success. As a final fling, however, the team ran in the Tasman races in New Zealand and Australia and at the wheel of a Lola powered

John Surtees

by the 2.5-litre Climax engine Surtees scored victories in the New Zealand Grand Prix and the Lakeside race. John was now looking for a Formula One drive and received an invitation to join Ferrari which meant that he also competed in Prototype racing, a category in which he soon became a leading exponent and at a time when Ferrari power was at its zenith.

For much of his time with Ferrari, however, John was driving Grand Prix cars that were no real match for the Lotus and BRM opposition. He started off the 1963 season well enough, leading in the *Daily Express* Trophy at Silverstone until his oil pressure fell and finishing fourth at Monaco and setting a new lap record on the hundreth and last lap of the race on a track that was well-coated with both oil and rubber. He took a good third place at Zandvoort and he finished second in the British race, passing Hill's BRM, which was running low on fuel, on the very last lap of the race. It was typical of Surtees's industry that he should have stayed up half the night before the race helping the mechanics make up a three-gallon reserve fuel tank for his car so as to be sure that he would not run out of fuel in this longer than average race.

At long last at the Nürburgring came the break for which John had waited so long. After battling in the early laps with Clark's Lotus which developed a misfire, John scored his first ever World Championship race victory in the German Grand Prix and Ferrari's first since the 1961 Italian race. An easy victory followed in the Mediterranean Grand Prix on the very fast Pergusa circuit in Sicily, a race in which there was not much in the way of opposition, and at the wheel of the latest and much improved Ferrari he led the Italian race until his engine expired in a vast cloud of white smoke. Another disappointment followed in the United States race which he was leading comfortably when his car developed engine trouble, and he retired again at Mexico City. The

Ferrari team then travelled to South Africa where Surtees won the Rand Grand Prix, but he retired with engine trouble in the South African Grand Prix proper.

In 1963 John enjoyed very mixed fortunes at the wheel of the 3-litre 250/P Ferrari Prototypes. Co-driving with Italian Lodovico Scarfiotti, he scored a good win in the Sebring 12 Hours race, but he crashed in the Targa Florio, team-mate Parkes crashed their car at the Nürburgring and it was team-mate Willy Mairesse who crashed at Le Mans.

For the 1964 Grand Prix season Ferrari produced a new V-8 Formula One which, it was hoped, would prove a match for the powerful British opposition. Surtees drove the new car to victory on its debut at Siracusa in April and although he failed to score any impressive run of victories, the 1964 season proved to be one of steady and consistent success, especially during the latter part. After retiring at Monaco, John took a second place at Zandvoort. He retired at both Spa and Clermont-Ferrand, but took a third place at Brands Hatch in July and won the non-Championship Solitude Grand Prix the same month. Then came the German Grand Prix at the Nürburgring. This difficult 14.2-mile course winding its way through the Eifel mountains, with a succession of difficult bends was a true driver's circuit, one which Surtees liked and one on which he excelled. He was fastest in practice and at the start of the race shot into the lead. Dan Gurney chased him hard with his Brabham and eventually squeezed by the red car, but fell back again when his Climax engine began to overheat. At the finish John was over a minute ahead of Graham Hill's BRM.

Another victory followed at Monza where after a battle with Jim Clark's Lotus and Bruce McLaren's Cooper, the Ferrari driver won by over a minute. A second place followed at Watkins Glen and he now held second place in the Championship with 34 points to the 39 of Graham Hill with only one race still to run. What happened at Mexico City was no fault of John's, but it was a pretty shameful affair

John Surtees

from Bandini's point of view and for Surtees took a lot of the pleasure out of his victory in the Championship. Graham Hill was holding a comfortable third place, sufficient to ensure him victory in the Championship, with the Ferraris of Lorenzo Bandini and John Surtees in fourth and fifth places. On several successive laps as the cars went through the hairpin bend on the far side of the circuit from the pits, Bandini tried to pass Hill, although it was obvious that there was simply not enough room for him to get by. Hill was shaking his fist at the Italian driver, but Bandini ignored him and on lap thirty-one the inevitable happened, Bandini taking the tighter, inside line refused to give way, the two cars collided and spun, and Hill, his exhausts crumpled by the Ferrari's wheels, was forced to stop at the pits. Bandini recovered from his spin, moved ahead of Surtees again to take third place, but in the closing laps, after Clark's leading Lotus had slowed right off, he eased his Ferrari and allowed Surtees to slip ahead into what was now second place and take the World Championship by the margin of one point. In Prototype racing in 1964 John's best performances were third places with Bandini at Sebring and Le Mans.

During 1965 John Surtees drove both the familiar V-8 Grand Prix Ferrari and the newer flat-12 model, but 1965 was definitely not a Ferrari year in Formula One racing. John's season was disappointing in the extreme and he failed to win a single Championship race. At East London in the South African Grand Prix at the start of the season he finished second and followed this up with other seconds at Siracusa and in the *Daily Express* Trophy and third places at Monaco, Clermont-Ferrand and Silverstone. He failed to finish in the first three in any other Grand Prix during the season. In Prototype racing he shared the second-place car at Monza in the 1000 kilometres race and won the Nürburgring 1000 kilometres race with Lodovico Scarfiotti.

A direct result of Surtees's season in 1962 at the wheel of

the Lola Grand Prix cars had been a close friendship with Lola designer and builder Eric Broadley. In 1965 Broadley had resumed in business on his own after eighteen months working on the Ford GT40 project and John Surtees was one of the first customers for Broadley's new T70 sports car, a type described by the Federation Internationale de l'Automobile as 'two-seater racing cars' and known from 1966 onwards as Group 7 cars. The new, low and very sleek T70 was powered by a Chevrolet 5.4-litre V-8 engine and with a power output of over 450 bhp its top speed was close to 200 mph. John had bought two of these cars which were entered in close liaison with the works under the name 'Team Surtees.' Surtees also drove Lola Formula Two cars during that year and his successes included a win in the Oulton Park Gold Cup race. With his T70 he finished second at Silverstone in March, won the Players '200' race at Mosport in Canada in June and the Guards Trophy race at Brands Hatch on August Bank Holiday Monday. In September he flew to Canada where he won a race at St Jovite and the following weekend he was competing with the Lola in the Canadian Grand Prix. In practice at Mosport one of the Lola's suspension uprights failed and Surtees crashed badly, suffering multiple injuries and a damaged kidney. It seemed that if Surtees survived his injuries, which at one stage seemed very doubtful, he would never race again and it is unlikely that any driver has suffered such bad injuries and succeeded in returning to racing. And the scars left on a driver by a serious crash are mental as well as physical; he has to get his confidence back, his judgment and reactions are often seriously impaired. If Surtees raced again, it seemed that he would be doing nothing short of committing suicide.

The Mosport crash was in September 1965 and in April 1966 he co-drove the latest P3 4-litre Ferrari Prototype at Monza with Mike Parkes and scored a fine victory in torrential rain. With the new 3-litre Grand Prix Ferrari he won the Syracuse Grand Prix, finished second in the *Daily Express* Trophy race at Silverstone and won the Belgian Grand Prix, a magnificent record for a driver whose injuries had brought him so close to death. Then came Le Mans. Ferrari team-manager Eugenio Dragoni announced that although Surtees would start the race, his car would be driven for the remainder of the twenty-four hours by Scarfiotti and Parkes. Dragoni and Surtees had always disliked each other, Surtees was too out-spoken, too single-minded, too independent for the Italian's tastes and, perhaps, showed his contempt too openly. John had always enjoyed excellent relations with Enzo Ferrari, but he now felt that he had endured more than enough of Ferrari internal political wrangles and left the team. If John had stayed with Ferrari, he would have probably won the World Championship, for the V-12 Maranello cars were amongst the most competitive that year. For the remainder of the season he handled the heavy and rather under-powered Cooper-Maseratis and with a second place at the Nürburgring, a third at Watkins Glen and a win in the Mexican Grand Prix he took second place in the Drivers' Championship.

Surtees and his Lola returned to the Can-Am series in 1966, the first year in which the major events were strung together in a series for the Can-Am cup. After the disaster the previous autumn, Surtees thoroughly vindicated himself, winning the races at Mont Tremblant, Riverside Raceway and Las Vegas to take the Cup with 27 points to the 21 gained by Mark Donohue.

Cooper's Jonathan Sieff wanted Surtees to stay with the team for 1967, but John thought, rightly enough, that the cars would not be competitive and said no. Instead he signed up to drive the Japanese V-12 Honda, a heavy car, but with tremendous development potential. For two years Surtees battled to make the Honda competitive and with the team's racing headquarters so far away from the Honda factory in Tokyo he was forced to take on responsibility for all the development work. But he had taken on too much, for all the development work. But he had taken on too much, for he was still involved with Lola in Formula Two and in both Prototype and Can-Am racing. Disappointment followed disappointment and all he could manage in 1967 with the Honda was a third in the South African race, a sixth in the British, one well-deserved win in the Italian Grand Prix with a new version with an improved chassis designed by Eric Broadley and a fourth place at Watkins Glen. It was much the same story in 1968 when his best results were a second place in the French Grand Prix at Rouen, a fifth place in the British Grand Prix and a third at Watkins Glen. At the end of the year Honda withdrew from racing, Surtees and the Japanese company parted on good terms, but with John still convinced that the Honda had the makings of a Grand Prix winner. There had been more disappointments in 1967 with the failure at the Nürburgring and at Le Mans of the new Aston Martin-powered Lola T70 Mk 3 coupés (painted dark green, but distinguished by Surtees's 'trademark,' a broad arrow-head on the nose) and by the failure of his Lola in the Can-Am series.

For 1969 Surtees involved himself in two more unsuccessful projects (and it was almost three); in Grand Prix racing he drove for BRM, in Can-Am racing he handled the new Chaparral 2H which he regarded as one of the worst cars he had ever driven and but for problems over tire contracts he would also have appeared for the Autodelta team at the wheel of the hopelessly unsuccessful Alfa Romeo Tipo 33/3 Prototypes. The V-12 BRMs proved both slow and unreliable to the point at which the team became little more than a subject for jokes in bad taste. Surtees did everything possible for the team, driving at his hardest, persuading engineer Tony Southgate to leave the Eagle team for whom he had been working in the States to join BRM and encouraging and helping the mechanics when the team's spirits were at

John Surtees

their lowest. All Surtees gained in return was a third place in the United States race and a fifth in the Spanish.

By 1969, however, Surtees had formed his own company at Edenbridge in Kent and that season introduced his new Surtees TS5 Formula 5000 car designed by Len Terry. For 1970 he decided to go Grand Prix racing on his own, fielding an ex-works McLaren until the new Surtees TS7 car was ready to make its debut in the British Grand Prix. His only success that year was a win in the Gold Cup race at Oulton Park, a victory which he repeated the following year when his improved TS9 was sponsored by Brooke Bond-Oxo. Surtees's only other successes in 1971 were third places in the Race of Champions at Brands Hatch and a non-Championship race at Hockenheim. John has now retired from Formula One racing to concentrate on running the business side of Team Surtees whose very full programme includes Formula One with cars driven in 1973 by Mike Hailwood and Carlos Pace, a Formula Two team sponsored by 'Matchbox' toys and the manufacture of Formula 5000 cars. In 1972 Hailwood drove Surtees cars to victory in the European Formula Two Championship.

John Surtees is probably the most dedicated and hardworking of all racing drivers, outspoken in his views, avoiding publicity, intolerant of other people's mistakes and almost excessively patriotic. With his wife Pat, whom he married in 1962, he lives in a large country house with spacious grounds at Limpsfield. Every day John and Pat travel to the works at Edenbridge and he still pushes himself just as hard as he did in his early racing days. Not much success in Grand Prix racing has so far come the way of Team Surtees, but John will keep persevering until it does.

11

The Kiwi King
DENIS HULME
1967

SLOW IN SPEECH and movement, looking older than his years, Denny Hulme is one of the fastest and safest of Grand Prix drivers and the most successful of the New Zealand 'Driver to Europe' award winners. Hulme was born at Motueka in in the Nelson province of the South Island of New Zealand on 18th June 1936. His father, Clive, was a farmer in a small way, but owning his own land, running a small dairy herd, as well as growing tobacco. Clive Hulme joined the army at the start of World War Two and for his exploits he was awarded the Victoria Cross before being invalided back to New Zealand in 1941. During his school days Denny's main interests were swimming and working on the lorries belonging to the trucking business that Clive Hulme had started in post-war years, but he played football, enjoyed trout-fishing and also took up shooting.

Denis Hulme had his first car at the age of nineteen, an MG TF bought for him by his father in appreciation of all the help that Denny had given to the family business. Soon afterwards he drove the car in the Papamoa hill climb, winning his class with ease; before long he was competing regularly and he moved on to an MGA. With the new MG,

Denis Hulme

Hulme soon had scored a whole string of successes and felt ready to graduate to something more ambitious. In early 1959, once again with financial assistance from his father, Denny bought a Formula Two Cooper with Climax engine enlarged to 2-litres from Mervyn Neil. Hulme spent the winter months working on the car and, driving in bare feet (as he did until the middle of 1960), a legacy from the days when he drove his father's trucks bare-footed because it gave better throttle control, soon showed a mastery of the New Zealand circuits that resulted in him winning the 'Driver to Europe' award for 1960.

In his first European season with a Cooper-Austin Formula Junior car Hulme achieved only a small degree of success, but he returned to New Zealand at the end of the year and drove a Yeoman Credit 2.5-litre Cooper in the Tasman series with sufficient success to win the New Zealand Gold Star award for local drivers. It was back again to Europe the following year when he raced a Ford-powered Cooper, again without much success, and his best performance was at Le Mans where he and Angus Hyslop drove a Fiat-Abarth into thirteenth place. By 1962 Denis Hulme was working for Jack Brabham, managing to get in a few drives in the elderly Cooper and hoping that he would soon be driving a new Brabham car. But the Brabham organisation was new, development work was slow and Hulme did not drive one of Jack's cars until the end of the season. During this season Hulme had been close to giving up racing, for he seemed to be waiting interminably at Brabhams for a drive and although he had been given a couple of try-outs by Ken Tyrrell, who ran the Cooper Formula Junior team, this entrant thought that he lacked the makings of a really good driver. Then the following season his fortunes changed. At the wheel of a Formula Junior Brabham he won seven races and also co-drove with Roy Salvadori the winning 3.8 Jaguar in the *Motor* 6 Hours race at Brands Hatch.

When Denny travelled home for the 1964 Tasman series

it could hardly have been a happier return. He returned to marry Greeta at Tauranga, and he was now a member of the works Brabham team with a car for the Tasman races and the promise of a regular drive with Formula Two cars in Europe. In the Tasman races Hulme's successes were limited to a win with his Brabham-Climax in the Levin race and third place in the Lady Wigram Trophy at Christchurch, but he enjoyed a thoroughly successful European season in 1964, winning a Formula Two race at Clermont-Ferrand and taking third place at Avus, and scoring a number of victories with the new Brabham BT8 sports car.

Denny remained as number two driver to 'Black Jack' himself in the 1965 Brabham Formula Two team and won the Formula Two race at Oulton Park and finished second at Karlskoga, Brands Hatch and Oulton Park later in the year and third at Albi. He drove the BT8 sports car, finished in the white and green colours of Irishman Sid Taylor, in a number of races during the year and scored a fine and rather surprising victory against much heavier machinery in the Tourist Trophy at Oulton Park. His stock was rising at Brabhams and at some races during the year the team fielded a third 1500 cc Climax-powered Formula One car for Denny. Hulme took fourth place in the French race at Clermont-Ferrand and finished fifth at Zandvoort.

At the end of the 1965 season Californian Dan Gurney, who had been the mainstay of the Brabham Formula One team for three seasons, left to run his own All-American Racers team of Eagle cars. So for 1966, the first year of the new 3000 cc Grand Prix Formula, Denny joined Jack Brabham in the Grand Prix team at the wheel of the new, but very simple and unsophisticated cars powered by Repco single cam per bank V-8 engines. At the beginning of the season Hulme had to make do with a car powered by the old 2.7-litre Coventry-Climax 4-cylinder engine, but by the French Grand Prix he, too, was at the wheel of a V-8-engined car. Although 1966 was very much Jack Brabham's 'come-back' year in which he scored a fine run of victories leading up to his third World Championship, Denny, driving with great skill, enjoyed a fair share of the spoils. With the older-engined car, he was out of luck, but he took a good third place in the French race, finished second at Brands Hatch and was third at both Monza and Mexico City.

The Honda-powered works Brabhams completely dominated Formula Two racing that year and although Jack himself enjoyed the lion's share of successes, Hulme won a race at Rouen and took six second places behind his team-leader. In Sports Car racing he appeared at the wheel of a works 7-litre Ford at Le Mans and in Ford's carefully staged three-abreast finish at the end of the twenty-four hours he and co-driver Ken Miles were officially classified second by a matter of feet—the organisers thwarted Ford's intended triple-tie by determining the finishing positions according to the cars' placing in the line-up at the start of the race. Denny continued to drive for Sid Taylor, but he was now at the wheel of a 6.3-litre Lola T70-Chevrolet and with this tremendously powerful car scored victories in the Scott-Brown Memorial Trophy race at Snetterton, at the *Daily Express* Silverstone meeting and in the Tourist Trophy for the second year in succession. Denny and the Taylor Lola also put in a tentative appearance in the Can-Am series, but although they achieved no success, his appetite was whetted for the future.

In 1967, as in the previous year, the consistent, reliable running of the Grand Prix Brabhams proved their strongest card and although the new Lotus 49, the V-12 Eagle and the H-16 BRM were conspicuously faster than the Repco-powered cars, they were also conspicuously less reliable. Because of brake troubles Hulme finished a poor fourth in the South African Grand Prix and he returned to Europe to take second place to Brabham in the Spring Cup at Oulton Park. Then Hulme's Grand Prix successes began to mount up; a fine win at Monaco, a third place at Zandvoort, but retirement with engine trouble at Spa. He finished second behind team-mate Brabham in the French race, was second to Clark's Lotus at Silverstone, won the German race and finished second again to Brabham in the inaugural Canadian Grand Prix. At Monza he retired with engine trouble, but he finished third in both of the remaining races at Watkins Glen and Mexico City to take the World Championship with 51 points to the 46 of Jack Brabham.

Denny also drove Lola-Chevrolet Prototype coupés for Sid Taylor in 1967 without success, but for the Can-Am series of races he teamed up with Bruce McLaren to drive his fellow-New Zealander's Chevrolet-powered Group 7 cars which for the first time were painted a striking orange colour. Of the six races in the series, the McLarens won five and Denny was at the wheel of the winning car on three occasions to take second place in the Can-Am Championship to team-mate Bruce.

The relationship between Denny and Bruce had proved near-enough ideal, they understood each other's temperaments perfectly, worked well together and despite his World Championship victory with Brabham, Hulme decided to throw in his lot with the McLaren team for 1968. At the 1967 Canadian Grand Prix, Bruce McLaren had appeared with his new M5A Formula One car powered by the BRM V-12 engine. Although work was progressing well on a new car, in the first race of the 1968 season, the South African Grand Prix at Kyalami, Hulme drove the M5A into fifth place. The new M7A car designed by Robin Herd and powered by the Ford V-8 engine was ready by the Race of Champions at Brands Hatch in March and with these new cars McLaren and Hulme took first and third places. The following month Hulme scored a victory with his M7A in the *Daily Express* Trophy race at Silverstone. The opposition in these races was not of the strongest, but once the European Championship season was under way, Hulme (and McLaren) and the M7A soon proved that they were a

Denis Hulme

formidable combination, even if not quite a match for either Stewart and the Matra or Hill and his Lotus on a good day.

In the Spanish race at Jarama, Hulme finished second behind Hill and he finished fifth and last at Monaco after a pit stop for a drive-shaft to be changed. McLaren won the Belgian race after Stewart's Matra ran out of fuel, but Denny was again the victim of drive-shaft trouble which caused his retirement. He retired with engine trouble at Zandvoort, took fifth place at Rouen and finished fourth at Brands Hatch. Next came the rain-soaked German Grand Prix, Hulme was far from happy in such atrocious weather conditions and trailed home in seventh place. In the next two races Hulme found the peak of his form and won at both Monza and St Jovite. He crashed at Watkins Glen when a drive-shaft broke again and retired with suspension failure at Mexico City. In the Drivers' Championship he took third place with thirty-three points.

Denny had appeared at Indianapolis with one of Dan Gurney's Ford-powered Eagles and drove a steady race to take fourth place. The Can-Am races, which were gradually increasing in importance, proved another Denny and Bruce benefit. McLaren cars won all six races in the series and Denis Hulme at the wheel of the latest and very potent M8A model with Chevrolet engine won the rounds held at Elkhart Lake, Edmonton and Las Vegas (the aptly-named Stardust Grand Prix) and in addition took second place in the race at Laguna Seca. It was Denny's turn to win the Championship with 35 points to the 24 scored by McLaren.

Denny's first season with McLaren had proved more than satisfactory, a gamble in the choice of car that had certainly paid off. By 1969 it was only too obvious that the McLaren team went Can-Am racing to make money and ran in Formula One because they enjoyed it. However the team's rather more relaxed attitude to single-seater racing never resulted in any fall-off in standards of preparation work and the orange cars were always as well turned-out as any of their rivals and as fast as most of them. The team's rather limited successes in Formula One were largely attributable to the fact that there were four teams using the Ford engine, performance differences between the marques were slight and neither Hulme nor McLaren was fast enough to beat Ickx, Stewart or Rindt when they were going well. It was, however, a different story in Can-Am racing in which the well-sponsored, well-financed Can-Am team had a definite 'edge' over its rivals and here the same pattern of McLaren domination persisted.

Throughout the 1969 Grand Prix season Hulme turned in safe, steady, unspectacular drives, consistently finishing well up the field, but only once wearing the winner's wreath. He started the season well with a third place at Kyalami, another third in the Race of Champions at Brands Hatch and a fourth place in the Spanish Grand Prix. At Monaco he took sixth place, he was fourth at Zandvoort and was in second place at Clermont-Ferrand until the front anti-roll bar sheared off and necessitated a pit-stop—he rejoined the race to take eighth place. He retired in the British and German races, finished a poor seventh at Monza, retired again at Mosport and Watkins Glen, but rounded off the season with a fine victory in the Mexican race. In the Drivers' Championship he took sixth place with a total of twenty points. In the BOAC 1000 kilometres sports car race at Brands Hatch, he drove the Alan Mann-entered Ford P68, but retired early in the race with low oil pressure and the enormous rear aerofoil loose and flapping.

The Can-Am series witnessed another McLaren landslide and the works orange cars won every race in the series and took the first two places in nine races out of the twelve. Denny won races at St Jovite, Edmonton, Lexington, Bridgehampton and Riverside Raceway, took second place at Mosport Park, Watkins Glen and Laguna Seca and finished second in the Can-Am Challenge Cup with 160 points and winnings of $146,000 to the 165 points of team-mate Bruce

Denis Hulme

McLaren. At Indianapolis in 1969 Hulme again drove one of Dan Gurney's Eagles, but it was an unsuccessful outing and although he was in second place at three-quarters race distance, because of clutch trouble he was unable to persuade his car to leave the pits after his final refuelling stop.

In 1970 Denis Hulme and the McLaren team achieved little success in Formula One but, despite the heaviest of odds against them again dominated the Can-Am series. Few drivers have ever suffered such an unhappy season as Hulme experienced in 1970, but persistent, courageous, apparently sometimes rather plodding Denny fought against disaster, disaster that would have wrecked many a lesser team, but in many ways helped to strengthen the bonds between the boys at the McLaren works at Colnbrook.

The season started well enough with a good second place by Denny with the new M14A McLaren at Kyalami, a third in the Race of Champions and a fourth at Monaco. Then during qualifying at Indianapolis where the McLaren team were fielding cars for the first time, Hulme's car caught fire and Denny was forced to jump out while it was still travelling at a fair speed. He suffered bad burns on his hands which gave him considerable pain all season. While Denny was still recovering from this accident, Bruce McLaren crashed and was killed in a testing accident at Goodwood with one of the latest Can-Am cars. As a result of this tragedy McLaren withdrew from the Belgian Grand Prix and because his hands blistered badly in the first of the year's Can-Am races at Mosport Park, Hulme was forced to miss the Dutch race.

On his return to racing in the French race at Clermont-Ferrand, Hulme finished fourth and he followed this up with a third place in the British Grand Prix, another third in the German race held at Hockenheim, a fourth at Monza and third place in the last race of the year at Mexico City. He took fourth place in the Drivers' Championship with 27 points.

Although Denny's last drive in a Sports Car had been short and not so sweet, he was induced to return to this form of racing on two occasions in 1970 and on both occasions showed that he was still a fine long-distance driver. After Kurt Ahrens had been injured in a testing accident, Hulme shared the wheel of a Porsche Salzburg 917 car with Vic Elford in the very wet BOAC 1000 kilometres race at Brands Hatch. He had been expecting that the 917 would prove a tremendous handful, but was pleasantly surprised by its docility and controllability, and Elford and he took a good second place behind the winning Wyer-entered 917 of Rodriguez and Kinnunen. After veteran Hans Herrmann had retired from racing following his Le Mans victory, Hulme was again asked to partner Elford in the Watkins Glen 6 Hours race. In this event they were plagued by tire trouble and eventually finished fourth.

There were ten rounds in the 1970 Can-Am series and nine of these were won by the works McLarens, a fine tribute to the high standards of preparation maintained at Colnbrook even after the death of the patron. Initially Hulme was partnered in the series by Dan Gurney, but then he dropped out and his place was taken by Peter Gethin. Hulme won six of the ten rounds, Gurney two and Gethin one and victory in the one race in which both the works McLarens retired went to Tony Dean at the wheel of his 3-litre Porsche.

Although Denis Hulme led the 1971 South African Grand Prix until four laps from the finish when a bolt dropped out of his McLaren's front suspension and he fell back to finish sixth, the team did not put such great efforts into Grand Prix racing that year and this showed itself only too clearly in the results. The only other races at which Hulme scored Championship points were the Spanish where he was fifth, the Monaco (fourth) and Canadian (fourth). As a result he was right out of the picture as far as World Championship placings were concerned. The reason for this apparent neglect of Formula One was the team's concentration on their new Indianapolis cars and, as usual, on the Can-Am races. In the 500 Miles race Hulme was forced out because of a water leak, but his Can-Am performances were up to their usual high standard and won three of the ten rounds and finished second in four others to take second place in the Cup rankings behind team-mate Peter Revson.

In 1972 the McLaren Formula One team was sponsored by Yardley and it was anticipated that a greater concentration of effort on this category of racing would bring much better results than seen in the previous couple of years. Denny started the season well enough with a second place in the Argentine Grand Prix and a win in the South African Grand Prix, but after that his best performances were a third place in the Race of Champions, a third place at Nivelles and a win in the Gold Cup race at Oulton Park. Later in the season Hulme finished second in the Austrian, third at Monza and Mosport Park and rounded off the season with yet another third place in the United States Grand Prix at Watkins Glen. On the strength of these consistent showings Denny took third place in the Drivers' Championship with 39 points. In Can-Am racing the McLarens were soundly trounced by the new Roger Penske-entered turbocharged Porsche 917-10 cars and Hulme succeeded in winning only two races in the series, at Mosport Park and Watkins Glen. McLaren realised that the long and successful career of their Chevrolet-powered Can-Am cars was drawing to a close and only with a completely new turbocharged engine could the team hope to defeat the German opposition. The design and development of such an engine was more than the McLaren team could possibly afford and reluctantly they did not compete in the 1973 Can-Am series.

For 1973 Grand Prix racing McLaren built a new and much improved Grand Prix car, still powered by the Cosworth engine, and this was designated the M23. Hulme and the McLaren team continued to enjoy a fine run of consistent success with the new contender from Colnbrook. After a fifth place in the Argentine race, Denny finished third in Brazil, won the Swedish Grand Prix after Ronnie Peterson suffered a last-minute puncture and was third yet again in the British race at Silverstone. At the end of the season Denny finished fourth in the United States race. He finished sixth with 26 points in the World Championship.

Despite Denis Hulme's many virtues as a driver and his many successes in the past, it now seems that he has passed his peak as a Formula One driver after but a very few seasons at the forefront of racing and although Grand Prix successes will continue to come his way, it is unlikely that he will again win the Championship.

12
A Champion of Our Times
JOHN YOUNG STEWART
1969, 1971, 1973

IN SIX SHORT seasons of racing Jackie Stewart rose from complete obscurity to World Champion, successful business man and the most vocal and convincing campaigner for safety improvements at racing circuits. When Jackie Stewart speaks, the motor racing world listens, far more impressed by his soft Scottish tones, tones that in themselves have a persuasive cogency, than it ever is by the bleatings of his professional body, the Grand Prix Drivers' Association, than it ever was by the statements of its late lamented President, Joakim Bonnier. For Stewart is a man who has proved himself the finest driver in the world at the present time, he has a natural stature stemming from achievement, but at the same time his public manner and business talents have been carefully groomed by high-powered business managers who are experts at the game. Stewart is the epitome of nineteen-seventies man, long-haired, fashionably, i.e. trendily, dressed, apparently breaking away from convention, but in fact helping to create one, projecting the image of a successful man of action and exploiting that image for its full commercial value.

As with the Moss family, motor racing was a familiar and

popular pursuit at the Stewart ménage. Both brother Jimmy and cousin Ian had been successful drivers in the 'fifties. James Stewart drove Ecurie Ecosse Jaguars and retired after a bad crash with a works Aston Martin at Le Mans in 1954. The family ran its own garage business in Dumbarton, they had the local Jaguar agency and were financially comfortable. Jackie drove his own Austin-Healey sports car and although he had always been a keen follower of motor sport, especially when his brother was racing, his main interest was shooting. He had a superb eye and excellent judgment and, shooting competitively, he enjoyed a fine run of successes. In 1959–60 he won five British National Championships and the Coupe des Nations. In 1960, at the age of twenty-one, he missed a place in the British Olympics team by a bad run of shots on the last day of the trials for the trap shooting team.

Whatever may have caused this unexpected failure—in later years Stewart attributed it to over-confidence—it proved a very bitter, but very worthwhile lesson that steeled him to take disappointment in his stride in later years. Although he continued to shoot competitively for another two years, Jackie began to take more interest in other sports. He helped one of the garage's customers, Barry Filer, who ran cars in Club events. Then came the chance to drive himself and he handled with remarkable skill and confidence a Ford-powered wooden chassis Marcos (a car that was built on much the same principles as Mosquito aircraft), an AC Ace and a Jaguar E-type that had started life as the garage's demonstrator. A test session at Oulton Park in early 1962 cast the die. With the fairly mildly modified E-type Jackie was able to turn in lap times as quick as Salvadori and Graham Hill had managed with much more modified Jaguars the previous autumn.

Not long afterwards Jackie married Helen McGregor whom he had known since his childhood. This pretty and intelligent, but perhaps rather unsophisticated girl, whose

John Young Stewart

character has been moulded and shaped by the same excitements, moments of ecstasy and tragedy as Jackie's, has changed into a mature woman, capable of handling the pressures of public life. She has lived through motor racing at its ghastliest when a friend's wife has stood completely broken at the news of her husband's death on the track, moments of the most terrible anxiety when Jackie's car has failed to come round and suffered the intrusions of press and public.

Jackie's very considerable natural ability had come to the notice of David Murray, patron of the Edinburgh-based Ecurie Ecosse team whose Jaguar D-types had won at Le Mans in both 1956 and 1957. After Jaguar's withdrawal from racing, Ecurie Ecosse fortunes had sadly declined. No major success had come the team's way for five years and the car the team now offered Jackie drives in a 2.5-litre Cooper Monaco sports car that was far from competitive. Later Stewart drove the team's Tojeiro coupés. These mid-engined sports cars, powered by Ford and Buick engines, were the creation of a most able designer, John Tojeiro, on whose 1953 Bristol-powered sports car the successful production AC Ace and Cobras were based. The new coupés were of beautiful conception and well ahead of their time technically, but they were plagued by a myriad of technical problems and neither they nor Stewart achieved the success they deserved.

Another driver might well have languished in obscurity with the Ecurie Ecosse team, but Jackie was lucky enough to have a reputation that went ahead of him, that of his very successful brother. When Ken Tyrrell, who had himself raced Cooper 500 and Formula Two cars and now ran the works Cooper Formula Three team, was looking for a driver partner for Warwick Banks for the 1964 season, Jackie's name was mentioned. At a test at Goodwood the young Stewart's times were so brilliantly quick that Tyrrell signed him up immediately. In 1964 Stewart won seven out of the nine races in which he was entered. During the season he received an invitation from Ron Harris who ran a Lotus Formula Two team on behalf of the works to drive one of his cars in the Circuit of Auvergne race at the difficult Clermont-Ferrand circuit. Stewart drove brilliantly, finishing second to Hulme's works Brabham and beating another rising star, Jochen Rindt, into third place.

By the end of the year Stewart had received invitations to drive for the Lotus, BRM and Cooper Formula One teams. Jackie decided to accept the BRM offer, for at this time the Bourne team was at the peak of its success—Graham Hill had won the Drivers' Championship for BRM in 1962 and finished second in both 1963 and 1964. In the meanwhile Stewart drove a Lotus for Colin Chapman in the Rand Grand Prix; a drive-shaft broke as Stewart accelerated away from the start of the first heat of the race, but he won the second heat.

Until the end of 1965 Stewart's career rose in a very steep crescendo and his success in his first year of Grand Prix racing far exceeded that a driver could reasonably expect. Then during the next two seasons he achieved little success, the acceleration curve of his career, rather like that of a child prodigy, had flattened out. Afterwards his success and ability continued to grow again, culminating in his 1969 World Championship victory. That his rate of development as a driver should slow off after such a brilliant start is in accordance with the pattern of ordinary human development, but it was largely attributable to the fact that BRM were passing through a period of technical difficulties, the cars were giving more than their fair share of trouble and, as Stewart later admitted, he perhaps stayed with the team a year too long.

In his first race for the BRM team, in the South African Grand Prix at East London, Stewart finished a satisfactory sixth and he followed this up by setting joint fastest lap (a record) and holding fourth place at Goodwood on Easter Monday before retiring with engine trouble, and he scored a fine victory over Surtees's Ferrari in the *Daily Express* Trophy race at Silverstone the following month. At Monaco he finished third behind team-mate Hill and Bandini with a flat-12 Ferrari. The Belgian Grand Prix was the first race in which Stewart had driven at Spa and the first in which he had driven a BRM in the wet. This circuit, with difficult fast curves that demand exceptional judgment and precision from a driver, proves more than some drivers can cope with even in ideal conditions, but in this miserable rain-soaked race Stewart drove like a Champion, trouncing team-mate Hill and finishing second only to Jim Clark.

At Zandvoort Stewart took yet another second place and at Clermont-Ferrand, another difficult driver's circuit with fast downhill bends and swoops, the two Scottish drivers, Clark and Stewart were head and shoulders above the rest of the entry. Clark won and Stewart was second, while demoralised BRM team-leader Graham Hill finished a poor fifth, as unhappy as most of his supporters with the ease with which young Stewart was running rings round him. He finished fifth with an engine that had gone off-song at Silverstone and was eliminated in the German race when he took to the grass on one of the corners and bent the front suspension on a hidden solid object. Both Hill and Stewart drove magnificently in the Italian race and when Graham made a slight mistake on the last lap but one, getting 'crossed up' at one of the corners, Stewart went ahead to score his first Championship race victory. Certainly Jackie would not have won the race but for Graham's mistake, but on the basis of his performances earlier in the season, the victory was thoroughly deserved.

At Watkins Glen Stewart was pushed off the track by Ginther at the wheel of a Honda and bent a suspension wishbone; although he carried on, his throttle linkage broke later in the race and after a pit stop he retired. In the final round of the Championship at Mexico City Jackie retired again with clutch failure. Hill and Stewart took second and third places in the Drivers' Championship, repeating the performance in 1963 when Hill and his then number two Richie Ginther had taken second and third places.

Jackie had continued to drive for Ken Tyrrell that year at the wheel of a Formula Two Cooper, but his car was no match for the works and Winkelmann Brabhams and his best performance was a second place at Oulton Park. At Le Mans he co-drove the Rover-BRM gas-turbine car with Graham Hill, but it was slowed by overheating and finished a disappointing tenth. Another interesting drive for Jackie that year was at Brands Hatch on August Bank Holiday Monday where he appeared at the wheel of a Lola T70-Chevrolet entered by Team Surtees, a monster of a car compared with the single-seaters he was used to handling. Despite his unfamiliarity with the Lola, Stewart finished third on the aggregate of the two heats behind 'Big John' at the wheel of the other Team Surtees car and Bruce McLaren with one of his own Oldsmobile-powered cars. In October 1965 the Sunday Times Colour Magazine ran a feature article on Jackie, with the emphasis on the stresses endured by a racing driver and his wife, and with a picture of a very short-haired Stewart and Helen in bed (*gewacht* for those days), but the public was still left with the impression that Stewart was just another racing driver with a more than passably pretty wife.

With the introduction of the 3000 cc Grand Prix Formula for 1966 onwards, BRM were developing a very complex H-16 car, a cylinder layout never before tried for a racing car engine, but at the thought of which older engineers with memories of the vibrations suffered by the H-24 Napier Dagger aero engine shuddered. The new BRM first turned its wheels in public at Monaco in 1966, but it was plagued by the expected vibration problems and also by transmission troubles—the latter apparently incurable—and while Tony Rudd and his colleagues battled to solve their problems, Graham Hill and Jackie Stewart were forced to race the 1965 cars with engines enlarged to 2-litres.

The first Formula One race of the 1966 season was the South African Grand Prix, but for this one year it was not a round in the Championship and BRM decided to give this race a miss and compete instead in the Tasman series in New Zealand and Australia. The dark green 2-litre cars completely dominated the series of eight races; Jackie won four and took second place in another, Graham scored two wins and Dickie Attwood one, leaving a solitary victory to Jim Clark and his rather under-powered Lotus.

The BRM team realised, however, that it was going to have a much more difficult time in the European Championship races until the new car was raceworthy, but despite giving away a litre to Ferrari, Brabham and Cooper, Hill and Stewart succeeded in keeping well in the hunt except on the fastest courses. Stewart took the lead at Monaco when Surtees retired his Ferrari with rear axle trouble and driving with intelligence held off a challenge, first from Clark's Lotus, and then from Bandini's Ferrari, to score a fine victory. At the end of the month Stewart drove a Lola at Indianapolis and was leading by a lap with only twenty miles to go to the finish when an oil scavenge pump failed. Such a brilliant performance by a 'rookie' was completely unknown in the fifty-four-year history of the 'Indy' race.

It was at Stewart's next race that the brilliant rise of his career received a severe check that nearly halted it altogether. In that notorious Belgian Grand Prix at Spa in which so many drivers went off the course when they ran into rain on the first lap, Stewart was among their number. Jackie's BRM went off the track at high speed and in pouring rain he lay trapped in his crumpled car, a shoulder broken, ribs cracked and petrol from the ruptured tanks soaking through his overalls and burning his skin. Graham Hill and Bob Bondurant, the driver of a private 2-litre BRM, both of whom had gone off the track, finally released him from the car.

A fit sportsman with a determined mind will always make a speedier recovery from an accident than less active men and Stewart re-appeared at the wheel of a BRM at the British Grand Prix at Brands Hatch. Now that rivals' cars were properly sorted, BRM were having a much harder time and Jackie did not win another Grand Prix until he was driving a Matra for Ken Tyrrell in 1968. In the British race he retired with engine failure. The German race was run on a wet track and Jackie, looking rather less confident than usual, which was hardly surprising after his Spa experience, trailed badly, moving up to finish fifth after the retirement of the works Ferraris. He failed to finish in the remaining three rounds in the Championship because of mechanical trouble with his cars.

For Stewart perhaps the most significant event of 1966 was Ken Tyrrell's decision to field Matra Formula Two cars. At a prize-giving in Paris in late 1965 Tyrrell had been persuaded by Jean-Luc Lagardère, Matra competitions chief, to give one of the French cars a testing. It was flown over to England and driven at Goodwood by a very sceptical Stewart who, understandably, had little confidence in the ability of a French company to build a good racing car. However, Jackie was very impressed with the Matra's handling which was better than that of any car he had driven previously and as a result of this test Tyrrell agreed to race Formula Two versions of the Matra in 1966. Little success came the team's way that year, partly because of the opposition from the Honda-powered Brabhams and partly because Stewart missed several races after his Spa crash. Although no one realised it at the time, Tyrrell's first association with Matra was to prove the starting point of a long and successful union leading to Jackie's first win in the World Championship in 1969.

John Young Stewart

Graham Hill left the BRM team at the end of 1966 to drive for Lotus and so Jackie remained as number one driver, partnered by Mike Spence who had come from Lotus. The BRM team was still struggling with the H-16 cars and at most races BRM was faced with the unhappy choice of fielding the underpowered and outdated 2-litre cars or the overweight and unreliable H-16s. The outcome was inevitable, but, even so, Stewart still managed to turn in some creditable drives during the year. At Kyalami his H-16 broke its engine on only the second lap and in the Spring Cup race at Oulton Park, the same circuit that Stewart had lapped so quickly with his E-type five years before, he made a very rare error of judgment, going off the track and damaging the BRM's front suspension.

That BRM were making progress with the development of the H-16 was apparent at the *Daily Express* Trophy race. Jackie drove a stirring race with the H-16, although it still looked a terrible handful, and he chased Mike Parkes's Ferrari hard until the transmission cried enough. At Monaco he had the choice of driving the H-16 or the older 2-litre car and opted for the latter which he thought was a better proposition on this tortuous course; he was leading the race when the back axle packed up after only fourteen laps. He retired again at Zandvoort, but in his next race, the Belgian Grand Prix at Spa, he turned in his best performance since his crash at the same circuit the previous year. Stewart could not match the speed of the new Ford-powered Lotus 49s, but when Jim Clark pulled into the pits with plug trouble, the BRM driver swept by into the lead. As the race progressed, however, Jackie experienced more and more trouble with the gear-selectors, the gears kept jumping out, the engine was shooting up to over 12,000 rpm (2000 rpm above the supposed limit) and he was having to hold the steering wheel with one hand and hold the lever in gear with the other. Steadily, but surely, Dan Gurney closed up with his Eagle, the blue and silver car swept by the ailing BRM and at the fall of the flag the American was just over a minute ahead of Stewart.

On the Bugatti circuit at Le Mans, scene in that one year only of the French Grand Prix, Stewart drove another good race to finish third behind the works Brabhams, but he did not make it to the chequered flag in any other Championship race that season. Retirement with mechanical trouble succeeded retirement and even in other fields little success came Jackie's way. At Indianapolis he had again driven a Lola, but retired with engine trouble. During the year Stewart visited Maranello on a couple of occasions to discuss the possibility of driving for Ferrari in 1968. While these tentative negotiations were taking place, he was invited to handle a P4 Prototype Ferrari in the BOAC '500' race at Brands Hatch—the only occasion in his career in which he has driven for Maranello—and his co-driver was Christ Amon. The race was won by the distinctive Chaparral with high-mounted rear aerofoil and driven by Mike Spence and Phil Hill, but despite a collision with a Porsche Amon and Stewart took second place. In Formula Two, 1967 was largely a Rindt year, but Stewart, still driving a Tyrrell-entered Matra, but now with 1600 cc Cosworth engine to comply with the new Formula, scored wins at Karlskoga in Sweden, Enna in Sicily, Oulton Park and Albi.

Dissatisfied with the continued failure of the BRMs, his discussions with Ferrari having proved abortive, Stewart talked to Ken Tyrrell about Formula One possibilities for 1968. It was agreed that Tyrrell should approach Matra to see whether they would be willing to supply a chassis to take the Ford-Cosworth V-8 engine that had proved so successful in 1967 and was now freely available to all constructors. Matra were planning their own Formula One programme with a car to be powered by their own V-12 engine, but Jean-Luc Lagardère was not slow to see the benefit of hedging the team's bets by co-operating with Tyrrell. The whole project was an enormous gamble for both entrant and driver, but they were confident that they would be racing the best chassis with the most competitive engine.

For a driver there is nothing more important than complete trust in his entrant and his car; a driver with the knowledge that everything has been properly screwed together, that there is no risk of structural failure, no mechanic's forgetfulness that will mean that a wheel will suddenly detach itself or the brakes fail can more readily give of his best, better concentrate on learning a difficult corner, and is more likely to knock a second off his lap time. He will jump into the car and drive off with confidence, not procrastinate over little details, while all the time there is a niggling worry at the back of his mind that something more basic is amiss. Four years of collaboration with Tyrrell had cemented a relationship of complete confidence and trust and the results soon began to speak for themselves.

In 1968 Tyrrell's team, which was known as Matra International, raced what were in essence modified versions of the familiar Matra Formula Two cars. There was a tremendous rush to get the first car ready in time and this, an interim model known as the MS9, was given only a brief testing at the Montlhéry track near Paris before it was flown off to South Africa, still unpainted and running in its natural green glass-fibre colouring. With the new car Stewart was fast enough in practice to gain a place on the front row of the grid and he led the race briefly before the Ford engine expired. By the Race of Champions the team had taken delivery of the first improved MS10 car, painted a striking French racing blue. After a pit stop to sort out trouble with the pedals, Jackie finished sixth at Brands Hatch. Then came a severe blow to Stewart's World Championship hopes. After scoring Formula Two victories at Barcelona and Pau, he crashed his Matra in practice for the Formula Two Madrid Grand Prix. Although the extent of the injury was not realised at the time, Stewart damaged his wrist badly enough to keep him out of Formula One until the Belgian race and he was forced to scratch from Indianapolis. Jean-Pierre Beltoise drove the Tyrrell Matra in the Spanish Grand Prix and Johnny Servoz-Gavin at Monaco and although neither achieved success, it was obvious that the car was the fastest Grand Prix model on the circuits that year.

On Stewart's return to racing at Spa, he was not really fit, his right wrist was in a plastic sleeve which had been specially made and although he could change gear with it, it was still not strong enough to grip the steering wheel. Despite considerable pain, Stewart built up a good lead in the race, only to run out of fuel. Somehow, for reasons which Tyrrell could never fathom out, a miscalculation as to the car's fuel consumption, had been made and the mistake cost Stewart the race. After a pit stop he rejoined the race to finish fourth. The Dutch race was run in continuous rain and with the track almost awash and Stewart, whose Dunlop tires seemed to give a far greater amount of controllability in these conditions than other makes, passed Graham Hill into the lead on lap four; only Stewart looked confident in these atrocious conditions and by the end of the race he had lapped everyone except Beltoise with the works V-12 Matra.

1968 was a season during which almost as many races were run in the wet as in the dry and the French Grand Prix at Rouen was another rain-soaked ordeal. In many ways the Tyrrell team was learning the hard way about Formula One racing and at Rouen Stewart found that the wet-weather Dunlops were not so effective as at Zandvoort. He looked unhappy throughout the sixty laps of the race and after a pit stop for the supplementary fuel tank retaining straps to be fixed, he finished third behind Ickx and Surtees, the latter at the wheel of a Honda. Ickx's win for Ferrari was to prove the last Grand Prix victory with a car powered by other than a Ford engine until the late Pedro Rodriguez scored a win for BRM at the 1970 Belgian race. The British Grand Prix was run at Brands Hatch, a tiring circuit that proved too much of a strain for Stewart's injured wrist; wracked by pain, completely exhausted and having steered with one hand for more than half the race, he crossed the line in sixth place to gain a single Championship point.

Jackie was lagging badly in the World Championship, his arm was still not healed and his doctors were predicting that it probably would not heal so long as Stewart failed to take a break from racing. Next came the German Grand Prix, yet another wet race with persistent rain throughout practice and on race day. Like Ascari, Stewart is a driver who likes to be out in front, setting the pace and controlling the race, and he tends to rise much better to the occasion if he is convinced that he has a car with an edge over its rivals. When the flag fell for the start of the German race, the rain was falling with the same intensity as many hours before, rivers of water were streaming across the track and parts of the circuit were thickly enveloped in banks of mist. Happy with his car and with his special Dunlop rain tires, Jackie was determined to make a good start, for if he could take the lead almost immediately, he would be driving with a clear track in front of him and not behind a vast bank of spray from other competitors' tires.

As the cars moved off Stewart roared through from the third row of the grid, halfway round the first lap he was in second place behind Ickx's Ferrari and by the end of the first 14.2-mile lap he had a lead of nine seconds. As the race progressed the blue Matra pulled further and further away from the rest of the field; Jackie was driving superbly in the worst conditions in which any major post-war race has been run. While others slithered and slid, hesitated when they were blinded by spray, Stewart out in front was able to drive a calm, collected race, with time in hand to allow for slight mistakes should he make them. At the end of this nightmarish 14-lap race Stewart was over four minutes ahead of Hill's Lotus and he was back in the running for the Championship, only four points behind Hill. This was the finest race in Stewart's career and in *Motor Sport*, Denis Jenkinson wrote: 'Caracciola may have been the *Regenmeister*, Rosemeyer the *Nebelmeister* and Fangio the *Ringmeister*, but surely Stewart topped the lot.'

Another victory followed in the Gold Cup race at Oulton Park, a short race that did not place much strain on Stewart's wrist and by the Italian race at Monza in September, this was healing well. In this race Jackie retired with engine trouble, Hill's Lotus lost a wheel and the leading positions in the World Championship remained unchanged. At the Canadian race Stewart finished sixth after a pit stop for repairs to the Matra's suspension and Hill was fourth. Stewart's third Championship race victory of the season followed at Watkins Glen, but Graham Hill was second and the outcome of the Championship would not be settled until the Mexican race in November. In practice at Mexico City a tire burst on the main straight when Stewart was travelling close to 150 mph and although he managed to bring the car safely to rest, the monocoque was damaged and the Matra was only just repaired in time for the race. Matra and Lotus battled for the lead until the blue car slowed off because of fuel pressure problems and Stewart, struggling on with a very sick engine, fell further and further back to take seventh place. Hill won the race and the Championship by a margin of twelve points.

1968 had proved Jackie's best season since he had joined the Grand Prix 'circus' and although he had failed to win the Championship, his disappointment was not too great. He had taken second place, despite missing two races because of his wrist injury, finished well down the field in another because of the pain and had lost another race through a silly error in calculating the Matra's fuel consumption. That he had been at the wheel of the best car, he was quite convinced, and for 1969 he would have a new Ford-powered Matra, the much-improved MS80, and greater support from the Matra works which was concentrating on Prototype racing and leaving its Formula One programme entirely in Tyrrell's hands.

Jackie's main rivals in 1969 were to prove to be Jochen Rindt and Jacky Ickx, but Stewart had a better car than either and with this knowledge he drove like a Champion from the start of the season, so often during the year setting fastest lap both in practice and in the race and dominating the race from the fall of the flag. As usual the first race of the season was the South African Grand Prix at Kyalami and although the Tyrrell team had taken delivery of the new car, it was suffering from teething troubles and it was decided to use the 1968 model in the race. He took an early lead, pulled out a good advantage over the opposition and set his own pace for almost the entire race to score a fine victory from Graham Hill's Lotus. Stewart's first victory with the new MS80 followed at the Race of Champions at Brands Hatch and in the *Daily Express* Trophy race, held at Silverstone on a wet track, he drove the MS10 into third place in its last race.

Stewart's second Championship race victory of the season followed at Barcelona, but although he drove well, it was a race in which other drivers' misfortunes paid off to his advantage. He made an atrocious start, slowly began to pick up places, but only moved up into the lead after the two Lotus 49Bs of Hill and Rindt had crashed with aerofoil failure and Chris Amon's well-driven Ferrari had disappeared in a cloud of blue smoke caused by engine trouble. At the finish Stewart was two laps ahead of Bruce McLaren with one of his own Ford-powered cars. The familiar pattern of Stewart and the Matra dominating the race from the start re-asserted itself at Monaco, but despite moving into the lead before the first corner and settling into a comfortable pace, taking great care not to over-strain the transmission, he retired with drive-shaft failure. Later it was discovered that this trouble, which also eliminated team-mate Beltoise, was caused by a batch of faulty components.

No mechanical troubles, however, interrupted Stewart's fine drives at Zandvoort, Clermont-Ferrand and Silverstone and he won all three rounds of the Championship. At Silverstone he had a lucky escape in practice, travelling at around 140 mph he struck a piece of concrete that dislodged itself from the edge of the road at Woodcote corner, the fast bend before the pits. A tire burst and the Matra spun into the barricades. Although the MS80 was badly damaged, Stewart was unhurt and drove team-mate Beltoise's car in the race.

In the next round of the Championship at the Nürburgring, Stewart was slowed by gearbox trouble and beaten into second place by Jacky Ickx at the wheel of his Brabham. During the last couple of laps Stewart was able to engage third and fifth gears only and when the car was being driven away after the race, the gearbox seized up altogether. Although Ickx was now second in the Championship with 22 points, Stewart, who had amassed a total of 51 points, was almost uncatchable and was already, to all intents and purposes, 1969 World Champion. At Monza there was the inevitable, close slip-streaming battle with nothing to distinguish one of the leading group of cars from another save who crossed the finishing line first at the end of the lap. Stewart led for 58 of the 68 laps and as the race progressed, one by one, cars fell back from the leading group, leaving only Stewart, Beltoise and Rindt battling it out for the lead. Despite a last-corner effort by Beltoise with the other Matra to snatch the lead, Stewart managed to hold on to a slight advantage and crossed the finishing line a few feet ahead of Rindt.

Now the Championship was definitely in the bag, regardless of the outcome of the three remaining races, and the Tyrrell team could afford to relax a little. Feted at Monza, inundated by telegrams and telephone calls, Stewart flew home in November to a civic reception at Dumbarton where, in heavy rain, he drove through the streets at the wheel of a Formula Two Matra. At Mosport, scene of the Canadian Grand Prix, Stewart was chased hard by Ickx with the Brabham and when the Matra was slowed, waiting to lap a tailender, the two cars collided. Unable to restart his car,

Stewart was out of the race, but Ickx carried on to win from team-mate Brabham. Naturally Jackie was upset by this incident, but it was a lot easier to accept Ickx's apologies and pass the incident over than if the World Championship had still hung in the balance. At Watkins Glen the new Champion retired because of an oil leak and he rounded off the season with a fourth place at Mexico City.

During 1969 Stewart had carried out comparative tests with two MS10 chassis, one fitted with the Ford engine and the other with the latest version of Matra's V-12 unit and had lapped as fast with the V-12. Matra, understandably enough, were anxious that Tyrrell should run the V-12-powered car in 1970, but neither he nor Jackie was convinced that it was a better bet than the Ford. A parting of the ways was inevitable and for 1970 Matra International became the Tyrrell Racing Organisation and with financial assistance from Ford to buy the cars fielded March 701s built at Bicester by a new company. The new car was the work of former McLaren designer Robin Herd and on paper at least there was every prospect that it would prove very competitive.

Jackie soon discovered, however, that the handling of the new car was inferior to that of his old Matra MS80 and that it was slower than the latest Lotus, Brabham and Ferrari designs. He started off the season well enough, with a third place at Kyalami, wins in the Race of Champions and at Barcelona, and second place in the *Daily Express* Trophy race, but as the season progressed, so his successes tailed off. Stewart retired at both Monaco and Spa-Francorchamps, but came back with a second place at Zandvoort. After a pit stop with ignition trouble in the French race, he finished ninth and retirements followed in the British, German and Austrian races.

For Stewart, Monza proved one of the greatest triumphs in his career, a triumph flowing from tragedy, a triumph of willpower and moral fibre rather than of racing success.

After Rindt's terrible death in practice for the Italian race, Ken Tyrrell urged Stewart, who was completely broken by the death of his friend, to go out and practice again. Jackie, feeling at the same time that he would never want to race again, yet that driving was the only thing he was capable of doing, took out the March and looking grey and strained turned in his fastest practice lap. In the race he drove himself without mercy, as though fighting not to be overwhelmed by the immensity of the tragedy. Every manoeuvre, every gear-change needed a conscious effort and although the Monza race, all over in little more than an hour and a half is one of the less strenuous of the season, Stewart, in second place finished completely enervated, mentally exhausted and soaked in perspiration.

Ken Tyrrell had never been too confident about the chances of doing well with the March cars and since the beginning of the season, almost as a sort of insurance policy, work had been steadily progressing on a new Tyrrell Formula One car to the design of Derek Gardner who had worked on the experimental Matra MS80 four-wheel-drive car that had been run at a few races in 1969. The Tyrrell was one of the best-kept motor racing secrets and few people knew of its existence before its announcement to the press just before the 1970 Oulton Park Gold Cup race. Stewart drove the new car in the last three Championship races of the season and although the car retired in all three, he had led both in the Canadian race at St Jovite and at Watkins Glen before being forced to withdraw. In the Championship he shared fifth place.

By the start of the 1971 season the new Tyrrell had been fully developed and a second car had been completed for Stewart's team-mate, young Francois Cevert. The strongest opponent to the Ford-powered cars was likely to be the new flat-12 Ferrari which had won four out of five races at the end of the 1970 season and the man most likely to beat the Maranello cars was Stewart. Throughout the season the

Tyrrell team received the maximum support from Ford and although all the latest Ford-Cosworth Grand Prix engines seemed to be equal, some were definitely more equal than others, some were hopelessly unreliable, but those used by Stewart were the most powerful and reliable of all. At only one race in 1971, the Italian Grand Prix, did Jackie retire with engine trouble.

It has already been commented that Stewart's knowledge and confidence that he has a faster car than his rivals always brings out in him the very best and throughout the year he seemed head and shoulders above his rivals, setting the pace in practice, going straight into the lead at the start of the race and controlling its pace, while his breathless rivals strove not to be left too far behind. He started the season gently enough with a second place in the South African Grand Prix and second places in the non-Championship Race of Champions (where the Tyrrell team gambled on the wrong tires) and the Questor Grand Prix held in California, but there was more than a small element of luck in the Ferrari victories in these races.

Then the Stewart dynamo began to hum. He out-drove Jacky Ickx to win the Spanish Grand Prix for the third year in succession and, undeterred by a crash in the *Daily Express* Trophy at Silverstone when the Tyrrell's throttles jammed open, he completely dominated the Monaco race, taking pole position on the grid, winning the race with ease and setting a new lap record. Only at Zandvoort did Stewart falter and disappoint his supporters by a rather apathetic drive in a wet race. Because of engine trouble in practice, there had been no chance to get Jackie's car set up for wet-weather racing and instead of displaying his usual domination, he trailed round at the back of the field, not bothering to make any sort of fight of the race, to finish eleventh. Such performances are best forgotten and Stewart's unfortunate lapse was soon overlooked in the excitement of his three successive victories in the French Grand Prix on the new Paul Ricard circuit, at Silverstone and the Nürburgring. Now, as in 1969, only Ickx could catch Stewart in the World Championship and although Jackie retired in the Austrian race when the Tyrrell lost a wheel, Ickx, too, retired and, with three races still to go, he had the Championship in the bag. At Monza he retired with engine trouble, another victory, his sixth of the season, followed in the Canadian race and in the last race of the season, at Watkins Glen, he came home fifth with a car that was handling badly.

In 1972 Emerson Fittipaldi found his form with the John Player Special and less success came Stewart's way. He started the season well, however, with a win in the Argentine race and subsequently took a fourth place at Monaco. He was forced to miss the Belgian Grand Prix at Nivelles because of ulcer trouble, but returned to racing to score a fine victory in the French race. He was beaten into second place in the British Grand Prix at Brands Hatch, allowed himself to be forced off the road by Regazzoni's Ferrari at the Nürburgring, but won the last two Championship races of the season at Mosport Park and Watkins Glen. Jackie took second place in the World Championship with a total of 45 points.

Although Emerson Fittipaldi made a brilliant start to the 1973 season with victories in the Argentine and Brazilian races, Jackie soon displayed that his skill had in no way diminished and made it clear that he was determined to win his third World Championship. After a slow start to the season with a third place at Buenos Aires and a second at Interlagos, Stewart's victories soon began to mount up. He scored a convincing victory in the South African race at Kyalami and won the non-Championship *Daily Express* Trophy race held at Silverstone in snow and sleet (despite a spin). Brake trouble caused his retirement in the Spanish race held over the Montjuich Park circuit at Barcelona. His second Championship race victory of the season came in the Belgian race at Nivelles and when he won at Monaco, not

John Young Stewart

only did he bring himself within four points of Fittipaldi's Championship score (41 to 37), but he had now knotched up twenty-five Championship Grand Prix victories, thereby matching Jim Clark's record.

Because of brake trouble Stewart fell back to finish fifth in the Swedish Grand Prix, a new addition to the Championship series, and he took fourth place in the French race at the Paul Ricard circuit near Marseille. Stewart was in second place at the British Grand Prix until he spun off and although he rejoined the race, he was now well down the field and finished a poor tenth. When Jackie won the Dutch Grand Prix held on 29th July, he made motor racing history for, with twenty-six victories to his credit, he had broken Jim Clark's record. A twenty-seventh victory followed in the German Grand Prix at the Nürburgring, a race that the Tyrrell duo of Stewart and Cevert controlled unchallenged from start to finish. Stewart now led the World Championship with 60 points to the 45 of team-mate Francois Cevert and 42 of Emerson Fittipaldi. He finished second to Ronnie Peterson's 'John Player Special' in the Austrian race and although he was only fourth in the Italian Grand Prix at Monza he now had the Championship in the bag. The results of the Canadian Grand Prix were clouded with doubt because of timekeeping confusion and Stewart was classified fifth after a pit stop for new tires.

At the end of 1973 Stewart was at the peak of his fame, his name was known in every household, featured in hundreds of advertisements, he was the slightly ageing George Best of motor racing; he had put all his efforts and talents into motor racing, he had brought the sport a lot of popular publicity that it would never otherwise have had, and, with the aid of his shrewd business managers, he has extracted from the sport every pound he could get. He has made hundreds of public appearances, organised his own Racing Car Show, appeared on British television to explain why he would not race at the Nürburgring, cut his own long-playing record, featured in a film, written three books (one narrating in almost ghoulish detail the events immediately following Rindt's death) and removed his shirt to advertise after-shave lotion.

No one can blame Stewart for having made as much money as possible from the dangerous profession he has loved, but he had now reached a cross-roads in his career. He has a beautiful wife, two splendid children and a magnificent home near Geneva in which to enjoy his very happy family life and the money he has earned. The longer he went on racing, the greater were the chances of a bad accident; the sooner he stopped racing, the quicker would dry up the very considerable income to be drawn from racing. A star's name quickly loses its impact and is forgotten.

By the final race of the 1973 season, the United States Grand Prix at Watkins Glen, Stewart had already make the irrevocable decision to retire from racing, a decision that had crystallised once his third World Championship was assured. But Stewart did not compete in what was intended to be his last race. In practice at Watkins Glen his teammate, brilliant young French driver Francois Cevert, a Champion in the making, crashed at high speed and was killed instantly. The Tyrrell team withdrew from the race and victory went to the 'John Player Special' of Ronnie Peterson.

Stewart's brilliant driving will be seen no more on the race tracks of the world, but he will continue to play an active role in motor racing. His promotional contract with the Goodyear Tire Company has been renewed, he has been appointed a consultant by Ford of Europe and he plans to continue his fight for greater safety in motor racing. Although not planning a full-time screen career, he will be seen playing the lead in *The Way to Dusty Death*, the film based on an Alistair Maclean novel and has a contract for commentating on sporting events with a leading American television company.

13
The Fastest Champion
KARL-JOCHEN RINDT
1970

DESPITE MANY A mumbled prediction that Jochen Rindt was too fast for his own good, driving too often on the ragged edge, too much a car breaker to win a Championship Grand Prix, doomed to kill himself by driving too fast, he lived to prove his critics wrong and enjoy a season of substantial Grand Prix success before dying at the peak of his fame in an accident, the causes of which are still wrapped in mystery. When Rindt was killed at Monza in 1970, he had already accumulated enough points to ensure his victory in the Drivers' Championship; so he became the only driver to win the award posthumously, as well as the only Champion to have died at the wheel of a Formula One car.

Born at Mainz on the River Main, not far from Frankfurt, Jochen Rindt was made an orphan when only fifteen months, for both his parents were killed in a bombing raid on Hamburg in 1943. The young Rindt was brought up by his grandparents at Graz in Southern Austria, but unlike so many other orphans, he was never short of money, for his father had run a very successful spice mill trading under the name of Klein & Rindt and Jochen was the only heir. Always keen on sport, especially tennis and ski-ing, he paid scant regard to school lessons. As soon as he attained the age of eighteen and old enough to hold a driving licence, he acquired first a Volkswagen and then a Simca which he used to pit in hard-fought duels with a Chevrolet driven by school-friend Helmut Marko, by 1972 a works Alfa Romeo and BRM driver. Marko's racing career was cut short, however, by a bad accident to an eye which he suffered during the 1972 French Grand Prix. Rindt's official racing career began with another Simca and he soon graduated to an Alfa Romeo Giulietta with which he scored a large number of successes.

That at this stage in his racing career his driving was wild in the extreme is beyond doubt, but at the same time he had a great deal of talent and was achieving lap times with the Alfa that were conspicuously quicker than more experienced drivers with similar cars. The next and obvious step was the acquisition of a single-seater and for the 1963 season he bought a second-hand Formula Junior Cooper-BMC. His driving that season was still wild and reckless, but the year was not without its compensations. On his first outing at the Vallelunga circuit at Rome he set fastest lap in the rain-soaked practice sessions, he won his second race, a minor affair at Casenatico, but he crashed at both Budapest and the Nürburgring. Despite, or perhaps because of these misfortunes, Rindt had progressed in vast strides during that year learning a great deal about racing techniques and tactics, taming his wild driving and the nerves that caused it, and realising for the first time that in motor racing, and not the spice mill, lay his future and that the business was only a means to an end.

Now Jochen felt ready to plunge into motor racing at which might be described as 'post-graduate' level. For 1964 the Federation Internationale de l'Automobile had introduced a new Formula Two for cars of up to 1000 cc unsupercharged and Rindt expended a sum in the region of £4000 on a new Formula Two Brabham powered by a twin overhead camshaft Cosworth engine. Rindt came to England to order the car, hired a mechanic and took up occupation in that famous flat in Pinner Road, Harrow, shared by many motor racing names including Frank Williams (whom he had got to know on the Continent the previous year), Piers Courage and Charles Lucas.

It was at Whitsun in 1964 that Rindt's name first made an impact with the motor racing public. There were Formula Two races at Mallory Park and the Crystal Palace and Rindt entered at both. At Mallory Park he set fastest lap in practice, but made a terrible start and then fought his way through the field to finish third behind the works Lotuses of Jim Clark and Peter Arundell. On the Monday at the South London circuit he won his heat and in the final made another bad start, but recovered superbly to come through to take the lead and win the race from Graham Hill whose Cooper was, admittedly, handicapped by the rear anti-roll bar coming adrift. Of Rindt's performance at the Crystal Palace, Mike Twite wrote in *Motor Sport:* 'Young Jochen Rindt drove his Brabham beautifully and hardly put a wheel wrong throughout the race, looking most relaxed all the time. Virtually unknown in Britain until this race and Mallory Park the previous day, Rindt should not lack works drives in future.'

For the rest of the 1964 season Rindt fought an uphill battle with the Brabham; the car was no real match for the works entries especially on the faster circuits, and after he lost his mechanic in mid-season, he was racing a car that was not as well prepared as it should have been. At the Austrian Grand Prix in August Rob Walker entered a new car for his usual driver, Joakim Bonnier and fielded his BRM-powered Brabham for Rindt. On the bumpy concrete-surfaced Zeltweg circuit Jochen disciplined himself to drive cautiously, lapping steadily well within the limits of both himself and the car so that at just over half race-distance he was in eighth place despite a pit stop because of brake trouble, and with a good chance of finishing in the money. But luck was not on his side and he was forced to retire with steering trouble.

There were no more Formula One drives for Rindt in 1964, but later in the year he tried to persuade Rob Walker to fix him up with a regular drive for the coming season. Walker felt unable to field a second team car and an additional problem was that Rindt had signed a contract with BP following his Whitsun successes and Walker was contracted to Shell. As it was, the link with BP was to prove more than worthwhile, for that company's competitions manager, Denis Druitt, had approached John Cooper whose Cooper-Climax team lacked a number two driver for the coming season and suggested that he should sign up the Austrian. The Cooper team was the least competitive of the Formula One contenders and had failed to win a single race in 1964. Furthermore Cooper's terms were less than generous and the team usually insisted on a three-year contract. But the offer of a place in any Formula One team was not to be sniffed at, Jochen could do little but accept the offer and for the next three years his fortunes were linked with Cooper's and hampered by their's. Almost equally significant from Jochen's point of view was the invitation to drive Formula Two Brabhams for the Winkelmann Racing Team whose cars were beautifully prepared.

So in 1965 Rindt gained his experience in Formula One with Cooper and his successes in Formula Two with the Winkelmann team. His first race of the season was the South African Grand Prix at East London on 1st January 1965. He was a satisfactory tenth fastest in practice, but retired in the race with electrical trouble. His next race for Cooper was at Goodwood where he was disqualified for taking a short cut through the chicane and in the *Daily Express* race at Silverstone his Climax engine threw a con-rod—and these three races set the pattern for his Formula One fortunes throughout the year. At Monaco he failed to qualify because of a defective car—the mechanic responsible was given his cards after the race which was rather too late to console an unhappy Rindt—and at Spa he came home eleventh, delayed by a pit stop when the tachometer fell out of the instrument panel! The French Grand Prix was held at Clermont-Ferrand, but Rindt had little chance to savour the delights of this true driver's circuit, for on only the fourth lap his brakes locked up, he collided with Chris Amon's Lotus and spun out of the race—and the press, not knowing the inside story, attributed the incident to over-enthusiasm. At Silverstone and Zandvoort he retired with engine trouble. Rindt's fortunes looked up at the Nürburgring and driving steadily within the limits of his uncompetitive car he finished fourth after the retirement of the faster cars. At Monza he was outpaced by the faster cars and took eighth place, which was satisfactory in all the circumstances, and he rounded off the season by finishing sixth at Watkins Glen and retiring with ignition trouble at Mexico City.

Despite the many frustrations suffered by Jochen during his first year with Cooper—and for a man with such a burning ambition to succeed, there was nothing more frustrating than driving an uncompetitive car—he derived a certain amount of satisfaction from success in other fields. For the 1965 Le Mans race Rindt was invited by Luigi Chinetti, boss of the North American Racing Team and American Ferrari concessionaire, to drive one of his entries. During the years 1964–7 Le Mans witnessed a titanic battle between the 4-litre works Ferraris and the 5- and 7-litre Fords, a battle won by Ferrari in 1964, by Ford in 1966 and with the honours fairly even in 1967 with a Ford winning the race and Ferraris finishing second and third. In such a hotly contested battle the chances of Rindt's car, a 3.3-litre Ferrari 275 LM coupé, a model built for sale to private owners and far less powerful than the works cars, seemed slight indeed. Nor did Jochen's co-driver, veteran American Masten Gregory, seem a likely candidate for victory; for Gregory, quiet and professorial behind his thick spectacles off the track, drove like a demon on it, throwing caution to the winds and to most onlookers it seemed something of a miracle that he had survived in one piece an accident-studded career dating back to 1953.

Early in the race the NART car was delayed by mechanical trouble which was eventually traced to a faulty distributor and by the time it was back in the race the Ferrari had lost more than ten laps and seemed to be well out of the running, even for a good placing. But first the works Fords, then the works Ferraris and finally the semi-works Ferraris entered by various agents ran into mechanical trouble and by half-distance the private yellow-painted Belgian-entered 275 LM Ferrari of Pierre Dumay, partnered by Gosselin, led by two laps from the dynamic duo of Rindt and Gregory who had been driving right on the limit to make up lost time. Whatever time the NART car made up on the road, it seemed to lose in pit stops for new tires, the price to be paid for such furious driving, with a deficit of sixteen miles on the leading car it seemed that Rindt and Gregory would have to settle for second place.

This was one race however, in which luck was on Rindt's side, for at lunchtime on the Sunday the yellow Ferrari burst a tire on the Mulsanne straight, crawled round to the pits for a wheel-change and body repairs and by the time it had rejoined the race, the NART car was in front. For the remainder of the race Rindt and Gregory switched tactics completely, nursing the car to the finish and at the end of the twenty-four hours they took the chequered flag for what Rindt regarded as one of the most pleasing victories in his career. It was the first time since 1949 that a private Ferrari had won at Le Mans and then the driver was Chinetti himself. And as the mechanic drove the car away after the race the final drive packed in! Like so many successful Grand Prix drivers, Rindt became increasingly disinterested in sports car racing and once he had become sufficiently estab-

Karl-Jochen Rindt

lished and felt that he could pick and choose his drives, he gave up racing sports cars altogether.

Although Rindt enjoyed far more success in Formula Two in 1965 than Grand Prix racing, the competition was strong, Rindt faced opposition from other Brabhams driven by Brabham himself, Hulme and Graham Hill and Jim Clark's Lotus and as all the entrants were using Cosworth engines, the cars were closely matched in power output and speed. Rindt took third places on the difficult road circuit at Pau and at Vallelunga, but his first win did not come until the Reims race in July. Early in the race Rindt lost a lot of time when he over-shot the Thillois hairpin bend but he soon made up lost ground and was battling for the lead with Jim Clark's Lotus, Frank Gardner's Lola and working in partnership with team-mate Alan Rees; at the last corner Rees was in front, as agreed before the race he eased off to let Rindt through to the front, but with the Austrian went Frank Gardner who forged into the lead. Just before they reached the finishing line Jochen whipped out of Gardner's slipstream to win the race by a fifth of a second. On the high-speed Pergusa circuit in Italy it was Alan Rees who won for the Winkelmann team and Rindt took second place.

At the end of 1965 the existing 1500 cc Grand Prix Formula came to an end and was replaced by a new Formula for cars up to 3000 cc. The change in Formula coincided with a complete reorganisation at Cooper that did much to raise Jochen's spirits and he looked forward to the coming season with optimism. During 1965 Cooper had become a member of the Chipstead Group of companies, headed by Jonathan Sieff, son of the chairman of Marks and Spencers. New works were acquired at Weybridge, former racing driver Roy Salvadori was appointed team manager and the team was much better financed than previously—although because of the restrictive terms of his contract, Rindt received little benefit from this change in financial fortunes.

Bruce McLaren, with whom Jochen had enjoyed an affable, but not particularly close relationship, had left the team to race his own cars and the Austrian was now number one driver, partnered in the early part of the season by Richie Ginther who left to drive the works Honda as soon as it was ready to test.

Former Connaught and Jaguar designer Derrick White had evolved a complete new monocoque and this was powered by a V-12 Maserati engine. On paper the new car matched its rivals in terms of both power and roadholding, but as the season progressed it became obvious that the Maserati engine was less powerful than its makers claimed and less reliable than expected and that the Cooper chassis was too heavy. Although Jochen failed to achieve the success he had hoped for and at the end of the year still had not won his first Grand Prix, he finished in the first six often enough and sufficiently high up to take third place in the Drivers' Championship.

In 1966 the works Cooper first appeared at the *Daily Express* race at Silverstone in May, but although Rindt got off to a good start, holding third place, all the team's testing had not resolved the sort of handling problems that can arise under actual race conditions and he gradually fell back to finish fifth. He tried hard again at Monaco, but still the Cooper was not handling as well as it should and Rindt was in fifth place when the engine broke.

Up until this time all Rindt's Formula One drives had been dull, uninteresting and generally unsuccessful; never at the wheel of a car that was competitive enough to challenge for the lead, he had been forced to drive sober, restrained races, hoping to pick up a place when faster cars retired and it was impossible to assess what progress he had made since the start of the 1965 season. It was at Spa in 1966, Cooper's next race, that Jochen displayed the first signs of the greatness that was to characterise his driving with Lotus in 1970. The Cooper was now a much improved car,

Karl-Jochen Rindt

its handling problems had been resolved and although the engine was still down on power, at this early stage in the first year of the 3000 cc Grand Prix Formula the only car that was more powerful was the Ferrari.

Rindt set second fastest practice lap at Spa, beaten only by Surtees with the Ferrari. As the cars formed up on the grid for the start, dense, dark rain-clouds lurked over the surrounding hills, and the cars roared off with Rindt well up with the leaders. Sudden rain that drenched one part of the long and difficult circuit, while other parts remained bone dry was always the driver's greatest fear at Spa. At the corner known as Burnenville, about a third of the way round the course, the pack ran into the rain, two cars went off at this corner, another five went off on the Masta straight and Rindt, losing adhesion while his Cooper was travelling at around 120 mph, spun twice on the straight, but succeeded in keeping his car on the road and at the end of the first lap, came round in fourth place. Rindt soon disposed of team-mate Ginther's Cooper, overhauled Bandini's Ferrari and on lap 4 thrust his car through the blinding wall of spray that marked the passage of race-leader Surtees. Despite trouble with his limited slip differential Jochen stayed in front for the next twenty laps, but now the rain had eased, the track was merely wet as opposed to awash and in these conditions the handling trouble resulting from the differential made itself more obvious. When Surtees forged by into the lead, there was nothing Jochen could do and at the chequered flag he was forty seconds in arrears, but with the satisfaction of having driven the best race of his career in the worst possible conditions.

By the French Grand Prix at Reims the Cooper team had been joined by Surtees who had left the Ferrari team after a disagreement and although two men more different in character, the fiery, effervescent Rindt and the so meticuluous, precise Surtees, would be difficult to imagine, they soon achieved a good working relationship. Reims was another high-speed circuit which favoured the Ferraris and Coopers, but the British cars were completely out of luck and in the race were plagued by overheating fuel pumps. Surtees retired early in the race but Rindt was able to keep his car going and he finished fourth, completely enervated by a difficult drive in excessively hot conditions.

Neither of the Coopers ran well in the British race at Brands Hatch and Rindt had to struggle to finish fifth and in the Dutch Grand Prix he spun off after missing a gearchange. At the Nürburgring the Coopers were no match for Jack Brabham's nimble Repco-powered car and Rindt drove a stolid race to finish third behind Brabham and teammate Surtees. At Monza he took fourth place, finishing with a flat tire which came off the rim and locked the wheel so that he crossed the line out of control and ended up on the grass. Rindt chased Clark's Lotus with BRM H-16 engine all the way in the United States race, waiting for the leader's complex engine to break; the BRM engine stayed in one piece, but on the last lap Rindt ran out of fuel and because of the time taken to complete the lap, it was disregarded under the regulations. Finally came the Mexican Grand Prix in which Surtees brought the Cooper team its first World Championship race win since McLaren's victory at Monaco in 1962, but Rindt retired with suspension trouble.

In the 1966 Le Mans race Jochen co-drove a privately entered 4.7-litre Ford with Innes Ireland, but until Pedro Rodriguez and Lucien Bianchi won the 1968 race for the Gulf team, a standard 'small capacity' GT40 had never survived the 24 Hours' race and after only sixty minutes of racing Jochen's engine blew up at Mulsanne. Although Jochen was still getting as much pleasure and satisfaction as ever from Formula Two racing, he now faced stronger opposition in this category. In 1965 the works Brabhams had appeared with new all-roller bearing twin-cam Honda engines especially built for Formula Two and much more powerful than the Cosworth engines used by the rest of the Formula Two contenders. In the first season these engines had suffered from teething troubles, but in 1966 they won race after race with almost monotonous regularity. Throughout the year Jochen battled to get to grips with the works Brabhams, his engine not always standing up to the strain of his press-on driving and having to settle for third places at Goodwood and Zolder. Only at Brands Hatch at the end of the year did he succeed in defeating the Honda-powered cars and by dint of sheer driving skill. After chasing Jack Brabham hard all the way, sitting only inches behind his exhaust pipes, he succeeded in boxing him in behind a slower car that they were lapping and held on to the lead to the chequered flag. That year he also drove saloon cars for the last time, racing Alfa saloons for the Autodelta team which won its class of the European Touring Car Championship.

Jochen Rindt had known Nina Lincoln, daughter of former amateur Finnish driver Kurt Lincoln since 1963. Although Nina was immensely attracted to the dashing Jochen and they were engaged for six months, her love was tempered by her apprehensions that he was too wild, too involved in motor racing and the people in the motor racing circus and too concerned with making money. The engagement was broken off, for a while they continued to see each other but all his overtures were rejected and for two years she ignored his letters while he pressed her to marry him. When they met again in New York in 1966 Nina realised how Jochen had changed, that he was no longer pre-occupied with himself and with racing and that he had strengthened in character. Jochen proposed again, Nina accepted and the wedding took place in Helsinki in March 1967 just before he embarked on this third full season of European Formula One racing. Jochen had kept a flat near Lake Geneva since 1965, he loved the country and at first the Rindts lived in rented accommodation in Switzerland where their first child, Natasha, was born in August 1968. They eventually moved into their own newly-built house near Geneva where they had the Stewarts as neighbours.

1967 was one of the least satisfactory Grand Prix seasons in Jochen's career. He was now an established driver of considerable experience and skill, whose services any one of half a dozen team managers would have been pleased to snap up. Instead of being free to drive for a team that would offer good financial terms and a competitive car, he was tied to Cooper on a less than satisfactory retainer for this third and final year. Although the Maserati engine had displayed much improved reliability in the later part of 1966, efforts by Maserati engineers in 1967 to improve the power output merely ruined the reliability of the V-12 engine and the appearance of Colin Chapman's new and brilliant Ford-powered Lotus 49 coupled with the improved speed and reliability of the latest Eagles and Hondas, resulted in the Cooper proving an uncompetitive also-ran, and at only two Championship races during the season did Jochen finish in the first six. He retired at Kyalami, where the South African Grand Prix was held for the first time, Monaco and Zandvoort, but at Spa a combination of Rindt's steady driving and a car that for once held together brought him one of his best results of the season and he took fourth place. He did not finish again until the Italian Grand Prix at Monza where he took fourth place, retired again at Watkins Glen and Cooper entered only a single car for his team-mate Pedro Rodriguez at Mexico City.

Whatever may have been Jochen's disappointments in Grand Prix racing in 1967, these were compensated for in Formula Two and so numerous were his successes during the year that the press was beginning to refer to him as 'King of Formula Two.' For that year the Federation Internationale de l'Automobile had introduced a new Formula Two with a maximum capacity limit of 1600 cc. Once again the Formula was monopolised by Cosworth-powered cars and Jochen was still driving for the Winkelmann team. Out of twenty-five Formula Two races held during the year, Jochen won nine and took four second places—his closest rival was Jackie Stewart with four victories. Rindt also drove for the Porsche team in 1967 Sports Car Championship races, but he achieved little success and when he parted company with the Stuttgart team, it was not on the best of terms because Jochen reckoned that the cars were not strong enough and Porsche thought he drove them too hard. In view of the many international successes gained by Porsche, this is an argument in which it is difficult to take Jochen's side!

At Indianapolis in 1967 Rindt appeared at the wheel of one of Dan Gurney's Eagle cars powered by a Ford twin overhead camshaft engine. With its four banked corners and simple oval shape, there seems nothing particularly lethal about the 'Indy bowl' and the very high speeds attained there appear at a casual glance much safer than on some of the faster European road circuits. Yet each corner because of surface variations and the effect created by surroundings, such as the enormous grandstands at the first turn, requires a different technique, it has always proved a difficult circuit for European road racing drivers to master and the race is often marred by multiple crashes which have cost the lives of many drivers. During qualifying for this race Rindt had the horrifying experience of the throttles jamming open at speed; the car ran into the retaining wall, the right-hand wheels were torn off, it careered along the track in a cloud of smoke and flames and Jochen was forced to jump out while it was still travelling at speed. The Austrian was lucky to escape with a shaking. In the race he drove another Eagle, but retired with piston failure.

One thing that was certain at the end of 1967 was that Jochen would transfer to a new Formula One team. There were plans for the Winkelmann team to run its own Formula One car, but these fell through. Eventually Rindt signed up to drive a Brabham, mainly because of his liking for 'Black Jack' and his complete trust in the tough Australian. On paper the decision could not be bettered. Although the Lotus 49s had been the sensation of the 1967 season in terms of both handling and speed, they had proved very fragile and it was a matter for speculation whether they would hold together better in 1968. Brabham himself won the Championship in 1966, Denis Hulme had won it at the wheel of a Brabham in 1967 (but had now left to drive the new McLaren car) and although the Australian Repco engine was less powerful than the Cosworth-Ford powering several of its rivals, it had proved itself the epitome of reliability and deficiencies in bhp should be more than made up in 1968 by the introduction of a new four-cam version of the V-8 engine.

Mechanical trouble, however, ruined the Brabham team's chances of success in 1968, for the new engine was far less reliable than its predecessor. At Kyalami, Rindt's older car ran well and he took an encouraging third place behind the Lotus 49s of Jim Clark and Graham Hill, but he was out of luck at the Spanish race, a new round in the Championship held at Jarama near Madrid, and his engine expired with overheating and loss of oil pressure. Still at the wheel of a car with the older engine at Monaco, he made an error of judgment while trying to overtake third-place man Surtees on the hill down from the Casino Square and crumpled the car up against the barrier. Although Jochen drove in a much more restrained manner than in past years, it was errors of this sort that revealed that he had not yet fully matured as a driver. Four days after the Monaco race he drove the new monocoque Brabham with Offenhauser engine at Indianapolis, but once again he retired with engine failure.

By the Belgian race at Spa one of the new four-cam Repco-powered cars was ready for Rindt to drive and for the first time the Brabhams were fitted with rear aerofoils, the start of a new trend in aerodynamic aids to adhesion that was to end in near disaster because designers did not fully appreciate the effects of using these devices. After only five laps Jochen was out of the race with engine trouble and he retired at both the French and British races the following month. Seven more Championship races were held in 1968, in six of these Jochen retired, mainly with engine trouble. His sole finish was at the rain-soaked and mist-enveloped German race; in such conditions the mechanics of a car are far less highly stressed because of the lower lap speeds, the ratio of finishers to starters is generally higher, and at the Nürburgring Rindt took third place.

In Formula Two Rindt enjoyed yet another fine year, scoring wins for the Winkelmann team at Thruxton, Zolder (in Belgium), the Crystal Palace, Hockenheim, Tulln-Langenlebarn (on home territory in Austria) and Enna. His victory at the Zolder circuit Rindt himself regarded as one of the finest in his career. The results were decided on the aggregate of two heats, the first of which he won from Chris Amon's Ferrari Dino. At the start of the second heat Jochen made a slow start and was rammed by an over-exuberant Brian Redman accelerating through from the second row with his Ferrari. Rindt's Brabham slewed round and eventually got away in tenth place. Now the Austrian was in his element and with every excuse to drive his car right on the limit to make up lost ground. By the end of the first lap he was in seventh place, nine laps later he was in fourth, but however fast Rindt drove, it seemed that his chances of catching the two leading Ferraris of Jacky Ickx and Chris Amon were nil. He closed right up on the leaders and at the start of the last lap Ickx was shown a signal by the Ferrari pit, indicating that he should let Amon through into the lead; this would ensure a Ferrari victory, for if Ickx won the heat with Amon second, Rindt would be the winner on aggregate, with a win and a third, as this would give a better score than Amon's two second places. Unfortunately Jacky failed to see the signal and although Rindt finished third on the road, unable to find a way round the two red cars, he had won the race!

During his four years in Formula One Jochen had seen other newcomers break into Grand Prix racing and although he knew that he was a driver of equal ability he had been forced to watch these newcomers, especially Jacky Ickx and Jackie Stewart, achieve greater success on the track and far greater financial rewards. For 1969 Rindt was determined to secure for himself the most financially favourable contract with the most competitive team. After Jim Clark's death at Hockenheim in April 1968 Colin Chapman had signed up Jack Oliver as number two in the Lotus team, but Oliver had now suffered the fate of so many other Lotus second-string drivers and was dropped from the team at the end of the year. Chapman was looking for a replacement for Clark, if possible a driver of equal ability; as long ago as July 1968 he had made approaches to Rindt, but at that time there were other possibilities including, once again, the idea that the Winkelmann team should run its own car, possibly a Matra. Brabham wanted Rindt to stay with him and had promised that his cars would use Ford instead of Repco engines in 1969, but he could not match Chapman's financial offer which was generous indeed. With some reluctance Rindt left Brabham to drive for Lotus, but on the understanding that he would be joint number one with World Champion Hill, just as Clark had been before his death.

For much of 1969 luck was still not on Rindt's side, he still had a terrible, almost inescapable reputation as a carbreaker and Britain's leading motor racing journalist promised to shave off his gnome-like beard if Rindt won a Championship race—and as that writer had sported his beard for twenty years, he must have had a great deal of confidence in his judgment. At the beginning of the year Team Lotus fielded a special 2500 cc version of the familiar 49B Lotus in the Tasman series of races in New Zealand and Australia. In the New Zealand Grand Prix the new Lotus driver was beaten into second place by Chris Amon's Ferrari, but in the next Tasman race at Levin Rindt's Lotus locked up its brakes and spun into an earth bank because the brake fluid reservoir had not been topped up. Despite the uneasiness that Rindt now felt about Lotus standards of preparation work, he scored a fine victory at Christchurch in the Lady Wigram Trophy race. Later in the series he won at Warwick Farm in Tasmania and was second in the Sandown Park race. In the Championship he took second place to Amon and he returned to Europe with his confidence in the Lotus set-up fully restored.

The first Championship race of the season was, as usual, at Kyalami and after his engine broke in practice, he ran in the race with a borrowed unit which also failed. At the Race of Champions at Brands Hatch in March there were the first murmurings of discontent within the team and to more perceptive observers it was obvious that Rindt wanted to pass Hill, but the reigning World Champion refused to make room for his team-mate to get by. A little later in the race Rindt was held up by slower cars that he was lapping and in his rush to make up lost ground he set a new lap record, but then retired with loss of oil pressure, almost certainly caused by over-driving. In the wet *Daily Express* Trophy race at Silverstone, his car ran badly during the opening laps because of wet ignition, but then the electrics dried out and Rindt drove a brilliant race to climb back through the field from tenth place to finish second, only three seconds behind his former team-mate Jack Brabham.

In 1969 the Spanish Grand Prix was held on the beautiful, but difficult Montjuich Park road circuit in Barcelona and both Hill and Rindt were at the wheel of cars fitted with very high rear aerofoils. Jochen went straight into the lead at the start of the race, heading Chris Amon's Ferrari and team-mate Hill. On only the ninth lap Hill's car went completely out of control on the rise between the start and the first left-hand hairpin bend and careered into Armco barrier, coming to rest a shattered wreck; Hill was lucky to step from the wreckage unharmed, but perhaps even luckier was Rindt who crashed at exactly the same spot ten laps later, his Lotus ricocheting off the Armco into the wreckage of Hill's car. The red and gold car overturned, trapping Rindt inside, but he escaped with a broken nose and jaw and injured ribs. In both cases the accidents were caused by the failure of the rear aerofoils and there is no doubt that the severity of the crashes was increased by the suspension incidence of the cars as they crested the rise at this point on the circuit. Rindt, as well as other drivers and some designers, had been very anxious about the safety of aerofoils, but all the teams were caught up in a vicious rat-race, none daring unilaterally to stop using these aerodynamic aids to adhesion because of the advantage they would be giving away to their rivals. At Monaco, where Rindt was not fit enough to drive, a ban was imposed on all aerofoils, a move for which Jochen had been campaigning, but this was later changed to restrictions limiting their size and prohibiting adjustable aerofoils.

At Zandvoort the rivalry between Rindt and Hill broke out into almost open aggression and Chapman must have despaired at his inability to control his headstrong drivers. The two Gold Leaf Team Lotus drivers roared away from the start, locked in combat, as though they were deadly rivals and not team-mates, nudging and shoving each other all the way round the circuit. Hill led initially, but then on lap three by dint of taking to the grass and kicking up the sand, Rindt forced his way in front and seared away into the distance. His car survived only sixteen laps before retiring with drive-shaft failure, the race was won by Stewart at the wheel of a Matra and Hill finished seventh after a pit stop.

By the French Grand Prix at Clermont, Chapman seemed to have sorted out the relationship between the two drivers, but his own understanding with Rindt was far from perfect and he was unable to persuade the Austrian to drive the new Lotus 63 four-wheel-drive car, the model on which Chapman pinned the team's future hopes. In the French race Jochen retired feeling ill and Stewart and the Matra scored their fourth victory of the season. Again before the British race Chapman tried to persuade Rindt to drive the new 63, but without success and Chapman was forced to change his mind about selling off the old 49 cars as he had intended. At Silverstone both practice and the race devolved into a duel between Rindt and Stewart and the Austrian, with all hopes of winning the 1969 Championship now gone, was more determined to prove that he was the faster driver than to win the race. In practice Stewart with the Matra lapped in 1 min 20.6 sec before going off the road at Woodcote (but this time was disallowed after he had switched to team-mate Beltoise's car for the race) and Jochen was a fifth of a second slower with his Lotus. The two drivers battled furiously for the lead in the race until Rindt's aerofoil came adrift and after two pit stops, the first for the aerofoil to be torn off and the second for extra fuel, the Austrian finished a disappointed fourth. For poor Jochen the race had proved nothing except that Lotus standards of race preparation did not match those of the rival Matra International team.

The next few races saw little improvement in Rindt fortunes. At the Nürburgring he retired with engine trouble. He offered to drive the 63 four-wheel-drive car in the Oulton Park Gold Cup race and finished second to Ickx's Brabham. This apparent volte-face surprised many people, but it was a decision in accordance with the simple Rindt philosophy that although new cars needed testing under race conditions, they should not be run in World Championship events for which tried and tested designs were essential. Jochen drove a good race at Monza, but after a race-long battle, furiously slip-streaming and chopping places with Stewart and Beltoise, he was pipped at the post by the Scot by less than the length of the Matra's nose. In the

Canadian Grand Prix at Mosport he finished third behind the Brabhams of Jacky Ickx and 'Black Jack' himself.

At long last the tide turned in Rindt's favour in the United States race, but it was a race of mixed fortunes for Team Lotus. Hill crashed badly, breaking both his legs and this accident did much to mar the pleasure of Jochen's first World Championship race win which had been gained only after a battle with Stewart's Matra. For Jochen this victory had taken four seasons of racing to achieve, whereas both Jackie Stewart and Jacky Ickx, his closest rivals, had achieved wins in their first full season of Formula One, Stewart at Monza in 1965 and Ickx at Rouen in 1968. In the final race of the season, the Mexican Grand Prix, Rindt retired because of a broken suspension wishbone. In the World Championship he took fourth place. Jochen had continued to race Formula Two cars for the Winkelmann team in 1969 and scored wins at Thruxton, Pau, Limbourg and Tulln-Langenlebarn.

At the end of the 1969 season Jochen was in a difficult no-man's land between notoriety and fame. After so many seasons of trying he had at last won his first World Championship race, in a season in which Jackie Stewart won six and Jacky Ickx in only his second full season of Formula One won two races. Stewart had a car that was conspicuously quicker than the Lotus 49B which was near the end of its racing life and allowing for this handicap, Jochen was probably the world's fastest Grand Prix driver. The Austrian had yet to prove however, that he was a consistent race-winner, using his very considerable intelligence to conserve his car and out-manoeuvre his opponents.

Soon after Graham Hill's serious accident at Watkins Glen, it was known that whether or not Graham fulfilled his vow to race again the following year, it would not be at the wheel of a works Lotus. Rindt was now unchallenged number one in the Lotus team, there would no longer be any inter-team squabbles and no doubts in Jochen's mind as to whether he would be getting the best-prepared car. After twelve months of uneasiness the relationship between Chapman and Rindt had become one of mutual trust and understanding. Chapman had a completely new Formula One car on the stocks, the hated four-wheel-drive 63 model had been abandoned and Rindt embarked on the 1970 season full of optimism.

At Kyalami Rindt was rammed at the first bend by a press-on Jack Brabham, but he struggled on despite a bent rear wishbone until his engine failed eight laps from the finish. The race was won by Jack Brabham who seemed to be enjoying a middle-aged renaissance. Jochen was bitterly disappointed and even more so at Jarama where the new 72 made its debut. The new Lotus, which was right on the minimum weight limit, with an appearance like a hammerhead shark, mid-mounted radiators and torsion bar suspension, represented a substantial technical advance over existing Formula One cars. That the new car still needed a great deal more development work soon became obvious. In practice at Jarama one of the shafts driving the inboard brakes failed and Jochen spun off; he retired in the race with ignition trouble, which was no fault of the 72s, but at both Jarama and the *Daily Express* Trophy race at Silverstone the following weekend it was obvious that all was far from well with the car's handling.

Two races had gone by, Jochen had failed to score a single Championship point and now he had to drive the old 49C again at the next round of the Championship at Monaco. Just as it was known that Jochen was prepared to take a risk if there was a chance of winning, Colin Chapman also knew that he would not drive his hardest if he thought his car was uncompetitive. At Monaco he drove leisurely for the first thirty-five laps of the race, at which point he was in fifth position, rather higher up the field than he expected and had forty-five laps of the race left in which to fight his way to the front. It was almost as though someone had switched on a motor, for Rindt, still fresh and not tiring as were other drivers in the race, conspicuously speeded up, passing Pescarolo's Matra and having no difficulty in disposing of Hulme's McLaren which was slowed by gearbox trouble.

With twenty laps to go to the finish, Jochen was fifteen seconds behind race-leader Jack Brabham and with a chance, albeit only a slight one, of catching him. The gap closed rapidly, but Brabham, warned by his pit of the danger, fought back to hold Rindt off and for several laps the gap stayed constant. Then Rindt turned on the pressure even more, cornering harder and braking even later, the gap was now being reduced at the rate of two seconds a lap and when the cars started their last lap Rindt was only a second behind. On that last lap Rindt was right behind Brabham, pressuring the tired, forty-six-year-old Australian every inch of the way. At the Gasworks hairpin, the last corner before the finish, Brabham passed Piers Courage's de Tomaso and decided to prevent any clever stuff on Rindt's part by cutting the corner instead of taking the usual wider line; Brabham left his braking fractionally too late, the brakes locked up and the turquoise Brabham slid on into the barricades, while Rindt swept by to win the race. On that last lap Rindt had set a new lap record of 84.56 mph, it was without doubt the finest drive in his career and it showed the wisdom of fighting hard all the way to the finish. Even after the race Rindt still had difficulty in believing that he had won, but he later admitted that he had never driven faster in his life than during the last laps of that race.

The 72 Lotus re-appeared in much revised form at the Belgian race at Spa, but Jochen opted to drive the older model, retiring early in the race with engine trouble. By Zandvoort Rindt had enough confidence in the 72 to drive it again and he led the race from lap three until the chequered flag at the end of lap 80. The Austrian now had a good lead in the World Championship, but what should have been one of his happiest days was turned into an occasion of tragedy and sorrow by the fatal crash of his close friend Piers Courage. Nina urged Rindt to retire, which he now clearly wanted to do, but Jochen said no, he could not possibly retire in mid-season and maintain any self-respect. He did, however, decide that 1970 would be his last season of racing.

Three more victories followed in quick succession, at Clermont-Ferrand, Brands Hatch and the German race which in 1970 was held at Hockenheim. In the British race Rindt had taken the lead from Brabham on lap eight and led for the next sixty-one laps until the Australian went ahead again when he made a slight mistake. Jochen realised that he would be unable to re-pass Brabham and had settled for second place when the turquoise car ran out of fuel on the last lap. Rindt won the race and Brabham coasted across the line half-a-minute later. At Monaco Rindt had beaten Brabham fair and square, but at Brands Hatch victory was snatched from the Australian by the worst possible luck and Rindt almost resented having won. After the race it was alleged that the rear aerofoil of the Lotus exceeded the permitted height and that Rindt would be disqualified. Two hours later after re-checking their measurements, the scrutineers reversed their decision. Whatever pleasure for Rindt there had been in this victory was now lost altogether and the little grey men of British motor racing had succeeded only in reducing the British Grand Prix to the level of a charade.

In August Rindt was beaten into second place by Jacky Ickx in the Austrian Grand Prix, the first race on the new Österreichring. Ickx's Ferrari had at last found its form after a season of failure and Rindt and the Lotus team were very anxious about the outcome of the Italian Grand Prix at Monza on 6th September—if Rindt won the race, he would have won the Championship, otherwise it was possible that his total of 45 points could be beaten.

In the final practice session at Monza on 5th September,

Jochen's world—and that of Nina too—came to an abrupt end. After half-an-hour's practice an eerie hush seemed to settle over the circuit. Denis Hulme stopped at the Lotus pit to tell Gold Leaf Team Manager Peter Warr what he had seen. He had been following Jochen into the South Curve when the Lotus driver weaved slightly and then swerved sharp left into the crash barrier. The nose of the Lotus passed under the rail and struck a supporting post and in the impact a wheel came off the car. Jochen was terribly injured and must have died almost immediately. The remains of the car were impounded, it was never possible for Team Lotus to carry out a thorough investigation of the crash, but Colin Chapman had no reason to suppose that there had been a structural failure.

Monza had witnessed the death of the fastest driver in motor racing. The king is dead. Long live the king. Team Lotus withdrew their entries from Monza and scratched from the Canadian Grand Prix. At Watkins Glen the Lotus team appeared with two new drivers Emerson Fittipaldi and Reine Wisell and Emerson won the American race. The only man who could have defeated Rindt's Championship score was Jacky Ickx if he won all three trans-Atlantic rounds in the Championship, but he failed at Watkins Glen. Rindt became the first—and one prays the last—posthumous World Champion. At Hockenheim in 1971 Ickx with a Ferrari won the Jochen Rindt Gedächtnis-Rennen.

14
The Black Prince
EMERSON FITTIPALDI
1972

TWO BROTHERS COMPETING simultaneously in Grand Prix racing, Emerson and Wilson Fittipaldi, is a unique event in the history of the sport and the nearest approach to this was in the 'thirties when both Luigi Villoresi (with Maseratis) and brother Emilio (for Alfa Romeo) competed in Voiturette 1500 cc racing. In 1972 and 1973 Emerson drove for the Lotus team and elder brother Wilson drove for the rival Brabham organisation. Equally unique has been Emerson's rise to fame and success and only two years exactly after his first Formula One drive he was well on the way to his first World Championship. And Emerson is the only Brazilian ever to reach the top in this high-speed sport, although a number of his countrymen, notably Ferrari exponent Chico Landi, drove fairly regularly in European Grands Prix in the early 'fifties.

Emerson Fittipaldi was born at Sao Paulo, centre of the Brazilian coffee trade, on 12th December 1946. His father, who is a motoring journalist and radio commentator, had already expressed his admiration for President Woodrow Wilson of the United States by naming his first son after him and Emerson's Christian name reflects his father's love of literature and in particular the work of the American poet and essayist of that name. At school Emerson displayed a lively interest in both engineering design and history, but what might well have proved an academic career was foreshortened by another of his talents, a sound approach to business matters. At the age of only sixteen he had started to make special steering wheels for motoring enthusiasts, the business boomed, two years later he left school to concentrate on the business in which he was joined by his brother. Emerson had started to compete in motor-cycle races, at first with diminutive 50 cc machines, but later with more powerful 125 cc bikes. A craze for karting was beginning to capture the enthusiasm of young Brazilians and the Emersons started to both race and manufacture go-karts. When Formula Vee for Volkswagen-powered cars took a hold in Brazil in 1967, the Fittipaldis began to make cars for this Formula and in their first year sold the impressive total of twenty-five.

At the age of eighteen Emerson began competing in saloon car racing with a Renault Gordini and a year later moved on to faster things in the shape of a Renault-Alpine coupé, a glass-fibre-bodied DKW which was a works-entered car and an Alfa Romeo which was also a works car. In 1967 in his third season racing young Fittipaldi drove in Formula Vee and raced a Porsche-engined Volkswagen. That year he won the Brazilian Formula Vee Championship and three sports car races. For the following year's racing he graduated to a 2-litre Porsche Prototype and continued to score success after success.

By this stage in his career Emerson knew beyond any doubt that motor racing was the career for him, that he was determined to succeed whatever obstacles were in his path, but if he was to further his career he would have to go to Europe to race. For 1969 he signed up with the Jim Russell Racing Drivers' School and raced a Formula Ford car.

Russell, himself a very successful driver in the days of 500 cc Formula Three, is a good talent-spotter and he soon recognised Emerson's considerable potential. Although the first three rounds had already been run, Russell decided to enter Emerson in the Lombank Trophy Formula Three Championship. By August Emerson had found his feet in Formula Three and after taking a second place with his Lotus 59 at Brands Hatch at the beginning of the month, he went on to score five victories, two at Mallory Park and three at Brands Hatch, and won the Championship with 57 points to the 49 of second-place man Alan Rollinson. In addition he scored Formula Three wins in non-Championship races at the Crystal Palace and Montlhéry in France.

Already Emerson was well on the way to fame and for 1970 he was offered a drive in a works-supported Lotus 69 Formula Two car. During the early part of the season he took a third place in the Barcelona race on the difficult Montjuich Park circuit and followed this up with a fourth place in the Eifelrennen at the Nürburgring and other third places at the Crystal Palace and Rouen; these successes coupled with a fifth at Enna in Sicily, a second at Imola and a fourth place at Hockenheim were sufficient to give him third place in the European Formula Two Championship for non-graded drivers.

In July Colin Chapman gave Emerson his first big chance by entering him with a Lotus 49C Formula One car, albeit an outdated model, in the British Grand Prix at Brands Hatch. Formula Two is a rather hectic class of racing, events are shorter and tend to take on the character of a flat-out sprint and it is often not until a driver is thrown into the deep end of motor racing with a Formula One that his true worth can be properly assessed—even the most experienced of team managers have made blunders in letting loose with such potent machinery drivers who have failed to tame their wilder instincts. It seemed, however, that once again Chapman had spotted a potential winner and despite losing the use of fourth gear, Fittipaldi drove a beautifully smooth, calm, restrained race, free of incidents, to finish eighth.

With this encouraging performance behind him, Emerson appeared with the same car at the German Grand Prix which in 1970 was held at Hockenheim. In practice he lapped faster than such notables as Francois Cevert, John Surtees and Denny Hulme and he drove a magnificent race with his obsolete car to take fourth place behind Rindt, Ickx and Hulme. He then drove the 49 in the Austrian race, but, slowed by mechanical trouble, finished at the tail of the field. For the Italian Grand Prix Emerson was provided with one of the latest Lotus 72 cars. In practice on the first day he was caught up by a bunch of much faster cars and at the South Curve he missed his braking point and crashed at high speed. The new car was a write-off, but Emerson stepped from the wreckage uninjured, knowing that the accident was entirely his own fault, to comment, 'I feel terrible.' The following day Rindt crashed with fatal results at the same part of the circuit—it seems that the two accidents were in no way connected—and Gold Leaf Team Lotus scratched from the race.

Lotus also withdrew from the Canadian Grand Prix to be held a fortnight later and when the team appeared at the next round of the Championship at Watkins Glen at the beginning of October, the Lotus 72s were driven by a pair of inexperienced drivers who, on paper at least, were unlikely to achieve much in the way of success. Leading the team was Emerson and he was backed up by Swedish driver Reine Wisell who earlier in the year had won three Formula 5000 races. In practice Emerson went well enough to take a place on the second row of the grid and for much of the race he held a fine third place. When Stewart's leading Tyrrell began to throw out clouds of white smoke and slowed off, Emerson, who had been lapped, put himself back on the same lap as the leader and he moved up into second place when Jackie's car expired. Just when Emerson seemed all set to take second place, with Wisell third, about thirty seconds behind him, Pedro Rodriguez, leading the race with his BRM, rushed into the pits for extra fuel. By the time the Mexican was back in the race, Fittipaldi had gone by in the lead. Emerson went on to score a fine, but lucky first World Championship victory by the comfortable margin of thirty-six seconds.

Both Emerson and Wisell stayed with Team Lotus in 1971, but it was one of the less successful seasons in Chapman's racing career. Throughout the year the team had difficulties because of its inability to retain mechanics, very often its efforts were divided between the 72s and the experimental 56B gas-turbine car which Lotus ran in a number of races and the 72s failed to prove a match for the Tyrrells, the March 711 driven by Ronnie Peterson and the Ferraris. At the South African race at Kyalami Emerson held second place in the opening stages, but gradually fell back to retire with engine trouble. He was plagued by mechanical trouble at Barcelona, finished a poor fifth at Monaco and then missed the Dutch race because of injuries suffered in a road accident. Emerson returned to racing to finish third in the French Grand Prix at the Paul Ricard circuit and in the British race. At the Nürburgring he was eliminated by engine trouble, but a second place, his best performance of a rather unhappy season, followed in the Austrian Grand Prix.

Because of possible repercussions from Rindt's accident in 1970 that could have resulted in the Lotus team cars being impounded, Lotus decided to give the Italian Grand Prix a miss, a decision that was easier to make at a time when the team was well out of the picture in the World Championship. Instead a single 56B gas-turbine car, painted in eye-catching black and gold colours, was entered by World Wide Racing and Emerson drove this far from competitive car into eighth place. Fittipaldi gained no success in the last two races of the Formula One season, but during the year he had won two European Formula Two races, finished second in two others and at the end of the year he won two of the four races in the Brazilian Torneio series. He had returned to his home country to find himself a National hero.

Emerson stayed with Lotus for 1972 and the season witnessed a complete transformation in his fortunes. After a season of disappointment the Lotus 72s, now known as John Player Specials and finished in a distinctive black and gold colour, were running superbly and, after a winter's hard work, proving as fast and as reliable as any of the opposition. In 1971 Emerson's driving had at times seemed mediocre and uninspired, but Chapman obviously had very great confidence in his ability and realised only too well that a driver is only at his best when his car is running to his complete satisfaction. Emerson's driving in 1972 was that of a true Champion; he drove with a new assurance and confidence and with the advantage of a full season of Formula One experience behind him. After retiring with suspension trouble in the Argentine at the beginning of the year and taking second place in the South African race, he enjoyed a fine run of victories in the Race of Champions at Brands Hatch, in the *Daily Express* Trophy race at Silverstone and in the Spanish Grand Prix at Jarama.

He was far from happy in the wet at Monaco, a rain-soaked miserable race in which Beltoise set the pace with his BRM and most of the other drivers slithered and slid unhappily in his wake. By not making mistakes, by not giving up or losing hope and despite almost nil vision through his visor, he moved up to finish third when Stewart's Tyrrell was slowed by wet electrics. Another victory followed in the Belgian Grand Prix on the new Nivelles circuit and he finished second to Stewart in the French Grand Prix at Clermont-Ferrand. He won the British race at Brands Hatch after a stiff fight with Stewart and Emerson now led the World Championship with forty-three points to Stewart's twenty-seven. Whatever the outcome of the season's remaining

Championship races, Emerson had proved that he was a true Champion in the making. At the Nürburgring he was in second place, chasing hard after Ickx's leading Ferrari, despite his gearbox jumping out of third and top gears, when his car retired with a small fire caused by the gearbox casing splitting and oil igniting.

Emerson's fourth World Championship race victory in 1972 followed in the Austrian Grand Prix held at the Österreichring on 13th August. His Championship points score now stood at 52 to the 27 of Jackie Stewart and this was almost, but not quite, uncatchable. Yet another victory followed shortly afterwards in the Rothmans' 50,000 race at Brands Hatch in which he came home ahead of Brian Redman's Yardley-McLaren.

Although it was essential that the John Player team ran in the Italian Grand Prix at Monza so as to clinch Emerson's Championship title, there were grave doubts whether Chapman would allow the cars to run. Because the legal investigation into Rindt's crash in 1970 had not been completed, Chapman was anxious in case he should be summoned before the Court of inquiry and the cars impounded. Eventually the race organisers gave the team an assurance that this would not happen and so two cars for Emerson were dispatched, but at this race the entry was made in the name of World-Wide Racing. One of the team's transporters crashed on the way to the race and so the Champion-to-be was forced to drive his spare car. In practice he took third place on the grid and he came through to take the lead after the retirement of the two Ferraris of Ickx and Regazzoni. Easing off in the closing stages of the race Emerson took the chequered flag and the 1972 World Championship with an unassailable score of 61 points (thirty ahead of the nearest rival Denis Hulme) over fourteen seconds ahead of second-place man Mike Hailwood. Emerson failed to score any points in the last two rounds of the 1972 Championship, but remained the clear victor, sixteen points ahead of Jackie

Stewart who won at both Mosport Park and Watkins Glen.

For 1973 John Player Team Lotus continued to race the now aging 72 design and Fittipaldi was joined in the team by Swedish driver Ronnie Peterson who ranked as equal number one. At the beginning of the year it seemed that Emerson was all set to win his second World Championship, and he kicked off to a good start to the season by winning both at Buenos Aires and Interlagos. His victory on home ground in the Brazilian race was particularly gratifying. But then the season began to turn sour. Jackie Stewart won at Kyalami and Emerson had to settle for a none too satisfactory third place. In the Spanish race at Barcelona the Brazilian was at peak form and scored a magnificent victory despite his left-hand rear tire deflating in the closing laps of the race. For Lotus this was an historic victory, the team's fiftieth World Championship Grand Prix win. Emerson finished third in the Belgian Grand Prix at Nivelles, second at Monaco after a spirited chase of race-leader Stewart in the closing laps and he was in second place in the Swedish race until slowed by transmission trouble that finally caused his retirement. He was now almost desperate to score Championship points as Stewart gradually whittled away his lead. In the French Grand Prix he was in second place with thirteen laps to go to the finish, but that was not good enough; he attempted to snatch the lead from young McLaren driver Jody Scheckter at a point on the circuit where there was clearly not room to pass, the two cars collided and both were eliminated from the race. Victory went to Emerson's team-mate, Ronnie Peterson. Emerson retired with drive-shaft failure at Silverstone and crashed in practice for the Dutch race, injuring his feet and was in so much pain that he was forced to retire at the end of the second lap of the race. He was still suffering from the effects of this accident at the Nürburgring the following weekend and drove what was a slow race by his standards to finish sixth.

Emerson Fittipaldi

In the Austrian race Emerson retired because of a broken oil pipe and at Monza he was beaten into second place by team-mate Ronnie Peterson. The Brazilian needed to win this race to remain in the running for the World Championship and it was a sad indication of the now strained relations between him and Colin Chapman that *le patron* failed to instruct the Swedish driver to ease his pace and allow Emerson to go ahead. Fittipaldi took second place in the Canadian Grand Prix, the results of which were confused and far from certain. After a collision between Cevert's Tyrrell and Scheckter's McLaren the pace car (an innovation in Formula One introduced in mid-season) was sent out and took up a position ahead of Howden Ganley's Iso-Marlboro instead of the leader, Fittipaldi's 'John Player Special.' The timekeepers lost track of the race order and although first place was eventually awarded to Peter Revson, Emerson could have been the winner . . . no one was really sure! Fittipaldi rounded off the season with a sixth place in the United States Grand Prix and took second place in the Championship behind Jackie Stewart.

For much of the 1973 season Emerson had to settle for the unhappy role of an also-ran to the Tyrrell team and his own team-mate Ronnie Peterson. He was far from happy with the team arrangement that he and Peterson received equal attention and as Peterson began to enjoy greater success in the latter part of the season, Emerson's resentment grew and relations within the team were not always the happiest. At the end of the year Chapman and Fittipaldi parted company and Emerson is now driving a Marlboro-sponsored car for the McLaren team.

Emerson Fittipaldi is married to Maria Helena, who has lived in Brazil since she was born, but has English parents. She is a true cosmopolitan, for she was educated at boarding school in England, went to a finishing school in Switzerland and can speak five languages. Twenty-three-year-old Maria gave birth to their first child in 1971. Emerson and she used to live in Norfolk, within easy reach of the Lotus works at Hethel, but have now settled in Switzerland.

Dubbed 'the Black Prince' by the *Daily Express,* Emerson is completely dedicated to motor racing and at this still early stage in his career has no intention of giving up racing in the foreseeable future. He is a shy, but friendly person, modest despite his now considerable racing success and experience and always helpful to the press.

Appendix

THE DRIVERS' WORLD CHAMPIONSHIP, 1950-73

THE CHAMPIONSHIP IS awarded on a points system on the results of specified major events. Up to and including 1959, eight, six, four, three and two points respectively were awarded for the first five places, with one point for fastest lap. In 1960 the point for fastest lap was abolished and, instead, one point was given for sixth place. In 1961 the winner's points were increased from eight to nine. Up to 1957, where more than one driver shared a car, they shared the points, but from 1958 onwards points were awarded only to a driver who handled the car throughout the race. A driver can count only a specified number of Championship rounds towards his personal total and the maximum number for each year is indicated in the results below. Until 1960 the Indianapolis 500 Miles race counted as a round in the Championship even though only one driver, Ascari in 1952, competed in both this and European events.

1950 (best four of seven events)

1st	G Farina (Alfa Romeo)	30 points
2nd	J M Fangio (Alfa Romeo)	27 points
3rd	L Fagioli (Alfa Romeo)	24 points
4th	L Rosier (Lago-Talbot)	13 points
5th	A Ascari (Ferrari)	11 points
6th	J Parsons (Wynne Friction Proof)	8 points

1951 (best four of eight events)

1st	J M Fangio (Alfa Romeo)	31 points
2nd	A Ascari (Ferrari)	25 points
3rd	J F Gonzalez (Ferrari)	24 points

4th	G Farina (Alfa Romeo)	19 points
5th	L Villoresi (Ferrari)	15 points
6th	P Taruffi (Ferrari)	10 points

1952 (best four of eight events)

1st	A Ascari (Ferrari)	36 points
2nd	G Farina (Ferrari)	24 points
3rd	P Taruffi (Ferrari)	22 points
4th	{ J M Hawthorn (Cooper-Bristol) R Fischer (Ferrari) }	10 points
6th	R Manzon (Gordini)	9 points

1953 (best four of nine events)

1st	A Ascari (Ferrari)	34½ points
2nd	J M Fangio (Maserati)	28 points
3rd	G Farina (Ferrari)	26 points
4th	J M Hawthorn (Ferrari)	19 points
5th	L Villoresi (Ferrari)	17 points
6th	J F Gonzales (Maserati)	13½ points

1954 (best five of nine events)

1st	J M Fangio (Maserati and Mercedes-Benz)	42 points
2nd	J M Hawthorn (Ferrari)	24 9/14 points*
3rd	J F Gonzalez (Ferrari)	24 1/7 points*
4th	M Trintignant (Ferrari)	17 points
5th	K Kling (Mercedes-Benz)	12 points
6th	{ H Herrmann (Mercedes-Benz) W Vukovich (Fuel Injection Special) }	8 points

1955 (best five of seven events)

1st	J M Fangio (Mercedes-Benz)	40 points
2nd	S Moss (Mercedes-Benz)	23 points
3rd	E Castellotte (Lancia and Ferrari)	12 points

* Fractions of points were due to shared fastest laps.

Appendix 249

4th	M Trintignant (Ferrari)	11⅓ points
5th	G Farina (Ferrari)	10⅓ points
6th	P Taruffi (Mercedes-Benz)	9 points

1956 (best five of eight events)

1st	J M Fangio (Lancia-Ferrari)	30 points
2nd	S Moss (Maserati)	27 points
3rd	P J Collins (Lancia-Ferrari)	25 points
4th	J Behra (Maserati)	22 points
5th	P Flaherty (John Zink Special)	9 points
6th	E Castellotte (Lancia-Ferrari)	7½ points

1957 (best five of eight events)

1st	J M Fangio (Maserati)	40 points
2nd	S Moss (Vanwall)	25 points
3rd	L Musso (Lancia-Ferrari)	16 points
4th	J M Hawthorn (Lancia-Ferrari)	13 points
5th	C A S Brooks (Vanwall)	11 points
6th	H Schell (Maserati)	10 points

1958 (best eight of eleven events)

1st	J M Hawthorn (Ferrari)	42 points
2nd	S Moss (Vanwall)	41 points
3rd	C A S Brooks (Vanwall)	24 points
4th	R Salvadori (Cooper-Climax)	15 points
5th	H Schell (BRM)	14 points
6th	M Trintignant (Cooper-Climax)	12 points

1959 (best five of nine events)

1st	J Brabham (Cooper-Climax)	31 points
2nd	C A S Brooks (Ferrari)	27 points
3rd	S Moss (Cooper-Climax and BRM)	25½ points
4th	P Hill (Ferrari)	20 points
5th	M Trintignant (Cooper-Climax)	19 points
6th	B McLaren (Cooper-Climax)	16½ points

1960 *(best six out of ten events)*

1st	J Brabham (Cooper-Climax)	43 points
2nd	B McLaren (Cooper-Climax)	34 points
3rd	S Moss (Lotus-Climax)	19 points
4th	I Ireland (Lotus-Climax)	18 points
5th	P Hill (Ferrari)	16 points
6th	O Gendebien (Cooper-Climax)	10 points

1961 *(best five of eight events)*

1st	P Hill (Ferrari)	34 points
2nd	W von Trips (Ferrari)	33 points
3rd	{ S Moss (Lotus-Climax) / D Gurney (Porsche) }	21 points
5th	R Ginther (Ferrari)	16 points
6th	I Ireland (Lotus-Climax)	12 points

1962 *(best five of nine events)*

1st	G Hill (BRM)	42 points
2nd	J Clark (Lotus-Climax)	30 points
3rd	B McLaren (Cooper-Climax)	27 points
4th	J Surtees (Lola-Climax)	19 points
5th	D Gurney (Porsche)	15 points
6th	P Hill (Ferrari)	14 points

1963 *(best six of ten events)*

1st	J Clark (Lotus-Climax)	54 points
2nd	G Hill (BRM)	29 points*
3rd	R Ginther (BRM)	29 points
4th	J Surtees (Ferrari)	22 points
5th	D Gurney (Brabham-Climax)	19 points
6th	B McLaren (Cooper-Climax)	17 points

1964 *(best six of ten events)*

1st	J Surtees (Ferrari)	40 points

* Hill awarded second place because of greater number of first places.

Appendix

2nd	G Hill (BRM)	39 points
3rd	J Clark (Lotus-Climax)	32 points
4th	{ L Bandini (Ferrari) R Ginther (BRM) }	23 points
6th	D Gurney (Brabham-Climax)	19 points

1965 (best six of ten events)

1st	J Clark (Lotus-Climax)	54 points
2nd	G Hill (BRM)	40 points
3rd	J Stewart (BRM)	33 points
4th	D Gurney (Brabham-Climax)	25 points
5th	J Surtees (Ferrari)	17 points
6th	L Bandini (Ferrari)	13 points

1966 (best five of nine events)

1st	J Brabham (Brabham-Repco)	42 points
2nd	J Surtees (Ferrari and Cooper-Maserati)	28 points
3rd	J Rindt (Cooper-Maserati)	22 points
4th	D Hulme (Brabham-Repco)	18 points
5th	G Hill (BRM)	17 points
6th	J Clark (Lotus-Climax and Lotus-BRM)	16 points

1967 (From 1967 onwards the season has been divided into two equal sections. If there is an uneven number of qualifying events, the first section contains one more event than the second section. Drivers may count the points obtained from all but one of the races in each section towards their final score.)

1st	D Hulme (Brabham-Repco)	51 points
2nd	J Brabham (Brabham-Repco)	46 points
3rd	J Clark (Lotus-Ford)	41 points
4th	{ C Amon (Ferrari) J Surtees (Honda) }	20 points
6th	{ G Hill (Lotus-Ford) P Rodriguez (Cooper-Maserati) }	15 points

1968

1st	G Hill (Lotus-Ford)	48 points
2nd	J Stewart (Matra-Ford)	36 points
3rd	D Hulme (McLaren-BRM and Ford)	33 points
4th	J Ickx (Ferrari)	27 points
5th	B McLaren (McLaren-Ford)	22 points
6th	P Rodriguez (BRM)	18 points

1969

1st	J Stewart (Matra-Ford)	63 points
2nd	J Ickx (Brabham-Ford)	37 points
3rd	B McLaren (McLaren-Ford)	26 points
4th	J Rindt (Lotus-Ford)	22 points
5th	J-P Beltoise (Matra-Ford)	21 points
6th	D Hulme (McLaren-Ford)	20 points

1970

1st	J Rindt (Lotus-Ford)	45 points
2nd	J Ickx (Ferrari)	40 points
3rd	C Regazzoni (Ferrari)	33 points
4th	D Hulme (McLaren-Ford)	27 points
5th	{ J Brabham (Brabham-Ford) { J Stewart (Tyrrell and March-Ford)	25 points

1971

1st	J Stewart (Tyrrell-Ford)	62 points
2nd	R Peterson (March-Ford)	33 points
3rd	F Cevert (Tyrrell-Ford)	26 points
4th	{ J Ickx (Ferrari) { J Siffert (BRM)	19 points
6th	E Fittipaldi (Lotus-Ford)	16 points

1972

1st	E Fittipaldi (John Player Special-Ford)	61 points
2nd	J Stewart (Tyrrell-Ford)	45 points

Appendix

3rd D Hulme (McLaren-Ford)   39 points
4th J Ickx (Ferrari)   27 points
5th P Revson (McLaren-Ford)   23 points
6th { C Regazzoni (Ferrari)
       F Cevert (Tyrrell-Ford) }   15 points

1973

1st J Stewart (Tyrrell-Ford)   71 points
2nd E Fittipaldi (John Player Special-Ford)   55 points
3rd R Peterson (John Player Special-Ford)   52 points
4th F Cevert (Tyrrell-Ford)   47 points
5th P Revson (McLaren-Ford)   38 points
6th D Hulme (McLaren-Ford)   26 points